JJ Wilson   with Antonia Clare

ADVANCED

Total English

Students' Book

PEARSON
Longman

Contents

LESSON 3	VOCABULARY	COMMUNICATION	FILM BANK
Grammar: perfect aspect **Vocabulary:** achievement **Can do:** talk about your achievements	Prefixes	Challenge yourself!	Ultimate challenge
Vocabulary: adjectives to describe places **Can do:** describe a place	Phrasal verbs	Start a club	Soho
Grammar: participle clauses/gerunds **Vocabulary:** humour **Can do:** tell a joke	Metaphors	Telling stories	A scary tale
Grammar: inversion **Vocabulary:** special abilities **Can do:** follow an extended piece of discourse	Two-part expressions	Great steps forward	Future world
Grammar: sentence adverbials **Vocabulary:** expressing quantity **Can do:** express priorities	Idioms 1	Spend a fortune	A new venture
Grammar: link words of time and contrast **Vocabulary:** personal characteristics **Can do:** write an autobiographical statement	Idioms 2	Who's the leader?	Hollywood icons
Grammar: *as ... as* and describing quantity **Vocabulary:** buying and selling **Can do:** write an ad for an object	Suffixes	Paradise island	In the wilderness
Grammar: fronting **Vocabulary:** cause and effect **Can do:** explain everyday problems	Academic English	Do you agree?	Pet hates
Grammar: unreal past **Can do:** respond to hypothetical questions	Confusing words	Business venture	Leonardo
Grammar: uses of *would* **Can do:** describe a childhood memory	Phrasal verbs and particles	Moan, rave, take a stand!	Close encounter

Writing Bank page 162   Tapescripts page 165

1 Read the text and match the parts of speech a–j below to each <u>underlined</u> word or phrase.

In 1967 Allen and Beatrice Gardner embarked on an (1) <u>experiment</u> to train a chimpanzee to talk. Realising that chimpanzees don't have the vocal apparatus to be able to speak like humans, but that (2) <u>they</u> can use gestures (3) <u>easily</u>, the Gardners decided to train (4) <u>the</u> animal in ASL, American Sign Language. Their subject was a chimpanzee called Washoe. The Gardners (5) <u>brought up</u> Washoe like a child, giving her regular meals and getting her to brush her teeth before sleep. At first Washoe made meaningless hand gestures, similar to the meaningless 'babbling' of baby children learning a language. But after four years Washoe had learned over 150 signs. She (6) <u>could</u> also combine the signs on some occasions, such as when she made the signs for 'water' and 'bird' on (7) <u>seeing</u> a swan on a lake. Linguists and scientists, (8) <u>however</u>, are (9) <u>sceptical</u> about the Gardners' (10) <u>research</u>, and question whether Washoe can really 'speak'. They say that her 'language use' is simply imitation.

a) present participle   f) phrasal verb
b) link word (contrast)   g) adjective
c) uncountable noun   h) adverb
d) countable noun   i) pronoun
e) article   j) modal verb

2 Find the grammar mistake in each sentence.

1 By this time tomorrow, we will have arrive in Peru.
2 We were hot because we'd run.
3 If I would have seen you, I would have stopped.
4 It's time we go home.
5 It mustn't have been John; John's tall and that man was short.
6 We haven't been knowing her long.
7 The conference will held in the theatre tomorrow.
8 I had my purse stole yesterday.
9 She persuaded me buying the car.
10 He climbed up the Mount Everest.

3 **a** Complete the word maps with words/ phrases from the box below.

half-sister   career path   uncharted territory
soulmate   culture shock   spending spree
be made redundant

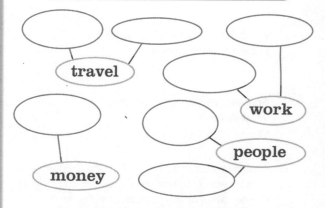

b <u>Underline</u> the main stress in each word/ phrase.

c Add three more words to each word map.

4 **a** Look at the dictionary extract below from the *Longman Dictionary of Contemporary English*. What does it tell you about each of the following: grammar, pronunciation, use and meaning?

dead·line /dedlaɪn/ *n* [C] a date or time by which you have to do or complete something: [**+for**] *The deadline for applications is May 27th.* | [**+of**] *It has to be in before the deadline of July 1st.* | **meet/miss a deadline** (=have or not have something finished on time) *working under pressure to meet a deadline.* | **set/impose a deadline** *They've set a deadline of Nov 5.* | **tight/strict deadline** (=a deadline that is difficult)

b Complete the dictionary extracts below by writing a definition for each one.

1 over·priced /ˌəʊvəˈpraɪst/ *adj*

_____:
The food was overpriced.

2 wan·der[1] /ˈwɒndə/ *v* [**+around**] [I, T]

_____:
We didn't know where to go so we wandered around.

3 ac·quaint·ance /əˈkweɪntəns/ *n* [C]

_____: *I don't know her well; she's just an acquaintance.*

4 i·ni·tia·tive /ɪˈnɪʃətɪv/ *n* [U]

_____: *You need to have initiative to do this job.*

1 Challenges

Lead-in

1 **Discuss.** What type of challenges are shown in the photos? Have you ever faced any challenges similar to these? What happened? How did you feel?

2 Complete the sentences by matching phrases 1–8 **in bold** to phrases/expressions a–h below.
   1 I like to **set achievable goals,**
   2 It's important to **face challenges,** but
   3 She usually **rises to the challenge,** even if
   4 If I succeed, it will **make my dream come true,** because
   5 I **couldn't have done it without** help, so
   6 It was a **burning ambition,** which
   7 It's important to **have the right attitude,** because
   8 It's quite a **daunting challenge,** but hopefully I

   a) I'd like to thank my family and my sponsors.
   b) can achieve it.
   c) so, before starting, I always think about my objectives.
   d) if you are a positive person, it will be easier.
   e) I've wanted to do this since I was a child.
   f) you mustn't be afraid of them.
   g) it's something very difficult.
   h) I finally managed to achieve.

3 **Discuss.** What are your goals on this course/in your career or studies/in your personal life? What challenges do you think you will face in achieving these goals?

Reading

1 Discuss.

1 How many languages do you speak? Why and how did you learn them?

2 What jobs require several languages? Do any of the jobs appeal to you?

3 Do you think it is easier to learn a new language when you already know other languages? Why/why not?

4 Do you know any polyglots (people who speak many languages)?

2 **a** Read about some amazing language learners and answer the questions.

1 According to Kenneth Hale, what type of talent do polyglots have?

2 Why do polyglots keep learning languages?

3 How is learning new languages sometimes 'easy', according to David Perlmutter?

4 How did Stephen Wurm first learn his languages?

5 What do polyglots sometimes worry about?

6 What bonuses and problems has Ziad Fazah experienced because of his linguistic abilities?

b Check your answers with other students.

3 Discuss.

1 What are the benefits of being a polyglot? Are there any drawbacks?

2 In your opinion, what personal qualities are necessary to become a polyglot?

3 Do you think it would be a good idea to have 'a universal language that would be written as it is spoken'? Will it ever happen?

Great language learners

1 Cardinal Giuseppe Mezzofanti (1774–1849), who spoke seventy-two languages, once learned a language overnight in order to hear the confession of two condemned prisoners the following morning. Modern linguists laugh at this story, but they admit that there are some phenomenal polyglots out there.

2 The greatest is probably Francis Sommer. Sommer, who died in 1978 and grew up in Speyer, Germany, used to amuse himself by inventing languages. While still a schoolboy, he learned Swedish, Sanskrit and Persian. On a visit to Russia, he picked up all the major European languages. By the late 1920s, after emigrating to the United States, where he worked as a research librarian, he had mastered ninety-four languages. David Perlmutter, Professor of Linguistics at the University of California, says, 'People like Sommer are amazing examples of human achievement.'

3 Many polyglots wince at being called superhuman. 'It's more like a musical talent than anything else,' says Kenneth Hale, a linguistics professor, who speaks about fifty languages. 'I didn't do very well as a student. I wanted to learn languages, and I let everything else slide.' Their motivation, they say, is the sheer delight of mastering a new form of expression. 'When I found I could speak Navajo at the age of twelve,' says Hale, 'I used to go out every day and sit on a rock and talk Navajo to myself.'

4 Perlmutter says, 'Each new language is like a fantastic puzzle and you want to learn how to do it. Sometimes it's easy because if you know English plus German, it's easy to learn Dutch. If you know Spanish and one other Romance language, Portuguese comes quickly.'

5 Stephen Wurm, linguistics professor at the Australian National University at Canberra, knows forty-eight languages. He believes the ideal way to learn a language is to have it spoken to you from the age of two.

6 'The members of my family all came from different backgrounds and spoke several languages,' he says. 'When I was growing up, my father, who was a

Vocabulary | learning languages

4 Match the words/expressions from the text to the definitions a–j below.

1 pick up (phrasal verb) (paragraph 2) ___

2 let (sth) slide (v + v) (informal) (para 3) ___

3 sheer delight (adj,n) (para 3) ___

4 master (v) (para 3) ___

5 garble (v) (informal) (para 7) ___

6 information overload (n) (para 7) ___

7 cram (v) (para 7) ___

8 on the ball (idiom) (informal) (para 7) ___

9 babble (v) (informal) (para 9) ___

10 unintelligibly (adv) (para 9) ___

a) speak in a way that is impossible to understand

b) put too much into a small space

c) neglect something or allow it to get worse

d) very attentive/aware

e) speak too quickly and not clearly

f) become an expert

g) too much to remember

h) learn without consciously studying

i) say something badly/in a confused way/nonsensically

j) pure pleasure

5 a Use one word/expression to complete each sentence.

1 It's easy to _____ foreign languages _____ if you don't use them regularly.

2 You have to be really _____ to understand foreign idioms.

3 The best way to _____ new vocabulary is by reading a lot.

4 It is impossible to _____ a foreign language completely.

5 For most students, more than ten new words per lesson equals _____.

Tick the sentences you agree with and compare your views with a partner.

Listening

6 [1.1] Listen to Mark Spina talking about his experiences as a language learner. Make notes about the following:

1 The number of languages he speaks

2 Where/how he learned the languages

3 Special techniques he uses

4 How he feels about language

5 Problems he has

7 Compare your notes with a partner. Listen again to check.

8 Discuss. Do you have any similar experiences of language learning to Mark?

---

linguist himself, insisted that each member of the family speak to me in only one language. So my father spoke to me only in English, his father in Norwegian and his mother in Finnish. My mother spoke to me only in Hungarian and her mother only in Mongolian. That way I never got confused. Then I travelled with my father to his postings in Germany, Russia, China, Argentina and Turkey, so that by the age of six, I spoke ten different languages.'

7 Some master linguists confess that they live in fear of garbling their various languages. Towards the end of his life, Sommer said he had given up learning new languages because he was experiencing information overload. 'I am afraid to cram any more words into my head,' he said. Similarly, Kenneth Hale says

8 sometimes he starts speaking in one language and finds himself unconsciously drifting into another. 'Unless I'm attentive and really on the ball, I can mix up languages like Miskitu and Sumu, both of which are spoken in Central America and are very similar.'

9 The greatest of today's polyglots is Ziad Fazah. Fazah, a Lebanese in his forties who has been living in Brazil for over twenty years, is fluent in fifty-six languages. Apart from Arabic, his mother tongue, and French and English which he learned at school, Fazah taught himself all the languages. He began with German and moved on to Mandarin Chinese, Cantonese and Japanese.

Fazah's abilities have had some unexpected uses. When police in Rio picked up an illegal alien babbling

10 unintelligibly, they turned to Fazah. 'I soon realised he was from Afghanistan and spoke a dialect called Hazaras,' Fazah said.

11 TV fame also arrived unexpectedly. He appeared on TV programmes in Spain and Greece, where his linguistic abilities were tested by people from Thailand, Hungary, Korea, Japan, China and other countries. The US consulate was less impressed. Because of his ability to speak Chinese and Russian, they feared he was a spy, and asked the Brazilian police to bring him in for questioning. 'After two hours I was let go,' he says.

According to Fazah, who can learn 1,000 words in a month, Mandarin Chinese is the hardest language to learn. His dream is to create a universal language that would be written as it is spoken.

Grammar | verbs/adjectives with prepositions

9 Match the cartoons with the sentences below.

1 Paco found he was very short of opportunities to use his English.
2 Olga tended to rely on translation when she learned new words.

10 Complete the tasks in the Active grammar box.

> ### Active grammar
>
> 1 There are many expressions which use a fixed preposition. Which of the sentences in Ex. 9 contains *verb + preposition* and which contains *adjective + preposition*?
>
> 2 Prepositions after verbs, nouns and adjectives always have an object. What is the object in the two sentences in Ex. 9?
>
> 3 When the preposition is followed by a verb, the verb is usually in the *-ing* form.
> *I look forward to <u>meeting</u> you.*
> *She apologised for <u>taking</u> the cake.*
> Rewrite sentence 2 in Ex. 9 to show this.

see Reference page 17

11 a Work in groups. Add the correct prepositions from the box to each sentence. Check any new expressions in your dictionary.

> from (x3)   to   in (x2)   about (x2)   for   with

1 Do you think you'll succeed _____ passing your next exam?
2 If you could improve your English by watching DVDs, by living in an English-speaking country or by studying from books, which would you opt _____?
3 Do your problems in English stem _____ poor grammar, or are there other problems?
4 Do you feel you are lacking _____ vocabulary?
5 Even at advanced level, some students' spoken English is riddled _____ errors. Does this matter or is fluency more important?
6 What distinguishes your first language _____ English?
7 What types of classroom exercises appeal _____ you?
8 Is pronunciation worth bothering _____ or are you happy to keep your accent?
9 Are you nervous _____ giving presentations in English?
10 How can your vocabulary benefit _____ using the media?

b Match questions 1–10 in Ex. 11a to the possible answers a–j below.

a) Some of the vocabulary is similar but the grammar is completely different.

b) I always make an effort with the sounds of English, but I know I'll never sound like a native speaker.

c) Yes, I think so. I've been studying hard and I really hope I achieve my goal!

d) I like class discussions best of all, and also role plays.

e) I think accuracy is important, too. It's difficult to listen to someone whose speech is full of mistakes, and it distracts you from the content of what they're saying.

f) I'd choose to immerse myself in the language and culture by living in Canada or Australia.

g) Listening regularly to the news or looking at websites is good for learning new words.

h) Yes. I don't know many idioms, phrasal verbs and informal expressions.

i) A lot of the difficulties come from the fact that I can't understand native speakers when they speak fast, but I also need to work on my grammar!

j) Speaking in public worries me a little bit, but I think it's a good thing to do in class.

Person to person

12 a Work in pairs. Discuss sentences 1–10 in Ex. 11a. Are the suggested answers true for you? If not, why not?

b Tell the class what you found out about your partner.

Vocabulary

1 Complete these sentences with a word from the box.

> nothing   sure   head   out
> positive   clue   of   hand
> know   heart   certain   idea

1 'Who won the match last night?' **'I haven't a _____.'**

2 'Who wrote *Silas Marner*?' '**I don't know off the top of my _____.'**

3 'Which state has the smallest population?' **'I'm pretty _____** it's the Vatican.'

4 'Where did Elisha Gray come from?' 'Who? **I've never heard _____ him.'**

5 'Do you know Paris?' 'Yes. I lived there for years so **I know it like the back of my _____.'**

6 'What date did Man first go to the Moon?' '**I don't _____ offhand,** but I can look it up.'

7 'Do you know Eliot's poem about Cats?' '**I know it by _____.** I learned it at school.'

8 'What do you know about company law?' '**I know it inside _____. I have a PhD in it.'**

9 'What do you know about Belgian politics?' '**I know next to _____** about it.'

10 'Which country has the biggest population?' '**I haven't the faintest _____.'**

11 'Are you sure Russia is the biggest country in the world?' '**I'm fairly _____** it is but it might be China.'

12 'Are you sure the Nile is the longest river in the world ?' 'Yes. **I'm _____** it is.'

2 a Put the expressions **in bold** in Ex. 1 into the correct column in the How to ... box.

b How are the expressions different? Which are the strongest? Which three expressions have the same meaning?

> **HOW TO ...**
>
> ## say how much you know/don't know
>
> | I know | *I'm pretty sure* |
> | --- | --- |
> | | |
> | I don't know | *I haven't a clue* |

Speaking

3 Ask a partner how much they know/don't know about the things in the box. Try to use the expressions in the How to ... box above.

> Antonio Meucci   the football World Cup
> global warming   jazz   the works of Shakespeare
> Alexander Graham Bell   the history of flight
> athletics   classical music   Leonardo da Vinci
> the North Pole   sailing   computers

Reading and listening

4 Work in pairs and do the quiz.

WHO DID IT FIRST?

1 Who was the first to fly a plane?
   (a) Alberto Santos Dumont
   (b) the Wright brothers
   (c) Von Zeppelin

2 Who invented the telephone?
   (a) Thomas Edison
   (b) Alexander Graham Bell
   (c) Antonio Meucci

3 Who first reached the North Pole?
   (a) Peary
   (b) Cook
   (c) Amundsen

4 Who invented the light bulb?
   (a) Edison
   (b) Bell
   (c) Leonardo da Vinci

5 Which country won the first football World Cup (and hosted it)?
   (a) Brazil
   (b) Uruguay
   (c) Germany

6 Which was the first country to allow women to vote?
   (a) Switzerland
   (b) New Zealand
   (c) the United States

7 Who was the first woman to sail solo around the world?
   (a) Ellen MacArthur
   (b) Amelia Earhart
   (c) Naomi James

8 Which country first held the Olympic Games?
   (a) Italy
   (b) France
   (c) Greece

5 〔1.2〕 Listen to extracts from a radio programme to find answers to the quiz.

6 Check your answers and discuss the questions below.
1 Is there anything surprising in the recording?
2 What extra information did you learn?
3 Why do you think people believe historical stories even if they are not true?

Grammar | passives

7 Read the Active grammar box and choose the correct answer (a) or (b).

Active grammar

1 We often use the passive to show that a statement is
   (a) not our own opinion.
   (b) a personal opinion.

   It is said that ...

   It is believed that ...

   It is claimed that ...

   If we aren't sure that the information is 100 percent true, we can use the passive to put 'distance' between ourselves and the statement.

   He is said to be the richest man in England (but I don't know if this is accurate).

   He was thought to have left the country (but I'm not sure if this is true).

   Other verbs for 'distancing':

   It appears/seems that

   It seems as if/though

2 *He appears/seems to have +*
   (a) Past Simple (b) past participle

see Reference page 17

8 Rewrite the sentences using passives and the verb **in bold**. Include adverbs if they are in the original sentence.

People say that Edison invented more machines than anyone else in history. **say**

Edison is said to have invented more machines than anyone else in history.

1 But the evidence suggests that Edison didn't invent as much as we thought. **seems**

But it _____ though Edison invented fewer things than we thought.

2 People believe that da Vinci invented the helicopter. **think**

Da Vinci _____ invented the helicopter.

3 North American historians assert that the Wright brothers flew first. **assert**

It _____ by North American historians that the Wright brothers flew first.

4 At that time, everybody in the US thought that the Wright brothers were the first to fly. **assume**

In the US it _____ that the Wright brothers were the first to fly.

5 A number of journalists in the late nineteenth century said that William Dickson had 'invented' the motion picture in 1891. **claim**

It _____ that William Dickson had 'invented' the motion picture.

6 We think Dutchman Joop Sinjou and Japanese Toshi Tada Doi invented the CD player at the same time. **believe**

Sinjou and Tada Doi _____ invented the CD player simultaneously.

7 Newspapers of the time reported that Felix Hoffman had invented aspirin. **report**

It _____ that Felix Hoffman had invented aspirin.

8 We now think that aspirin was first used by ancient Egyptians. **believe**

It _____ that aspirin was first used by ancient Egyptians.

Listening

9 **a** `1.3` Listen to some radio news headlines. What achievements do they talk about?

b `1.4` Listen to the first lines again and write down exactly what you hear.

c Check in pairs. Now look at the tapescript on page 165. What problems did you have?

Lifelong learning

Reading aloud and listening

The rhythm of English may be very different from your language. To help your listening and pronunciation, look at the tapescript and read aloud at the same time as you listen. Notice where there are pauses and where the speaker speeds up.

Speaking

10 Work in pairs. Look at the cartoons below and answer the questions.

1 Which story is the most interesting?
2 Which is the most likely/unlikely?
3 What preparation or lifestyle would be required to do these things?

FIRST MAN TO LIVE WITH LIONS

FIRST WOMAN TO SKATEBOARD AROUND THE WORLD

FIRST TWINS TO REACH 125 YEARS OLD

Writing

11 **a** Write a news bulletin based on one of the cartoons in Ex. 10 (about 100–150 words). Use at least two passive constructions for distancing information.

b Practise reading your news bulletins in pairs. Concentrate on putting stress on the most important words.

c Read your bulletins to the rest of the class.

Reading

1 Look at the activities in the box below and answer the questions.

1 Who generally does each activity better: women, men or neither? Why?

2 Are there any other activities which you think men or women do better?

> driving   cooking   gardening   doing jobs around the house
> expressing emotions   looking after children   being alone
> teaching   tolerating pain   listening to other people

2 Work in pairs. Student A: read the text on page 13. Student B: read the text on page 145. Make notes in the table.

Name?		
What is/was their ambition?		
To what extent have they achieved it?		
What challenges have they faced?		
Who has helped them achieve their ambitions? How?		
Other information		

3 Tell your partner about your text and complete the tables with any missing information. What similarities are there between the two stories?

4 Discuss.

1 Do you think that women have limited opportunities in the world of sport? Is this changing?

2 '… there is a prejudice that cooking is not for boys.' Do you agree with this? Is it the same in all countries?

3 Do you think sport could help reduce levels of delinquency in teenagers and young people?

4 What do you think of the fathers' behaviour in these two cases? Would you have reacted similarly? Do you believe that parents should influence the ambitions of their children?

Vocabulary | achievement

5 **a** What do the following words/ expressions from the texts mean? Use the context to help you establish the meaning.

1 head (straight for the top)
2 pursue (a dream)
3 deal with (chauvinism)
4 face (barriers)
5 believe in (what you can achieve)
6 have the potential (to do something)
7 persevere (with something)
8 keep pushing someone (to do something)

b Complete the sentences using the words/expressions in Ex. 5a.

1 It was obvious that Venus Williams had the _____ to become a tennis champion when she was very young.

2 Ralf Schumacher had to _____ with criticism from his colleagues.

3 Ellen MacArthur _____ her dream of sailing solo around the world.

4 McManus is _____ the biggest challenge of his career.

5 If you _____ yourself, you can achieve almost anything.

6 Woods found the course tricky at first, but _____ and came through to the final.

7 If you win this championship, nothing will stop you from _____ straight for the top.

8 Encourage your kids to try new things, but don't _____ them too hard.

Fast female heads for Formula 1

Is Formula 1 ready for its first female star? Matt Rendell travelled to São Paulo to meet Bia who, at the age of nineteen, is tipped to join the ranks of her country's greats – Senna, Piquet, Barrichello. She has already beaten the boys from Brazil at their own game. Now she's ready to take on the world.

As the swarm of go-karts completes its final warm-up lap and hurtles across the starting line, the race is on. Thirty minutes later, when the winner's helmet is removed, a wave of dense dark hair flows freely. For the champion is a girl, Ana Beatriz Figueiredo – Bia, for short – and she is heading straight for the top.

I first met Bia Figueiredo in May 2001. She was sixteen and her rivals in São Paulo's kart scene – all male – had been suffering the obvious taunt for eight years: 'Beaten by a girl ... again?'

Now she is nineteen and still winning. One day soon, the image of her long hair spilling out of her helmet could open motor sport to new audiences, sponsors and perhaps a whole new lease of life. For in Brazil she is being spoken of as the possible future of Formula 1, the woman to transform an increasingly predictable sport.

The Ayrton Senna Kartodrome in Brazil is a theatre of dreams, and Bia Figueiredo is pursuing hers in the Brazilian Formula Renault Championship. 'The first time I went to the kartodrome,' she tells me, 'I was five or six. I begged my father to take me and became fond of the noise and the crashes. He told me I had to be seven before I could learn to drive. Somehow I managed to wait.'

Money pressures are inherent in motor racing, even for a family that is well-off, by most standards. Compared with other drivers at this level, Bia is disadvantaged. Bia's father, Jorge, says that Bia was already dreaming of Formula 1 at the age of six. And having encouraged his daughter's passion, he has accepted the financial burden with good humour. 'I once heard a Formula 1 team boss say it costs $10 million to become a Formula 1 driver. I said to myself, 'Okay. I'm only $9,990,000 short!'

Because of the expense, Bia could only do two fifty-minute tests before each race, when other drivers did four. She went to one of the best schools in São Paulo, which meant she was doing school work when other drivers were on the track. 'Given these constraints, she has done very well,' her father says. 'She was born with a forceful personality and, today, she's still forceful and has a caustic sense of humour. I feel a little sorry for anyone in her way!'

Motor racing would not be every father's chosen career for his daughter. 'Yes, it can be dangerous,' Jorge concedes. 'But the element of risk can be controlled. I'm much more afraid of Bia not doing what she likes. By pursuing what they enjoy, I think people have more chance of being happy.'

Yet Bia will have to deal with chauvinism. Not the least of the barriers facing her is whether motor sport is prepared to accept a genuine female contender. 'A beautiful woman is always welcome,' Alex Dias Ribeiro says, smiling and then adds: 'But she will have to be quick and mentally tough, because Formula 1 is a pressure cooker'.

One man who believes in Bia's potential is her mechanic and mentor of nine years, Naylor Borigis de Campos, who is better known simply as Nô. Nô has worked closely with most of Brazil's best drivers. He compares Bia favourably with the best of his protégés. 'She's as cool, aware and determined as Rubens Barrichello and as any other driver I've ever worked with.'

As for Bia herself, she believes in the future and in what she can achieve: 'I have a lot to learn, but my temperament is right: I've got plenty of animal instinct. I believe I have the potential to reach Formula 1, and perhaps one day be a great driver.'

Listening

6 Discuss. How difficult would it be to run a marathon/work abroad/start your own business? Would you ever consider doing any of these activities? How would you attempt/prepare to achieve them?

7 **1.5** Listen and answer the questions.

1 Which things has each speaker achieved?
2 What did each person say about their experience?
3 What challenges did they face?

Grammar | perfect aspect

8 Complete the tasks in the Active grammar box.

Active grammar

Verbs used in their perfect forms link two times. The perfect aspect is used to refer back from one point to a point in time before that. Match the examples from the listening to the time lines below.

a) *I'll have been here for three months.* (Future Perfect)

b) *Now my fiancée has come out to join me.* (Present Perfect)

c) *I'd never done anything like that before.* (Past Perfect)

1 Past and Present

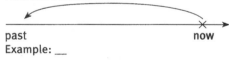

past   now
Example: __

2 Two points in the past

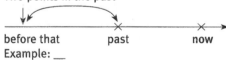

before that   past   now
Example: __

3 A point in the future

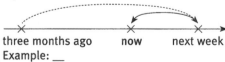

three months ago   now   next week
Example: __

Perfect tenses can be used in the simple or continuous forms. Perfect Continuous tenses, like other continuous tenses, focus on an event which continues, or is temporary.

Next March I'll have been playing with the team for five years.

I've been doing voluntary work all my adult life.

see Reference page 17

9 **a** Correct the mistakes in sentences 1–8.

1 Jake, this is my friend Amy, who I've been knowing for absolutely ages.
2 I asked what had been happened, but nobody could tell me.
3 I chose this school because I'd hear it was the best.
4 He should have finish by the time we get back.
5 Before I came to the US, I never been abroad.
6 I'm so exhausted. I'd been working really hard.
7 By the time she retires, she'll have be working there for more than fifty years.
8 I'll phone you as soon as we will have arrived.

b **1.6** Listen and check your answers.

c Practise saying the sentences.

Speaking

10 **a** Complete the How to ... box with the words in the box below.

> expect   decided   expectations   challenge

HOW TO ...	talk about an achievement	
Background information	*I've always ...* *I'd never done ...*	
Details	*We set up ...* *We _____ to organise ...*	
Problems	*I didn't know what to _____.* *The whole thing was quite a _____.* *It was very tough.*	
How it felt	*It exceeded my _____.* *We felt we'd accomplished something.* *It was a fantastic learning experience.*	
Results/ follow up	*I've learnt a lot* *I'm planning to ...*	

b Spend a few minutes thinking about your greatest achievement. Make notes using the headings in the How to ... box and then tell the class about your achievement.

1 Vocabulary

Prefixes

1 **a** Read the text and underline twelve prefixes.

On Saturday Mick Johnson, the multi-talented Londoner – previously a semi-professional basketball player – rescued a sub-standard performance by the unimpressive league leaders. With a superhuman effort, Johnson scored two goals in two minutes against arch-rivals Blackbridge Rovers. Trailing by one goal until the sixty-eighth minute, Johnson's overcautious team had looked tired and under-prepared. Johnson, probably the best footballer ever to play for Sidcup United, single-handedly brought his side back from the brink of disaster. Johnson's manager, Paul Deacon, said, 'They outplayed us. I don't know why we misfired so badly, but it's irrelevant. We got the goals and we took home the points.'

b Read the text again and answer the questions.

1 Which six prefixes are related to degree, size or quality?

2 Which three are related to numbers?

3 Which three give words the opposite or negative meaning?

c Write the prefixes in the table.

DEGREE, SIZE OR QUALITY	NUMBERS	OPPOSITE/ NEGATIVE
sub-	multi-	un

d Now add the prefixes **in bold** in sentences 1–4 below to the table.

1 Johnson had an early chance to score, but was **in**decisive with his shot.

2 'Winning the league isn't **im**possible for us,' said Deacon.

3 'Yeah, we won,' said the **mono**syllabic Johnson.

4 The team looked **de**motivated.

2 Add a synonym using a prefix. Use the root word in brackets.

A: He's a little bit rude!

B: Pardon?

A: He's rather _impolite_. (polite)

1 **A:** Our interpretation of the instructions was completely wrong.

 B: Pardon?

 A: We completely _____ the instructions. (understand)

2 **A:** I didn't know that you were a vegetarian.

 B: Sorry?

 A: I was _____ that you were a vegetarian. (aware)

3 **A:** I'm seventy years old. I quit my main job but I still work part-time.

 B: Pardon?

 A: I'm _____. (retire)

4 **A:** We lost the match because they had more players! There were ten of them, and only six of us.

 B: Really? So the numbers weren't equal?

 A: That's right. We were completely _____. (number)

5 **A:** I must go on a diet. I weigh too much.

 B: What?

 A: I'm _____. (weight)

6 **A:** My estimate was wrong. I thought there would be only ten people here, not fifty.

 B: Really?

 A: Yes, I _____ the numbers. (estimate)

3 **a** Work in pairs. Look at the opposites below. Where do you fit on a scale of 1–5?

	1	2	3	4	5	
1 super-fit	☐	☐	☐	☐	☐	totally unfit
2 talented	☐	☐	☐	☐	☐	untalented
3 imaginative	☐	☐	☐	☐	☐	unimaginative
4 overpaid	☐	☐	☐	☐	☐	underpaid
5 political	☐	☐	☐	☐	☐	apolitical

b Compare your position with other students.

Challenge yourself!

1 a Do the questionnaire. When you have finished, work with a partner and think of another question to add.

   b **1.7** Listen to someone describing what the answers say about your personality.

2 Discuss.

   1 Which would be the most difficult/easiest challenge for you? Why?
   2 What preparation would you need for each challenge?
   3 Do you think challenge involves being in extreme situations? Or are there more challenges in day-to-day life?
   4 Which do you think are the tougher – mental or physical challenges? Give examples.

DO YOU LIKE A CHALLENGE?

1 You are climbing a mountain with some friends. It is cold and wet and you are halfway up. You
   (a) feel like turning round and going home to a hot bath.
   (b) keep going. Nothing will stop you once you've started.
   (c) see what your friends want to do. It doesn't really matter if you reach the top.

2 You get an offer to work abroad for a year. But it means you have to learn a diffcult new language and live in an isolated place with no cinemas or cafés . You
   (a) refuse politely. Only a madman would live in the middle of nowhere.
   (b) accept. Who needs restaurants and cappuccino? And you may like it.
   (c) ask all your colleagues, friends and family what they think.

3 You are asked to perform in a local play. You will have to learn some lines and act in front of a large audience. You
   (a) say no. You might come and watch, but you aren't going to make a fool of yourself in public.
   (b) jump up on stage and start singing. This is your chance of fame and fortune.
   (c) ask exactly what you'll have to do, then say you'll think about it.

4 Your friends decide to do a parachute jump for charity. They want you to join them. You
   (a) refuse, saying you're too young to die.
   (b) immediately book lessons. What fun! And what a great view you'll have too!
   (c) find some statistics on the mortality rate of parachutists before committing yourself.

5 You are asked to cook for fifteen people. You
   (a) immediately find out the name of a good takeaway food restaurant, and make sure they'll be able to take your order on the night.
   (b) start dreaming of the delicious feast you will prepare. It could be a great night.
   (c) consult your parents' cookery books and work out how much it'll cost.

6 You are offered a place on a sailing boat that will go around the world. You
   (a) say no. You can't take the time off work and all that sea gets annoying after a while.
   (b) buy some large rubber boots and a sailing hat immediately. Nothing will stop you!
   (c) ask about the exact schedule and if there's Internet access on board and what the food will be like.

7 You are asked to be the babysitter for six young children for one evening. You
   (a) quickly think of a brilliant excuse – for example, you have tickets for a game or you need to wash your hair that evening, so you won't be available.
   (b) buy a large bag of balloons, chocolate cake and lots of children's games – it's going to be the party of the century!
   (c) ask for details of the children's behaviour, exact ages, and dietary requirements, then think about it.

8 A magazine wants you to write a piece about your hobby. You
   (a) explain that you're far too busy doing it, so you don't have time to write about it.
   (b) jump up and down with excitement, write three different drafts and offer them all to the editor the next day.
   (c) read twenty back copies of the magazine to see if you like it, then arrange a meeting with the editor to discuss the piece.

Verbs/adjectives with prepositions

There are many fixed phrases which use prepositions.

Verb + preposition: *opt for, distinguish from, succeed in, stem from, appeal to, bother about, rely on, benefit from*

Adjective + preposition: *short of, riddled with, lacking in, nervous about*

See page 8 for a full description of preposition use.

Passives

Passives can be used for 'distancing'. This means that the speaker/writer doesn't want the whole responsibility for the ideas they express. The passive is often used:

to make a statement less personal and slightly more polite.

We don't allow that. → *That isn't allowed.* (It isn't the speaker's decision; it is an impersonal rule).

You must hand in the essay by Friday. → *The essay must be handed in by Friday.*

in formal writing when the focus is on achievements and events rather than the people who were responsible.

The vaccine was discovered by chance.

There are some common passive expressions to show that we are not certain of a statement.

It is believed that the thief was an ex-employee.

It is said that he was able to speak more than twenty languages, but there is no proof.

It was claimed that the President had not seen the documents before the scandal broke out.

She was thought to have come from Germany originally, but there was little evidence.

He was reported to have been living in Brazil, but there was only one sighting of him.

Perfect aspect

We use the perfect aspect to refer from one point in time to another point in time before that. It shows that the speaker sees one event as (1) linked to a later event, or (2) finished by a certain time.

She'd lost her ticket so she missed the show.

By 6.00 I will have finished work.

We use the Present Perfect to describe something that happened:

during a period that includes past and present.

We've been here since 8.00a.m.

in the past but when the exact time isn't relevant to this discussion or isn't known.

She's lived in over twenty countries.

in the past but has a result or effect in the present.

Oh no! I've lost my passport.

in the very recent past (especially with *just*).

I've just heard the news.

We use the Past Perfect to talk about completed actions that happened before another action in the past.

She wanted to go to the castle, but we'd already been there.

We use the Future Perfect with time phrases with *by*. E.g. *by that time, by this time next week, by the end of February, by the end of the day*, etc.

By June we will have finished the project.

We often use the perfect aspect with *for*, *since* and *just*.

By January, I will have been here for a year.

I've just been speaking to Mickey.

I felt it was time to move because I'd been living there since 1967.

Challenges

set achievable goals   face challenges
rises to the challenge   make my dream come true
couldn't have done it without   burning ambition
have the right attitude   daunting challenge

Phrases about language

pick up   let (sth) slide   master   garble   on the ball
information overload   cram   babble   unintelligibly

Saying how much you know

I haven't a clue   I don't know it off the top of my head
I'm pretty sure   I've never heard of him   by heart
I know it like the back of my hand   inside out
I don't know offhand   next to nothing
I'm fairly positive   I haven't the faintest idea

Achievements

head (straight for the top)   pursue (a dream)
deal with ... (chauvinism)   face (barriers)
believe in (what you can achieve)
have the potential (to do something)
persevere (with something)   learning experience
keep pushing someone (to do something)
exceed expectations   quite a challenge

Prefixes

super-fit   unfit   multi-talented   polyglot
monolingual   underpaid   overpaid   apolitical
monosyllabic   demotivated   arch-rival   indecisive
single-handedly   outplayed   semi-professional
sub-standard   misfired   irrelevant

1 Choose the correct word/expression below to complete the text.

The language, Hawaiian Creole, was invented through necessity. In 1880, thousands of immigrants from Europe and Asia went to work for the English-speaking owners of sugar plantations in Hawaii. Among all the other challenges these immigrants (1)_____, the most (2)_____ was to understand each other, to understand their bosses, and to understand the Hawaiian people. To these immigrants, other ethnic groups must have sounded as if they were (3)_____. After a short time, they were able to (4)_____ some English, but barely enough to communicate. Instead, they (5)_____ body language and a simple code of sounds.

However, things changed fast, and by 1910 a new language had emerged: Hawaiian Creole. This included words and sounds from other languages, but could be (6)_____ all of them by its different grammar. Hawaiian Creole, a simple dialect, is (7)_____ complex structures. With this new easily-understood language, everybody (8)_____ increased communication.

Many years later, Derek Bickerton studied the origins of Hawaiian Creole. He was amazed that within one generation, the immigrants had (9)_____ creating a language that was (10)_____ to all. In fact, in his book *Roots of Language*, he says that the children invented the language while playing together.

1 (a) made (b) knew (c) faced
2 (a) daunting (b) definite (c) harsh
3 (a) babbling (b) garbling (c) cramming
4 (a) discuss (b) pick up (c) pick out
5 (a) persisted in (b) appealed to (c) relied on
6 (a) riddled with (b) distinguished from (c) defined by
7 (a) reminds you of (b) stemming from (c) lacking in
8 (a) benefited from (b) benefited (c) mastered
9 (a) opted for (b) succeeded to (c) succeeded in
10 (a) intelligible (b) unintelligible (c) intelligibly

2 Add one word to each bulletin to make it correct.

1 Giant multinational research centre Sci-Corps seems to abandoned its research into cloning after pressure from the government.
2 Ex-President Michael Nkrumah is said be recovering well from the stroke he suffered last Thursday.
3 Michaela Kritzkoff, the explorer who disappeared for a month while canoeing along the Amazon, has been found in a village in Brazil. It believed that she had drowned during a storm.
4 British Commonwealth boxing champion Roderick Bland appears to finally retired, at the age of forty-six.
5 And finally, it seems if summer really is coming. Sarah Smith reports on tomorrow's weather.

3 One of these sentences is correct. Rewrite the others using a perfect tense.

I've never seen the man before yesterday, when he knocked on my door.

I'd never seen the man before yesterday, when he knocked on my door.

1 By the time she finishes her degree, she will be at the university ten years.
2 He was delighted when they told him he got the job.
3 I feel healthier now that I took up kickboxing.
4 Where were you? I've been waited here for at least an hour!
5 It was a shock when I saw him. I would expected to see a big man, but he was tiny.
6 When she got to work, she found out she was fired. Her desk was empty, everything gone.
7 Hi, John! We've just talked about you!
8 It's 9.00. Mandy will land at Heathrow Airport by now.
9 I'd been running for years before I entered my first competition.
10 We'll have use up all the world's oil long before 2100.

4 Put B's words in order to complete the dialogues.

A: What is Pelé's real first name?
B: pretty I'm Edson it's sure.

I'm pretty sure it's Edson.

1 A: Have you ever been to Prague?
B: yes, I of the hand like my back it know.
2 A: How many women have succeeded in Formula 1 racing?
B: I many know not but don't offhand.
3 A: Can you help me with my homework? I need some information about space travel.
B: know nothing it to next about I.
4 A: When's the best time to go there?
B: far as concerned as never, I'm.
5 A: Who's Michael Vaughan?
B: never him heard I've of.
6 A: Who's the President of Colombia?
B: head I top tell off the can't of my you.

2 Community

Lead-in

1 Discuss. What types of community are shown in the photos? What are the positive/negative aspects of each?

2 **a** Unjumble the <u>underlined</u> words/expressions in the sentences below to find out what makes a place good/bad to live in. Mark each sentence positive (+) or negative (−).

1 reasonable <u>octs</u> of <u>glinvi</u> – not too expensive
2 <u>onactsilopom</u> – has people from many countries
3 good transport <u>rftersauurtnci</u> – well-organised buses, trains, etc.
4 <u>ldim</u> climate – not extreme weather; not too hot or too cold
5 personal <u>ermefod</u> – you are allowed to do what you want
6 efficient <u>ecraehalht</u> system – plenty of good hospitals
7 good <u>addsarnt</u> of <u>ilgniv</u> – you can have a good lifestyle
8 interesting historical <u>emmusntno</u> – ancient buildings, etc.
9 high <u>emcir</u> <u>reta</u> – many crimes per year
10 high level of <u>pnmletouneym</u> – many people don't have jobs
11 traffic <u>noncsogtei</u> – too many cars for the amount of space
12 <u>ooitpulln</u> – dirty air
13 racial <u>nnesito</u> – people of different races don't like/trust each other
14 no-go <u>rseaa</u> – places where it's too dangerous to walk around
15 no <u>utllruac</u> life – lack of theatres, cinemas and art galleries, etc.

b Discuss. Which four positive/negative things are the most important to you? Why?

| Grammer | verb patterns 1 |
| Can do | give advice/make recommendations about places |

Listening

1 Discuss.

　1 Have you ever (or do you know anyone who has ever) lived abroad?

　2 What were your/their impressions?

　3 What problems might there be for people living in a foreign country?

2　a　**2.1** Listen to three speakers discussing their experiences and make notes in the table.

	SPEAKER 1	SPEAKER 2	SPEAKER 3
1　Where did he/she live?			
2　What was he/she doing there?			
3　What did he/she like about the host country?			
4　Was there anything he/she didn't like, or that was difficult?			
5　What are his/her favourite memories of the country?			

b　Which of the speakers (1, 2 or 3):

1 pretended something?

2 got a few surprises?

3 was there at the wrong time?

4 is from a small town?

5 would like to return?

6 learned about the culture by talking to the local people?

7 says the place was multicultural?

8 has lived in many countries?

9 doesn't mention the scenery?

10 describes a special type of cooking?

c　Listen again to check.

3　Discuss.

1 Which of the places in Ex. 2 would you most like to live in? Why?

2 Would you like to live abroad for a while? Why/why not?

3 Why do you think the speakers talk mainly about food, scenery and people? Which of these is the most important in a place?

Grammar | verb patterns 1

4 a Work in pairs. Find and correct the grammatical mistakes in sentences 1–15.

A

1 I'm **thinking** take a break.
2 If you can't **afford** eating in expensive restaurants, Vancouver has lots of cheaper ones.
3 I can't **imagine** live there.
4 We **look forward** to see you.
5 You can **avoid** to offending people by learning the host country's customs.

B

6 I don't **mind** to queue, but it took hours to get into the museum!
7 I don't **fancy** live there.
8 She doesn't **want** that she misses out on 'fusion cuisine'.
9 I can't **stand** to travel on the Tokyo underground.
10 If you **object** to pay lots of money for clothes, don't go shopping in Ginza, Tokyo.

C

11 I **advise** you going to the Salzburg music festival.
12 I'd **encourage** all foreigners to try some real sushi.
13 I'd **urge** you seeing Stanley Park in Vancouver.
14 I'd **recommend** to go to Tokyo Art Gallery.
15 She **persuaded** us visit Austria in the spring.

b Answer the questions.

1 Which group of sentences is connected with
   (1) recommendations?
   (2) likes or dislikes?
2 Which of the verbs in group B have a very similar meaning? Which is/are the strongest?
3 Which of the verbs in group C have a very similar meaning? Which is/are the strongest?

5 Complete the table in the Active grammar box using the verbs **in bold** in Ex. 4a.

Active grammar

Verb + -ing	Verb + infinitive	Verb + object + infinitive with to	Verb + preposition + -ing

see Reference page 31

6 Rewrite the sentences below using the verbs **in bold**. Begin each sentence with *I*, *I'd* or *I'm*.

You really must go to the National Gallery. **urge**

I'd urge you to go to the National Gallery.

1 I don't have the money to go to the theatre. **afford**
2 You should go to Brixton Market on Sunday. **advise**
3 I think people ought to use the parks more. **encourage**
4 It will be good to see you next weekend. **look forward**
5 You should buy tickets early for Buckingham Palace. **recommend**
6 I never take Intercity trains because they're too expensive. **avoid**
7 I'd like to take a short trip to Paris. **fancy**
8 I may go to Thailand in February. **think**

Speaking and writing

7 Put the words below into the correct place in the How to ... box.

> wary   were   out   found   value   sure   all

HOW TO ... give advice/make recommendations about places

Saying it's good	It's a must/a must-see.
	It's good _____ for money.
Saying it's not so good	It's a bit overrated/overpriced.
	It's not _____ it's cracked up to be.
	I _____ it a bit dull/touristy.
Recommending	If I _____ you, I'd go to ...
	Don't miss .../Make _____ you go to ...
	You should try -*ing* ...
	I suggest going .../that you go there.
Warning	Watch _____ for ...
	One thing to be _____ of is ...

8 Choose an aspect of life in your country, e.g. customs, food, places to go and write a web page of advice for visitors. Try to use the expressions from the How to ... box.

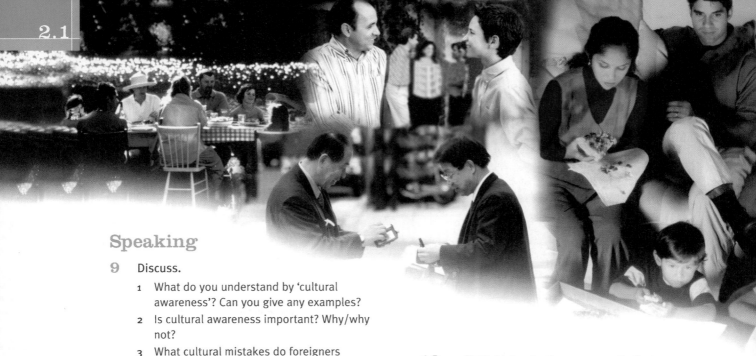

Speaking

9 Discuss.

1 What do you understand by 'cultural awareness'? Can you give any examples?

2 Is cultural awareness important? Why/why not?

3 What cultural mistakes do foreigners sometimes make in your country?

4 Are there any customs/habits that are acceptable in your country but impolite in other countries?

10 Make sentences 1–8 more polite using the words in the box below.

> possibly   mind   were   was   wouldn't   wondering   think   possible

1 Open the window. → Would you _____ opening the window?

2 Be quiet. → Could you _____ be a bit quieter?

3 Slow down. → Do you _____ you could slow down a bit?

4 I thought you could come earlier. → I _____ hoping you could come earlier.

5 Can you give me a hand with this? → I was _____ if you could give me a hand with this.

6 Can I come back later? → Would it be _____ for me to come back later?

7 You should take a coat. → If I _____ you, I'd take a coat.

8 No, you're wrong. → I _____ have thought so.

11 Rewrite sentences 1–8 so they sound more polite. Use the words in brackets.

1 Shut the door. (mind)

2 Can you give me a lift? (wondering)

3 Pass the salt. (possibly)

4 Can I use your phone? (possible)

5 I disagree. (wouldn't)

6 Keep the noise down. (think)

7 Help us with the luggage. (hoping)

8 Leave a bit earlier. (if/were)

12 a **2.2** Listen to the answers. Notice the intonation.

b Listen again and repeat.

13 Match the different ways to avoid criticising too directly in 1–4 to sentences a–d below.

1 Give a negative opinion in the positive or vice versa.

2 Use modal verbs *could*, *may* and *might* to sound less direct.

3 Use opinion words to make the criticism 'only' an opinion, not fact.

4 Use understatement (making the criticism sound less serious than it is).

a) Why don't you do more exercise? → You could think about doing more exercise.

b) You aren't good enough for this class. → You aren't quite the right level for this class.

c) It's the worst essay you've ever done. → It's not the best essay you've ever done.

d) That's not the best way to fix it. → In my view, that's not the best way to fix it.

14 a Work with a partner to make B's sentences less direct.

1 A: What do you think of the new restaurant?
   B: It's terrible.

2 A: I want to get fitter.
   B: You should smoke less.

3 A: I can never remember new vocabulary.
   B: Why don't you study a bit harder?

4 A: Do you like his new book?
   B: No, it's rubbish.

b In pairs, write a few more lines of dialogue and then act them out in front of the class.

Listening

1 Discuss.

1 How often do you use the Internet? What do you use it for?

2 Are there any websites that you use frequently? What do you like about them?

3 Do you trust what you read on the Internet? Why/why not?

4 Has the increased use of computers and the Internet been a good thing (a) for you (b) in general?

2 **2.3** Listen to two people discussing some of the questions above. Which issues do they discuss? Are their views similar to yours?

3 Listen again and tick (✓) the phrases you hear.

1 (It's) miles easier

2 (It's) far easier

3 (It's) nowhere near as ... as

4 (It's) nothing like as good as

5 rather than + -ing, I'm better off + -ing

6 the less we ..., the less we ...

7 the more we ..., the more we ...

8 I'd prefer to ...

9 I'd rather ... than ...

10 It's not quite as ... as ...

11 It's definitely not as ... as

12 It's considerably + comparative (formal)

13 It's marginally + comparative (formal)

14 (It's) much the same

15 (It's) much + superlative

16 I'd sooner go ...

Grammar | comparatives review

4 Complete the table in the Active grammar box using the phrases in Ex. 3.

> ### Active grammar
>
> | | |
> |---|---|
> | 1 A big difference | |
> | 2 A little difference | |
> | 3 Describing preference | |
> | 4 *The* + comparative + *the* + comparative | |
>
> Add the words/expressions *in italics* to the table above.
> *slightly   a tiny bit   far   decidedly*

see Reference page 31

5 ⃝Circle the incorrect alternative in each sentence.

1 *I'd rather/I'd sooner/I'd quite prefer to* communicate by email than telephone.

2 Buying things in shops is *not like/nowhere near/nothing like* as cheap as shopping online.

3 *You're much better off/It's best/It's considerably easier* writing on a computer than doing it by hand.

4 The more you know about using computers, *the easier/easier/the simpler* it becomes.

5 Buying things online is *marginally/extremely/slightly* more risky than face-to-face transactions.

6 It's *a mile/considerably/far* easier to find information on the Internet than in books.

7 *The more we rely on/The more we use/As much as we use* computers, the more vulnerable we are to hackers and computer viruses.

8 *I'd better off playing/I'd sooner play/I'd rather play* games outside than computer games.

Person to person

6 **a** Look at the sentences in Ex. 5 again. How do you feel about each issue on a scale of 1–5 (1 = completely disagree and 5 = agree completely)?

b Discuss your views with other students.

The Internet's largest encyclopaedia

Reading

7 Discuss. Have you ever heard of or used Wikipedia? If so, what is special about it? If not, what do you think it is?

8 Read the text and match the paragraphs to the headings below.

a) THE ORIGINS OF THE WIKI WORD

b) WIKIPEDIA'S BIG NUMBERS

c) GETTING STARTED

d) WIKIPEDIA – A DEFINITION

e) CAN YOU TRUST WIKIPEDIA'S FACTS?

f) JIMMY WALES – ONE HAPPY CHAP

g) THE WEIRD AND WONDERFUL THINGS JIMMY FINDS IN HIS INBOX

9 Answer the questions.

1 What is Wikipedia?

2 What is a wiki?

3 Who is Jimmy Wales and what's he like?

4 What problems has Wikipedia had?

5 What criticisms has it faced?

10 a Read the article again quickly. Is it formal or informal in style? How do you know?

b Put the headings from the box below next to the correct examples in the How to ... box.

> Humour   Informal vocabulary   Style (spoken English)
> Ellipsis (omitting words)

HOW TO ...

recognise features of an informal writing style

A) Headings   B) Examples

	guy (paragraph 1) *kooks* (paragraph 1)
	say (paragraph 1) *Oh my God* (paragraph 1) Short forms: *who've* (paragraph 1), *you'll* (paragraph 5)
	Need to solve a thorny business problem ... (paragraph 3). The full question = *Do you need to solve ...* 'And the name?' (paragraph 3)
	An Encyclopaedia Britannica editor once likened Wikipedia to a public toilet seat because you don't know who used it last. (paragraph 2)

c Answer the questions in pairs.

1 What are the formal words for 'guy' and 'kook'?

2 Are there other examples in the text of (a) informal vocabulary (b) spoken English (c) humour?

3 What is the full version of: 'And Wikipedia's growth?'

1

Being the founder of the Internet's largest encyclopaedia means Jimmy Wales gets a lot of bizarre emails. There are the correspondents who assume he wrote Wikipedia himself and is therefore an expert on everything – like the guy who found some strange chemicals in his late grandfather's attic and wanted Wales to tell him what to do with them. There are kooks who claim to have found, say, a 9,000-year-old fifteen-foot human skeleton and wonder if Wales would be interested. But the emails that make him laugh out loud come from concerned newcomers who've just discovered they have total freedom to edit a Wikipedia entry at the click of a button. 'Oh my God,' they write, 'you've got a major security flaw.'

2

Wikipedia is a free open-source encyclopaedia, which basically means that anyone can log on and add to it or edit it. And they do. It has a stunning 1.5 million entries in seventy-six languages – and counting. Academics are upset by what they see as info anarchy. An Encyclopaedia Britannica editor once likened Wikipedia to a public toilet seat because you don't know who used it last. Loyal users claim that collaboration improves articles over time.

3

But what exactly is a wiki and how does it work? Wikis are deceptively simple pieces of software that you can download for free. You then use them to set up a website that can be edited by anyone you like. Need to solve a thorny business problem overnight and all the members of your team are in different time zones? Start a wiki. And the name? Believe it or not, the name came about because the inventor of the wiki had his honeymoon in Hawaii, where you catch the 'wiki wiki' (quick) bus from the airport.

4

Anyway, just five years ago, Jimmy Wales was looking for a way to combine his two major hobbies: perusing the Encyclopaedia Britannica and surfing the Internet. 'I met all these great people online,' he says, 'and we were all discussing things on mailing lists no one ever looks at. I thought, why not build something more long-lasting, more fun and entertaining?'

5

Ah, fun. Spend enough time talking to Wales – a confessed 'pathological optimist' – and you'll believe his life has been one long riot of laughter. Options and futures trading, which he did in Chicago in the 1990s, was 'fun and cool'. Quitting his job to start an Internet company? Delightful. Paying the mortgage purely from investments? Fantastic. And Wikipedia's growth? Simply amazing.

6

Wikipedia is the cumulative work of 16,000 people, the bulk of it done by a hard-core group of around 1,000 volunteers. Its 500,000 entries in English alone make it far larger than the Encyclopaedia Britannica. And Wales pays just one employee who keeps the servers ticking.

Naturally there are a lot of idiots, vandals and fanatics, who take advantage of Wikipedia's open system to deface, delete or push one-sided views. Sometimes extreme action has to be taken. For example, Wales locked the entries on John Kerry and George W. Bush for most of the 2004 Presidential election campaign. But for the most part, the geeks have a huge advantage: they care more. According to an MIT study, obscene comments randomly inserted on Wikipedia are removed within 100 seconds, on average. Vandals might as well be spray-painting walls with disappearing ink.

7

As for edit wars, in which two geeks with opposing views delete each other's assertions over and over, well, they're not much of a problem these days. All kinds of viewpoints co-exist in the same article. Take the entry on, er, Wikipedia: 'Wikipedia has been criticised for a perceived lack of reliability, comprehensiveness and authority.' Indeed, Larry Sanger, Wikipedia's former editor-in-chief (now a university lecturer), still likes the site but thinks his fellow professionals have a point. 'The wide-open nature of the Internet encourages people to disregard the importance of expertise,' he says. Sanger doesn't let his students use Wikipedia for their papers, partly because he knows they could confirm anything they like by adding it themselves.

11 Are the following generally used in formal or informal texts: full verb forms, lots of phrasal verbs, sentences beginning with *and* or *but*, repeated use of the passive?

12 Read the two formal emails below. Some of the words/phrases used are too informal. Replace them with a more appropriate word/phrase from the box below.

> regards   attend   don't hesitate to   concerning   following
> will be very happy to attend   will be unable to attend
> a previous arrangement   we would be grateful if you could
> could you please confirm your attendance   queries   requested

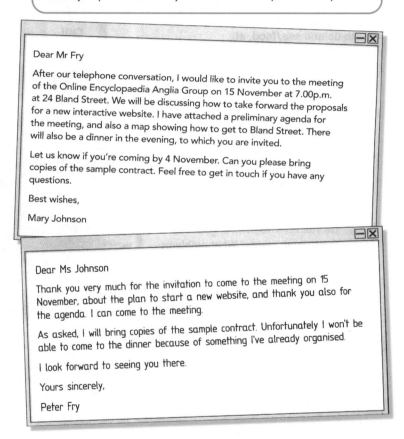

Dear Mr Fry

After our telephone conversation, I would like to invite you to the meeting of the Online Encyclopaedia Anglia Group on 15 November at 7.00p.m. at 24 Bland Street. We will be discussing how to take forward the proposals for a new interactive website. I have attached a preliminary agenda for the meeting, and also a map showing how to get to Bland Street. There will also be a dinner in the evening, to which you are invited.

Let us know if you're coming by 4 November. Can you please bring copies of the sample contract. Feel free to get in touch if you have any questions.

Best wishes,

Mary Johnson

Dear Ms Johnson

Thank you very much for the invitation to come to the meeting on 15 November, about the plan to start a new website, and thank you also for the agenda. I can come to the meeting.

As asked, I will bring copies of the sample contract. Unfortunately I won't be able to come to the dinner because of something I've already organised.

I look forward to seeing you there.

Yours sincerely,

Peter Fry

Writing

13 a Read the formal email in the Writing bank on page 162 and do the exercises.

b Read the information in the box and write a formal email. Pay particular attention to greeting and signing off, coherence and cohesion, punctuation, spelling and style.

> You are a famous person. You read your entry in Wikipedia. It made some rude comments about you and contained a number of factual errors. You tried to edit the Wikipedia entry, but it was 'locked' so you were unable to change it. Write to Wikipedia complaining about this. Make sure you include corrections of the facts and explain why you think the comments about you are unfair. Ask for the changes to be made as soon as possible.

Cali

Reading

1 Discuss. What do you know about the places in the photos? What do you think they are like? Would you like to visit them? Why/why not?

2 Work in groups. Student A: read the text about Cali. Student B: read the text about Cape Town and Student C: read the text about Corsica. Make notes about the atmosphere/things to do and see/food, etc.

3 Describe the place to the other members of your group.

4 Discuss.

1 Each place is described as a type of 'paradise'. Which aspects of these places sound perfect to you? What makes them unique?

2 Which place would you prefer to go to for a holiday? Why?

3 Do you think tourism is good for these three places? What problems might it bring them?

Cape Town

TEXT A

Cali

1 In Cali, they say, even the ghosts play guitar. Music can be heard in cafes on buses, along the avenues of Juanchito and Plaza Caicedo, and here too, in a taxi moving at the speed of light, taking me to the heart of the bustling city. The driver slows down at a traffic light, turns to me and says, 'Our people are the happiest men in the world!' And we're off again, driving past gangs of *mulato* men laughing in the street.

2 My hotel is a run-down old building whose blue skin is peeling in the heat. It has a stunning view from the balcony, and I gaze down on the square. The guidebooks tell you to visit the Gold Museum and the Museum of Colonial Art, the churches of San Antonio and La Merced.

3 The *musicians* don't get busy until night so instead I stop at a restaurant serving typical Colombian food: *sancocho* – a stew made with chunks of beef, vegetables, cassava (a tropical plant with edible roots) and plantain (a type of banana but not so sweet) served with rice. Then I must choose from the amazingly diverse selection of Colombian fruit. I settle for guanabana and maracuya, and I'm not disappointed. I stroll for a while, tempted by dark smoky cafés, the fans spinning weakly on the ceilings. This is the old, unspoilt Cali, which lives side by side with a newer version, the Cali of junk food, Internet cafés and vast touristy places. I walk past the trees and sculptures that line the river, and into San Antonio park, a tranquil spot off the beaten track.

4 Later, on Avenida Sexta – Sixth Avenue – I find what I'm really looking for: a *guitarist*. Some charming young Colombians teach me a few notes of a famous tune and we chat about Cali. They say that when times are tough, they play guitar to forget their worries. By 10.00 p.m. the place is packed, and I know one thing for sure: I've found the Cali that I was looking for – the musician's paradise.

TEXT C

Corsica

1 'Day in, day out, they're always watching: the shepherd on the hillside, the road workers resting under the shade of a tree, the old man on the bench in front of his house, his wife airing the sheets at the window, the boules player next to the war memorial. They hardly move their heads but they see everything. It's a survival instinct moulded out of two thousand years of dangers coming from across the sea.'

2 The stereotypical Corsican community is introverted, family-based, dignified and shy. The truth behind the stereotype is that Corsicans like Corsica so much that they don't want the outside world to ruin it. Tradition is important; Corsica is one of the last McDonald's-free zones in Europe. It is also simply stunning; the ancient Greeks called it 'Kalliste', meaning 'the most beautiful one'.

3 The island is famed for its diverse landscape. You can find magnificent mountains, long stretches of Mediterranean coastline, and thick forest almost side by side, as well as charming villages, perfect for long, slow days in the sun. The island belongs to France but it has an atmosphere all of its own.

Corsica

4 A good place to start is Ajaccio. In this charming town, you can sit outside the cafés and watch fishermen mending their nets, or stroll in the bustling market which sells delicious seafood and Corsican specialities: *macchia* honey and *brocciu* cheese. Old run-down houses stand proud on the side of the hill, overlooking modern yachts and wooden boats. Stroll along the streets and you will notice something interesting as you gaze at the monuments, the street signs and restaurant names: the town stands in the vast shadow of its greatest son, Napoleon Bonaparte. His influence is everywhere, and in the Musée Napoléonien you can see his baptism certificate and his death mask.

5 Although Napoleon is at the heart of Corsican history, it is Corsica's natural beauty that you'll remember. Fishermen, surfers, sailors and hikers all find everything they need here. And for the less energetic, there is always the pleasure of a wander along some of Europe's most tranquil scenery. Despite the tourists, the island is unspoilt. You won't find any packed clubs here, but there are plenty of cosy cafés off the beaten track, where you can taste the atmosphere of Europe's own natural paradise.

XT B

Cape Town

1 The first thing I can tell you about Thabo, my South African guide, is that he is the world's worst driver. From the airport to the heart of the city, he does 100 km per hour, swerving around lorries, motorbikes and taxi-vans crammed with people. The second thing is that he knows everybody and everything about Cape Town. This is good, because I am trying to complete *Mission Impossible*: see Cape Town in just three days.

2 On the first day, Thabo takes me to the posh areas: suburbs with unpronounceable names – Tamboerskloof and Oranjezicht – from where you can watch the sun go down on Africa. The views are stunning. 'This is all very pretty,'

I tell him that evening, 'but show me a community. Show me something the tourists never see.' So the next day we go off the beaten track to Cape Flats, the run-down township where the buildings are made of cardboard and corrugated iron. It is the poorest part of the city and it is truly vast – nearly a million people live here, side by side. Skinny pets slide out of the way as Thabo zooms along roads of mud and rotting rubbish. Some people wave, others stare. Children run barefoot by the car.

3 Later that night we walk around the bustling Victoria and Alfred Waterfront, Cape Town's most stylish area. The contrast from the township could not be greater. As we stroll, the smells of cooking drift up from the kitchens – Asian, French, Italian and of course the wild animals of South Africa that

end up on your plate. The cafés and restaurants are packed, and I soon find out why. Cape Town is a paradise for people like me, who just like eating seafood. We go into a charming little bistro, and Thabo tells me I can't leave Cape Town without trying some Cape seafood, so I do. It's delicious.

4 On my final morning, we spend a tranquil hour sitting outside a café. I gaze at Table Mountain, which forms the backdrop to the city, while Thabo shouts greetings to everyone that passes by. Then we are driving again, experiencing the diverse landscape – sandy beaches, mountain slopes and green valleys unspoilt by tourism. It's a great way to say goodbye to a place I've known only too briefly. I promise myself, and Thabo, that I'll be back.

Vocabulary | adjectives to describe places

5 Work in groups. Find words in the texts on pages 26–27 that mean:

1 not damaged in character or atmosphere_____ (text A: para. 3, text B: para. 4, text C: para. 5)

2 having variety _____ (text A: para. 3, text B: para. 4, text C: para. 3)

3 look at something interesting for a long time _____ (text A: para. 2, text B: para. 4, text C: para. 4)

4 peaceful _____ (text A: para. 3, text B: para. 4, text C: para. 5)

5 the centre _____ (text A: para. 1, text B: para. 1, text C: para. 5)

6 next to each other (3 words) _____ (text A: para. 3, text B: para. 2, text C: para. 3)

7 in areas people don't normally go to (usually outside the city) (4 words) _____ (text A: para. 3, text B: para. 2, text C: para. 5)

8 extremely large _____ (text A: para. 3, text B: para. 2, text C: para. 4)

9 in poor condition, uncared for _____ (text A: para. 2, text B: para. 2, text C: para. 4)

10 amazingly beautiful _____ (text A: para. 2, text B: para. 2, text C: para. 2)

11 so attractive and pleasing that you admire it/them _____ (text A: para. 4, text B: para. 3, text C: para. 3)

12 very busy, crowded _____ (text A: para. 4, text B: para. 3, text C: para. 5)

13 energetic and noisy, full of life _____ (text A: para. 1, text B: para. 3, text C: para. 4)

14 walk in a relaxed way _____ (text A: para. 3, text B: para. 3, text C: para. 4)

6 a Use the vocabulary in **Ex. 5** to complete the sentences.

1 The roof is falling off and the windows are broken; the old house looks very _____.

2 It's hard to find the little villa in the countryside because it's _____.

3 You can hardly move during carnival time because the streets are absolutely _____.

4 There are many different nationalities living there, so the culture is very _____.

5 My favourite holiday activity is lying on a beach and _____ at stars all night.

6 The Sahara Desert is 9,100,000 square kilometres. It's absolutely _____.

7 We're going to spend a _____ few days camping, far from the noisy city.

8 The town remains _____ even though there are lots of tourists now. It hasn't changed at all.

b Now use the vocabulary to describe the places in the photos above.

Speaking and writing

7 Work in pairs. Think of a place you have been to that (a) has stunning views, (b) is off the beaten track, (c) serves delicious food, (d) is in the heart of the town/city, (e) is tranquil, (f) is bustling at the weekends, (g) is good to stroll around. Tell your partner about them.

8 a Decide on a favourite place. It could be another country or another city. Think about atmosphere, landscape, things to see/do and food. Make some notes.

b Write a short paragraph (100–150 words) about your favourite place.

c Read your paragraphs to the rest of the class. Decide which would be best for a group holiday.

Phrasal verbs

1 Read the texts below. Would you like to join any of these communities? Why/why not? Would you like to join them temporarily or permanently?

1
They said it was a passing trend that would never catch on. They were wrong. When I turned up at the Chrysalis Hippy Commune forty years after I'd left it, nothing had changed. Living here, you can still get by on $50 a week, and you'll have no problems fitting in. Everyone is welcome.

2
We decided to do up a small barn in a tiny rural village. No water, no electricity, no Internet! We filled in some forms to get planning permission, and this took months. Then the terrible weather held us up so we couldn't start renovating. Finally, a year later, the house was finished. We knew nobody in the community except John, who had carried out most of the work.

3
I first came across Claudio and the surfing community in São Paulo. I'd never surfed before, but I took to it immediately. Claudio told me they were expecting giant waves at the end of the summer, so I practised every day and saw to it that I was ready. When the big waves came, I got through it OK.

4
I came up with the idea of starting an online book community. It seemed like a good way to keep up with the latest books. Anyone is welcome to write reviews and post them on the site. It really comes down to democratising the process, because we wanted to get away from the idea that you need a degree in order to write and read reviews.

2 Find four phrasal verbs in each text and match them to the correct meaning.

Text 1
a) arrive
b) feel comfortable in a social group
c) survive financially
d) become stylish

Text 2
a) complete paperwork
b) restore/redecorate
c) delay someone
d) put ideas/instructions into practice

Text 3
a) finish successfully
b) meet/find by chance
c) organise/manage
d) like something/someone

Text 4
a) escape/avoid
b) be essentially
c) invent/think of
d) know about recent developments

3 There are four types of phrasal verb and each text in Ex. 1 contains one type. Match a–d to the correct text and definition.

Text 1 _____ (verb + particle) – no direct object.

*The plane **took off**.*

Text 2 _____ (verb + particle) – with a direct object. If the object is a noun, it can come between the verb and the particle or after the particle.

*I **paid back** the money. I **paid** the money **back**.*

Text 3 _____ (verb + particle) – with a direct object that always goes after the particle.

*She **looked after** me. NOT: ~~She looked me after~~.*

Text 4 _____ (verb + particle + preposition) – with a direct object that usually goes after the preposition.

*I went on a spa break to **get away from** it all.*

a) transitive (1)
b) transitive (2)
c) intransitive
d) three-part phrasal verbs

4 **a** Ask and answer the questions in pairs.

1 Did you take to your partner or best friend immediately? Why/why not?
2 Do you have to come up with ideas at work/school?
3 Have you come across any interesting people/books/places in the last few months?
4 Do you usually turn up early, on time or late for appointments? What does it depend on?
5 Do you do anything special to get away from your daily routine? What?
6 Do you keep up with new developments in your work/hobby? How?
7 When was the last time you filled in a form? What was it for?

b Tell the class one thing you learned about your partner.

Lifelong learning

Personalise phrasal verbs

When you learn a new phrasal verb, write it in a sentence about yourself or your friends/family. This will help you to remember the form and meaning of the phrasal verb. Choose five of the phrasal verbs above and do this.

Start a club

1 **a** Read about a club. Do you think the club is
    (a) silly? (b) funny? (c) a good idea?

THE NOT TERRIBLY GOOD CLUB

IN 1976 STEPHEN PILE formed 'The Not Terribly Good Club'. To qualify for membership, you had to be not terribly good at something and then attend meetings. During these meetings people gave public demonstrations of things they couldn't do, such as painting and singing, and gave awful presentations on things they knew nothing about. Stephen Pile kept a record of these unsuccessful events, and then published them as 'The Book of Heroic Failures' in 1979. The stories included epic examples of incompetence, such as the World's Worst Tourist, who spent two days in New York, believing he was in Rome; 'the slowest solution of a crossword' (thirty-four years); and the burglar who wore metal armour to protect himself from dogs – the armour made so much noise that he got caught, and it was too heavy for him to run away. Included in 'The Book of Heroic Failures' was an application form for membership to 'The Not Terribly Good Club'. Amazingly, within two months of the book's publication, the group had received 20,000 applications to join, and the book appeared on various bestseller lists. As a result of his sudden fame, Pile was kicked out of his own club, and the club itself soon disbanded: it had become too successful.

CAN YOU TELL ME THE WAY TO THE COLISEUM?

b If you were joining The Not Terribly Good Club what would your presentation be about?

2 **a** **2.4** Listen to the man describing the club he belongs to. Complete the notes as you listen.

   1 **Old boys' club**
      The main idea of the club:
      Other things that it does:
      Type of meeting:
      Who can be a member:
      Problems:

   b Compare your notes with a partner.

3 Work in groups. You are going to form a club. Think about the following questions.
   1 What type of club is it?
   2 What events will you organise?
   3 How will you know if the club is successful? (What are your goals?)
   4 What is the name of the club?
   5 Where will you meet?
   6 How often?
   7 How many people can join the club?
   8 What do people have to do to join?
   9 What rules will the club have?
   10 What will the club's symbol, logo, motto or song be?

4 Present your ideas to the rest of the class. Which clubs would you like to join?

Verb patterns 1

When one verb follows another, the second verb is either *-ing* form or infinitive.

Some of the verbs which use an *-ing* form after them are related in meaning. These verbs show personal tastes:

adore, fancy, don't mind, detest, can't stand

I *adore living* here.

I *can't stand listening* to their music all night.

Other verbs take an object + infinitive. (*I told her to come here.*) Some of these verbs are also related in meaning. These verbs show one person (or thing) influencing the actions of another:

warn, tell, advise, urge, order, persuade, encourage, force, forbid, allow

I *persuaded her to visit* me.

She *warned him not to go* there.

Verbs which are followed by a preposition use the *-ing* form:

I *look forward to meeting* her.

He *succeeded in finding* a job.

We *insist on paying*.

Some verbs can only be followed by the infinitive or the *-ing* form. See page 21.

Comparatives review

There are many expressions we can use to show if the difference between two things is big or small.

For a small difference we can use:
slightly, a little bit, a tiny bit, marginally (formal), etc.

I'm *slightly taller* than Peter.

The population is *marginally larger* than that of Ghana. (formal)

For a large difference we can use:
much, far, miles (informal), *considerably* (formal), etc.

They're *far better* than us at football.

The government was *considerably more* corrupt a hundred years ago. (formal)

as + adjective + *as* means the two things are equal.

I'm *as intelligent as* my sister.

It took me *as long* to drive to Cardiff *as* it did to travel there by train.

If we want to say two things aren't equal, we can say:

She's *not as big as* me. (= she's smaller)

The new menu *isn't as nice as* the one they had during the summer.

There are many expressions with *as* + adjective + *as* which show whether the difference is big or small.

For a small difference we can use:
not quite as

This bed *isn't quite as comfortable as* the other one. (= It's nearly as comfortable)

For a big difference we can use:
nowhere near, nothing like

He is *nowhere near as good as* me at tennis.

To express preference, we can use a number of verb constructions:
would sooner + infinitive without *to*, *would rather* + infinitive without *to*, *rather than* + *prefer to*, *would prefer*.

I'd *sooner leave* now than tomorrow.

I *would prefer* tea to coffee, if you have any.

Rather than eat potatoes, I'd prefer to have a steak.

We can use double comparatives with *the* to say that one thing causes another.

The longer you take, *the less* chance we have of catching the plane.

The more you write down, *the more* you'll remember.

Key vocabulary

Qualities of communities

cost of living   cosmopolitan   infrastructure   mild climate   freedom   healthcare system   standard of living   monuments   crime rate   unemployment   traffic congestion   pollution   racial tension   no-go areas   cultural life

Recommending places

a must   a must-see   good value for money   overrated   overpriced   not all it's cracked up to be   found it a bit dull/touristy   Don't miss …   If I were you, I'd go to …   Make sure you go to …   You should try *-ing* …   be wary of   watch out for

Describing places

off the beaten track   unspoilt   diverse   tranquil   the heart   side by side   vast   run-down   stunning   charming   packed   bustling   gaze   stroll

Phrasal verbs

catch on   turn up   get by   fit in   do up   fill in   hold up   carry out   come across   take to   see to   get through   come up with   keep up with   come down to   get away from

1 Complete the sentences using a verb from the box in the correct form (infinitive or *-ing* form). You may need to add a preposition.

> take pay spend apply consult
> hear make wear buy live

1 I encouraged the architects _____ the community about their new project.

2 We didn't mind _____ a few days in the town, but we didn't want to live there.

3 I look forward _____ from you soon.

4 We urged them not _____ a house in that area because it's very expensive and noisy.

5 She's thinking of _____ for a job as a tour guide.

6 I object _____ such a high rent in such a horrible part of town.

7 They persuaded us _____ an effort and actually see some of the city.

8 I can imagine _____ here for the rest of my life. I like it.

9 Members of the ski club are advised _____ helmets while skiing, for their own protection.

10 To relieve stress, I recommend _____ a long holiday in a quiet community!

2 Add one word to complete each sentence.

Chile is pretty as Argentina.

Chile is as pretty as Argentina.

1 You'd be off going to Texas in the spring than in the summer.

2 Paraguay is nowhere as big as Brazil.

3 I sooner go to Cartagena than Bogotá for a holiday.

4 Fiji is nothing as rich as New Zealand.

5 Switzerland is much the as it always has been: safe, clean and expensive.

6 The more cars we use, the polluted our environment becomes.

7 Poland quite as cold as Norway, but its climate is similar in the north-east.

8 Honduras is a tiny bigger than Guatemala.

9 China is by far most populated nation in the world.

10 Rather getting a job in Madrid, why don't you travel around Spain?

3 Put the lines in the correct order. The first two have been done for you.

a) Paris is one of the great tourist destinations. Its mild ☐1☐

b) tension in some areas of the city. The crime ☐

c) out for exorbitant prices in the cafés along the Champs Elysees. These aren't good ☐

d) infrastructure makes it easy to get around. As for atmosphere, there has been a lot of racial ☐

e) life. There are so many wonderful things to visit. Of these, the Eiffel Tower is a must- ☐

f) rate is rising, but there are few no-go ☐

g) congestion in the centre of the city, the outstanding transport ☐

h) of pickpockets on the metro. Also, watch ☐

i) areas. One must, however, be wary ☐

j) climate is perfect for relaxing and strolling along the wide streets. Although there is traffic ☐2☐

k) living is not too high, compared to most of western Europe. Paris is famous for its cultural ☐

l) value for money, but the general cost of ☐

m) see. ☐

4 Complete the text using the words/expressions in the box.

> ~~heart~~ stunning came up with
> charming come across keep up with
> side by side get away from turn up
> held up run-down carried out
> bustling vast

In 1883, Italian priest Don Bosco dreamed of a futuristic city in the *heart* of Brazil. Seventy-seven years later, his dream came true. Brasilia was completed in 1960, the construction of this specially designed city (1)_____ in just three and a half years. Brasilia has never forgotten Don Bosco: a cathedral in the city bears his name.

The city was commissioned by President Kubitschek to house the government and its buildings. Brasilia's supporters say the city promotes growth in the whole of Brazil, which is a (2)_____ country (easily South America's biggest), not just on the famous east coast. Its detractors say it was built so that politicians could (3)_____ the high crime rates of Rio and São Paulo, and so they wouldn't have to live (4)_____ with the population in (5)_____ areas.

Instead of a (6)_____ city centre full of people, Brasilia seems quite empty and almost like a machine. Its architects (7)_____ a rigidly organised design, with designated areas for government buildings, housing, etc. In the original design, there were no traffic lights; cars would go through tunnels and bridges in the sky, never getting (8)_____ by excess traffic. In order to (9)_____ a growing population, however, Brasilia eventually had to install traffic lights.

It isn't a (10)_____ city, compared to other parts of Brazil as it is very regimented and lacks pretty little streets. But if you (11)_____ in the centre of Brasilia you will (12)_____ some excellent restaurants. You should also pay a visit to the futuristic cathedral built by Niemeyer, the television tower with its (13)_____ views, and the zoo near the airport.

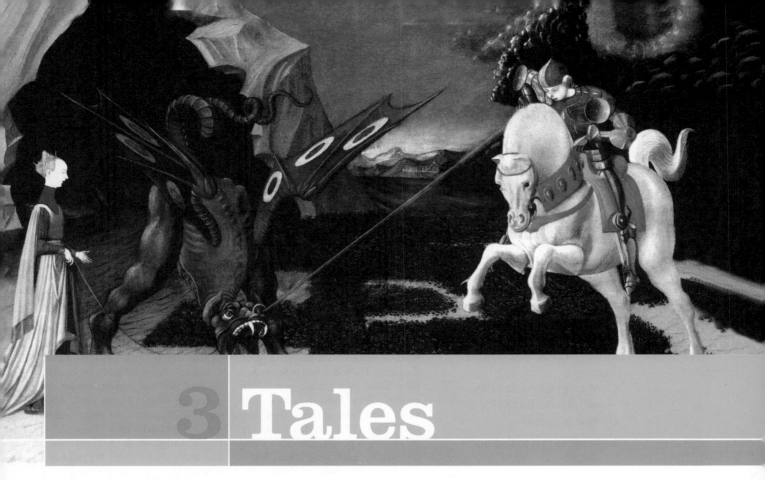

3 Tales

Lead-in

1 Discuss. How are the pictures connected? What types of story do they illustrate? Do you ever tell stories? Are you good at storytelling? What makes a good storyteller?

2 **a** Work in pairs. Discuss the difference between the words/expressions. Use your dictionary to check the meaning of any words you do not understand.
1 a plot / a biographical sketch
2 a fake / a myth
3 a tall story / a fairy tale
4 a legend / an anecdote
5 a punch line / a joke

b Can you think of any examples of the words/expressions above?

3 Check you know the meaning of the phrases **in bold**.
1 Do you think it's OK to **tell a white lie** if it makes life easier?
2 What would you do if you heard that someone had been **spreading rumours** about you?
3 Are you sometimes a **bit of a gossip**?
4 Have you ever taken part in (or heard about) an **elaborate hoax**?
5 When you describe things, are you **prone to exaggeration**?
6 Do you know any **good storytellers**?
7 Did you listen to **bedtime stories** when you were a child? Which were your favourites?

4 Discuss the questions in Ex. 3 in pairs.

Manuel Elizalde

Reading

1 **a** Look at the photos and discuss the questions.

1 Where are the people in the main photo?

2 What do you think they are doing?

3 What is their relationship with Manuel Elizalde?

4 What is a hoax?

b Read the text to find out.

2 Write questions for sentences 1–4 below. Read the text again to check if they are correct.

1 It was completely isolated from the modern world.

2 The tribe became world-famous immediately so reporters and academics wanted to study it.

3 Because Elizalde lost power and left the country.

4 None of them existed. They were all hoaxes.

3 Discuss.

1 Why do you think people were so excited about the discovery of the Stone Age tribe?

2 Why do you think the people in the text created these hoaxes? Did Elizalde, Shinichi, Plimpton and Boyd have different reasons?

3 In general, why do hoaxers do it? What type of person would you need to be?

4 Why do intelligent people such as journalists and academics fall for hoaxes, i.e. believe them?

HOAXES THAT FOOLED THE WORLD

In 1971, while he was working as a government minister in the Philippines, Manuel Elizalde announced a great discovery. He had found a Stone Age tribe living in a remote part of the country. They lived in caves, used stone tools, and ate any food they could find. This isolated tribe, just twenty-seven people, had been living this way for many generations, and in fact they didn't even speak the same language as other people in the area. Journalists arrived from all over the world, a documentary about the tribe was filmed for TV, and thousands of dollars were spent on research trips. The Philippines government, however, not wanting to destroy a way of life that had existed for thousands of years, allowed only a few people to visit them.

It was only years later, when the government (and Elizalde) lost power, that the truth came out. Researchers found the tribe living in villages, wearing Levi's jeans and communicating happily with other people. They explained that they had been pretending all along; Elizalde had paid them to act like a Stone Age tribe. And, what's more, Elizalde had left the country, with all the money.

Elizalde's hoax was just one in a long line. Anthropology has been a particularly rich field for hoaxers, with stories ranging from the famous Piltdown Man hoax – a supposedly ancient skull that was actually made of the bones of a medieval human and an orangutan, and chimpanzee teeth – to Fujimura Shinichi, the Japanese archaeologist who faked vital discoveries for years before being found out in 2000.

But perhaps the most interesting hoaxes are those that involve fictitious people. Piotr Zak was a Polish composer. An avant-garde modernist, he was not well-known among the public. At least not until 1961, when the BBC broadcast his piece *Mobile for Tape and Percussion*. Some music critics hailed it as a great work. Unfortunately for them, the piece had consisted of BBC staff making silly noises edited by BBC technicians. It was a classic hoax.

Nearly a quarter of a century later, another great hoax was to shake the world of American sports. It was 1 April, April Fools' Day, which is a day for playing practical jokes. *Sports Illustrated* ran an article about Sidd Finch, a truly extraordinary baseball player. The subheading of the article read: 'He's a pitcher, part yogi and part recluse. Impressively liberated from our opulent lifestyle, Sidd's deciding about yoga – and his future in baseball.' Read the first letters of these words again, carefully. They spell out 'Happy April Fools' Day'. On 15 April, the magazine came clean: Finch was an invention. The writer of the article, George Plimpton, then extended his article into a novel, published in 1987.

Just a year later, British writer William Boyd published *Nat Tate: American Artist, 1928–1960*, the tragic biography of a New York painter. A number of prominent critics claimed to remember Tate's work, claiming that he had been one of the greatest artists of the century. He'd never existed. The name Nat Tate is derived from two of Britain's most famous art galleries: The National Gallery (Nat) and the Tate Gallery.

Grammar | narrative tenses

4 Complete the tasks in the Active grammar box.

Active grammar

1 Read the first paragraph of the text in Ex.1 again. Find examples of the Past Simple, Past Continuous, Past Perfect Simple and Past Perfect Continuous.

2 Explain the difference in meaning (if any) between the pairs of sentences below. Why might one verb tense be more appropriate than the other in this context?

  1 a) *When the truth came out, Elizalde had already left the country.*

     b) *When the truth came out, Elizalde left the country.*

  2 a) *People believed the tribe had been living the same way for centuries.*

     b) *People believed the tribe had lived the same way for centuries.*

  3 a) *When researchers arrived, the people from the tribe weren't living in caves any more.*

     b) *When researchers arrived, the people from the tribe didn't live in caves any more.*

3 Complete the rules by adding the words below.

> progress   length   chronological   before

a) Use the Past Simple for past finished actions. Use it to describe a sequence of events in _____ order.

b) Use the Past Continuous for actions in _____ when something else happened.

c) Use the Past Perfect Simple for actions completed _____ other events in the past. Use it when you are already talking about the past.

d) Use the Past Perfect Continuous for progressive actions that started before the main events happened. Use it to emphasise the _____ of the action.

---

see Reference page 45

5 **a** Read about some famous hoaxes and put the verbs in brackets into the correct tense.

¹ In 1957 a news programme called *Panorama* broadcast a story about spaghetti trees in Switzerland. While the reporter told the story, Swiss farmers in the background (1)_____ (pick) spaghetti from trees. Following this, thousands of people (2)_____ (call) the show, asking how to grow spaghetti trees.

² In 1998 large numbers of Americans went to Burger King asking for a new type of burger. The food company (3)_____ (publish) an ad in *USA Today* announcing the new 'left-handed Whopper', a burger designed for left-handed people. The following day, Burger King (4)_____ (admit) that they (5)_____ (joke) all along.

³ Swedish technician Kjell Stensson (6)_____ (work) on the development of colour TV for many years when he (7)_____ (announce) in 1962 that everyone could now convert their black and white TV sets into colour. The procedure was simple: you (8)_____ (have) to put a nylon stocking over the TV screen. Stensson demonstrated and fooled thousands.

⁴ Pretending that it (9)_____ (develop) the product for some time, a British supermarket announced in 2002 that it (10)_____ (invent) a whistling carrot. Using genetic engineering, the carrot grew with holes in it, and, when cooked, it would start whistling.

b **3.1** Listen and check your answers.

Pronunciation

6 **a** **3.2** Listen and write the sentences you hear. Which words are contracted?

b Look at the tapescript on page 167 and practise reading the sentences aloud in pairs. Can you hear the contractions?

Speaking

7 **a** Prepare to tell a story about something that has happened in your life, e.g. a time you were cheated/got into trouble/did something funny/learned an important lesson/made a silly mistake. Think about the following:

  1 What were you doing when it happened?

  2 How long had you been doing it?

  3 Where were you? Who were you with?

  4 What had happened before this? Why?

  5 What happened next? How did you feel?

b Now invent two or three minor details to add to your story and go over the whole story again until you can tell it fluently.

c Tell your story to a partner. As you listen to each other, think of questions to ask and try to guess which details are invented.

Vocabulary | synonyms

8 **a** Read the newspaper extracts below. Think of synonyms for the <u>underlined</u> words/phrases.

1 The President is under pressure to <u>combat</u> illegal migration after another state took <u>drastic measures</u> to <u>deal with</u> the problem yesterday.

2 Two men have been <u>detained</u> by police in connection with a bank robbery. The police stopped a lorry <u>loaded</u> with cars that may have been <u>purchased</u> by the thieves.

3 In order to <u>keep track of</u> cows, which are <u>considered</u> <u>sacred</u> in India, authorities in Delhi are <u>placing</u> microchips in the animals.

4 The government has <u>initiated</u> a series of <u>talks</u> to <u>settle</u> the dispute which <u>led to</u> chaos in the rail service.

5 A <u>PROMINENT</u> doctor <u>claims</u> that Britain's failure to <u>prevent</u> the yearly outbreak of flu <u>arises</u> from a lack of hygiene in schools.

b Match the words in the box to the <u>underlined</u> words/phrases with similar meanings above.

stop   fight   resolve
follow the movements
extreme actions   asserts
arrested   stems   packed
putting   thought to be
formal discussions
cope with   caused
bought   started

9 Work in pairs and complete the crossword below. All of the words are from the text on page 34.

1 faking (v)
2 well-known and usually well-respected (adj)
3 alone (adj)
4 imagined/invented (adj)
5 extremely important (adj)
6 freed (adj)
7 expand (v)
8 extremely old (adj)
9 ruin (v)
10 extremely sad (adj)
11 a big, elaborate trick (n)
12 tricked (v)

Lifelong learning

In your own words ...

When telling or writing a story, try to put it in your own words. Think of synonyms and other ways to show the ideas. Try working with other students and summarising articles that you read. When you record vocabulary, make a note of opposites or synonyms.

10 Work in pairs and re-tell some of the stories from the text on page 34 using the key words below. Try to use your own words too.

minister   tribe   journalists   jeans   Piltdown Man   bones
composer   BBC   technicians   baseball   April Fools' Day
artist   Nat Tate   critics

3.2 | A good read
Grammer | compound words
Can do | describe a person in detail

Vocabulary | books

1 Discuss.

1 What sort of books do you like reading?

2 What three books would you take to a desert island?

3 Would you like to be a writer? Why/why not?

2 a Match the sentence halves 1–8 with a–h below.

1 I couldn't

2 It's very

3 It's a page-

4 I found the

5 The characters

6 It's based on

7 I'm a real

8 It's a

a) turner

b) best-seller

c) story quite moving

d) readable

e) bookworm

f) a true story

g) are one-dimensional

h) put it down

b Which expressions from Ex. 2a have a similar meaning to the expressions 1–8 below?

1 I'm an avid reader.

2 I was hooked.

3 It was gripping.

4 It depicts real events.

5 It has a nice, easy style.

6 It has sold many copies.

7 I was emotionally involved in it.

8 They didn't really come alive for me.

3 Think of different books which could be described by the words in the box. Have you read any of them? If so, tell other students about them.

> a page-turner   based on a true story
> moving   a best-seller   readable

The Da Vinci Code is a best-seller. It's very readable but I wouldn't describe it as a page-turner.

Listening

4 a 3.3 Listen to three people answering some of the questions below. Which questions do they answer and what do they say? Make notes in the table.

	SPEAKER 1	SPEAKER 2	SPEAKER 3
1 Who is your favourite fictional character?			
2 How do you visualise them (what do they look like)?			
3 What personal traits do they possess (type of character)?			
4 What memorable things do they do?			
5 What problems do they overcome?			
6 Do you know anyone like them in real life?			

b Listen again to check.

5 Who is your favourite fictional character? Spend a few minutes thinking about your own answers to the questions in Ex. 4a. Discuss them with other students.

Reading

6 Read the book extracts 1–6 opposite and answer the questions. There may be more than one possible answer.

a) Which extract describes a dangerous character?

b) Which extract describes a middle-aged and not very handsome character?

c) Which extract describes a probably very bossy and talkative character?

d) Which extract describes a character who is a very active child?

e) Which extract describes a character who probably has a tough job outside?

f) Which extract describes a character who is old but has a young mind?

7 **a** Work in groups. Read the extracts again and answer the questions.

1 What type of person is being described in each extract?

2 What physical details are included? Do they show the person's character?

3 What actions are shown? How do these reveal character?

4 Do any of the people sound attractive? Which words tell you this?

5 What type of book is it (funny, serious, etc.)?

b Discuss.

1 Which person do you think is the most/least attractive? Why?

2 Would you like to read any of the books?

1

For one thing he was unlike any other man we'd ever seen – or heard of, if it came to that. With his **weather-beaten** face, wide teeth-crammed mouth, and **far-seeing** blue eyes, he looked like some wigwam warrior stained with suns and heroic slaughter.

(*The Edge of Day* – Laurie Lee)

2

My father is still living, but less and less. Judge James Charles Endicott Jackson ... that tall, lean, **hollow-cheeked** man who had made such a religion of the law, preached from the head of our dining-room table each evening of my young life.

(*The Best Revenge* – Jane Riller)

3

Nola is a tomboy, a **hell-raiser**, a maverick, and she's captured my heart like no other. She's got the broad choppy legs of an athletic boy and the scowl of an old maid. No matter how many baths she takes, she manages to smell unwashed. She stands in the sunlight, an amber specimen in a glass jar, still as an Indian or a stone. Then quick as an insect, she sparks into action, running down the hill where the wasps won't follow, stepping on the dried brown grass.

(*The Stuntman's Daughter* – Alice Blanchard)

4

He was fifty-five, but he could have been ten years either side of that. Thin sandy hair, a big awkward mouth. Bad teeth, crooked and dark when he smiled, jug-handle ears. As a **self-conscious** boy he'd tried different things with those ears. He'd made an elasticised band with elaborate leather flaps to flatten his ears while he slept. He'd tried his hair short. He'd tried it long. He'd tried all kinds of hats. Eventually he'd grown the moustache as a kind of diversionary tactic, and he'd kept it.

(*The Idea of Perfection* – Kate Grenville)

5

The tribesman was small and thin, with tiny hands and feet – **fast-moving** feet the size of a child's – and **washed-out** red frizzy hair that he dyed the colour of Red Delicious apples. He had disappearing lips, painted large, twice their size, the colour of plums. All his life, he'd been a performer of the tribe's ceremonies. Even now, at seventy-seven, he'd put on colourful garments and perform the ceremony in front of his tribespeople.

6

He was just a **hot-headed**, twenty-year-old kid at the time, but he was greasy-fast with a gun. The problem was that he was spoiling for a fight and got it. At over six feet and one hundred and ninety pounds, he was a big boy and he had set out to prove to everyone that he was a man to reckon with.

(*Slade* – Robert Dyer)

Grammar | compound words

8 Complete the tasks in the Active grammar box.

> ### Active grammar
>
> 1 We often use compound adjectives, e.g. kind-hearted, to describe people. All of the extracts on page 38 except one contain compound adjectives. Which one contains only a compound noun?
>
> 2 Which compound adjectives in the extracts on page 38 a) describe someone's character? b) describe something physical?
>
>   Compound adjectives frequently use a hyphen (-) between the words. Often the second word ends in a participle, usually -ed or -ing.
>
> 3 Sometimes we can guess the meaning of compound adjectives. What is the compound adjective for a person who works hard? keeps an open mind? looks good? thinks freely? loves fun?

see Reference page 45

9 a Read sentences 1–8 below. With a partner, try to explain in your own words what the compound adjectives **in bold** mean.

1 He's very **single-minded**. It took him ten years to learn the violin and he never gave up!

2 She's very **self-sufficient** for a child. She makes her own food and entertains herself for hours.

3 Writers have to be **thick-skinned**. Lots of people criticise their work, but they try not to get upset.

4 He's so **kind-hearted**. He always helps everybody even if he's busy.

5 They can be rather **stand-offish**. At the party they refused to talk to anybody.

6 He's very **career-orientated**. He even reads about law when he's on holiday.

7 They're really **level-headed**. Even when they won all that money they didn't get too excited.

8 I'm a bit **absent-minded**. I keep forgetting where I put my glasses.

b Are the compound adjectives positive, negative or neutral?

Person to person

10 a Look at the photos above and write down as many compound adjectives that you can think of to describe each person.

b Compare your opinions of each person with a partner.

Speaking and writing

11 Read the How to ... box below and prepare to write a short description of someone you know well. Make notes about the following: first impressions/physical details/character. Try to use as many compound words as you can.

HOW TO ...	describe people	
	First impressions	She comes across as ... (adjective) ... but once you get to know her, she's ... (adjective)
		The thing that strikes you about ... is that ...
	Character – good things and bad things	The thing I (don't) like about ... is ...
		What I (don't) really like about ... is ...
		He's so + (adjective)
		He's such a (+ adjective) + person/man, etc.
		He can be a bit ... (negative adjective)

12 Describe your person to the rest of the class. Did any of the descriptions sound similar?

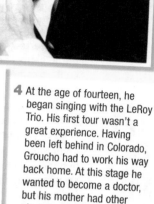

Reading

1 Discuss. Do you have any favourite comedians? Which comedians are famous in your country? Have they made any films?

2 Read about Groucho Marx. Guess the answer to the question at the end of each section.

1 Julius Henry Marx was born in New York into a poor but happy family on 2 October 1890. His father worked at home as a tailor and his mother, Minnie, worked as a promoter for her brother, comedian Al Shean. Growing up with a comedian in the family would have important consequences later. But, as a child, Groucho's first hobby was reading. He was also an extremely good singer.

What happened next?
(a) *He became a singer.*
(b) *He wrote a book.*
(c) *He started performing with his uncle.*

Go to 4 to find out. ➡

2 Groucho became host of a radio show called *You Bet Your Life*. It was so popular that they moved it to TV. Groucho would interview the contestants and ad-lib jokes. Some of the more memorable questions included: 'What colour is the White House?' and 'Who is buried in Grant's Tomb?' Returned now to national prominence, Groucho embarked on his solo film career, with a string of films throughout the 50s and 60s. But by now he was entering his seventies.

What happened next?
(a) *Groucho went to live in the Bahamas, for health reasons.*
(b) *Groucho started writing fiction.*
(c) *Groucho returned to fame in the Seventies.*

Go to 8 to find out. ➡

3 Desperately attempting to win some money, Groucho met Irving Thalberg, a big name in Hollywood, during a chess game. Thalberg, impressed with his new friend's act, helped the Marx Brothers to get established in the movie business. In the 30s and early 40s, the brothers made their most famous films: *A Night at the Opera* (1935) and *A Day at the Races* (1937).

What happened next?
(a) *Groucho got sick and then retired.*
(b) *The Marx Brothers disbanded.*
(c) *The brothers set up their own production company, which made them rich.*

Go to 5 to find out. ➡

4 At the age of fourteen, he began singing with the LeRoy Trio. His first tour wasn't a great experience. Having been left behind in Colorado, Groucho had to work his way back home. At this stage he wanted to become a doctor, but his mother had other plans for him.

What happened next?
(a) *He ran away to study medicine.*
(b) *Groucho and his brothers formed a musical act.*
(c) *Groucho won a TV competition.*

Go to 7 to find out. ➡

King of the Jokers

5 Following a film called *The Big Store* (1941), the Marx Brothers disbanded. It seemed as though Groucho was going to fade into obscurity, when suddenly another opportunity arose.

What happened?
(a) *He started a radio show.*
(b) *He became a politician.*
(c) *He was invited to perform in front of the British royal family.*

Go to 2 to find out. ➡

6 After suffering a severe stroke, Minnie died. Then the stock market crashed, signalling the beginning of the Great Depression. After hitting the heights of fame and fortune, suddenly Groucho and his brothers had lost everything. Depressed by the situation, Groucho began to suffer from insomnia, a condition that would plague him for the rest of his life.

How did the Marx Brothers recover in the 1930s?
(a) *They invested in property.*
(b) *They toured the world, playing in small theatres.*
(c) *They started making films.*

Go to 3 to find out. ➡

7 Groucho and his brothers, encouraged by their ambitious mother, formed a group called The Six Mascots. Having been no more than a moderate success, one day they suddenly started cracking jokes on stage. The audience liked it. Being funny came naturally to them. Soon the Marx Brothers were performing in the best venues all over the country. Groucho, with his fast-talking characters, chicken-walk, painted-on moustache, big glasses, and a cigar that he never smoked, was the star. Then everything changed in 1929.

What happened in 1929?
(a) *The brothers' mother died and Groucho lost all his money.*
(b) *Groucho went to live on a Pacific island.*
(c) *The brothers argued about money and split up their act.*

Go to 6 to find out. ➡

8 Groucho made a comeback in the Seventies, with a live one-man show. But with his health failing, he retired. He died of pneumonia in 1977 at the age of eighty-six, three days after Elvis Presley. Voted the fifth greatest comedy act ever by his fellow comedians in a 2005 poll, Groucho lives on, at least in memory. His films may not be watched much these days, but everyone recognises those famous glasses with the fake nose and moustache.

THE END

3 **a** Do you think the following statements about Groucho Marx are true? Write a number next to each statement:
1 = definitely, 2 = probably, 3 = probably not,
4 = definitely not.

1 He had a hard life.

2 He had a great relationship with his mother.

3 He had a great relationship with his brothers.

4 He had a long career.

5 He was a lucky man.

6 His type of humour is still funny today.

b Compare your answers with a partner. Give reasons for the numbers you wrote.

4 **a** [3.4] Listen to someone describing Groucho Marx's life. How many mistakes does she make?

b Compare your answers with a partner.

Grammar | participle clauses/gerunds

5 Complete the tasks in the Active grammar box.

> ### Active grammar
>
> The text on page 40 contains several examples of participles and gerunds. There are two types of participle: past participles (-*ed* forms) (for regular verbs) and present participles (-*ing* forms). The -*ing* forms are called gerunds in some cases.
>
> 1 We often use participles to add extra information to the idea in the sentence. The past participle sometimes acts as an adjective. The present participle sometimes gives background information.
>
> *Returned now to national prominence, Groucho embarked on his solo film career ...* (section 2)
>
> Find an example with a past participle and one with a present participle in section 3.
>
> 2 '*Having* + past participle' shows the cause of a second action (or a sequence of actions).
>
> *Having been left behind in Colorado, Groucho had to work his way back home.* (section 4)
>
> Find another example in section 7.
>
> 3 We often use the -*ing* form (the gerund) after conjunctions (*after, before, when*) and prepositions.
>
> *After suffering a severe stroke, Minnie died.* (section 6)
>
> Find another example in section 6.
>
> 4 We can use the -*ing* form (the gerund) as the subject of the sentence.
>
> *Being funny came naturally to them.* (section 7)
>
> Find another example in section 1.

see Reference page 45

6 Correct the mistakes in the sentences below using participles.

1 When tell a joke, timing is very important.

2 Work as a comedian must be a great job because you make people laugh.

3 Have become famous, comedians get depressed.

4 Making to look out of date by modern comics, old comedians like Chaplin and Groucho Marx are not funny these days.

5 Tell jokes in a foreign language is extremely difficult.

6 On been told a joke, you should laugh even if you don't think it's funny.

7 After to watch Mr Bean and Chaplin, etc., I think physical humour can be as funny as verbal.

Person to person

7 Do you agree with the statements in Ex. 6? Compare your views with a partner.

Vocabulary | humour

8 Match the types of humour in the box below to the people or ideas associated with it in sentences 1–8. Use your dictionary to check any words you don't understand.

> farce puns cartoons
> black humour surreal
> irony exaggeration
> satire

1 bizarre (very strange) humour
2 a series of things go wrong, and the situation gets funnier and funnier
3 Tom and Jerry
4 jokes about death and other serious issues
5 word play
6 not saying exactly what you mean, or saying the opposite of what you mean
7 saying something is much more than it is (sometimes for comic effect)
8 laughing at politicians and 'important' people

9 Discuss.

1 Do you know any famous actors/comics/writers/films associated with these types of humour?
2 Which types of humour do you like?
3 Do you ever tell jokes a) in your own language b) in English?
4 In your country, are there any special days when people play jokes on each other? What happens?

Listening

10 a 3.5 Cover the text below and listen to someone telling a joke. Do you find it funny?

b Why do you think the speaker pauses at certain moments? Listen again and read the joke. Mark the pauses. The first one has been done for you.

Three colleagues, a photographer, a journalist and an editor are covering a political convention. | One day, during their lunch break, they walk along a beach and one of them sees a lamp. He picks it up and rubs it and a magic genie suddenly appears. The genie says 'You can each have one wish.' So the photographer says, 'I want to spend the rest of my life in a big house in the mountains with a beautiful view, where I can take photographs.' Bazoom! Suddenly the photographer is gone to his home in the mountains. Then it's the journalist's turn. 'I want to live in a big house in the countryside with an enormous garden where I can sit and write for the rest of my life.' Bazoom! The journalist is gone. Finally, the genie says to the editor, 'And what about you? What's your wish?' So the editor says, 'I want those two back before lunch. We've got a deadline at 6.00 tonight.'

Speaking

11 a Work in groups of three. You are going to tell a joke. Student A turn to page 147. Student B turn to page 149. Student C turn to page 150. Read your joke two or three times and try to memorise it.

b Tell the joke to the other students in your group. Whose joke was the funniest? Who told it best?

Metaphors

1 **a** Look at the picture below and discuss.

1 What kind of relationship do the people have?

2 What do you think the story is about?

b Read the text and answer the questions. Who is the narrator describing? What made them the way they were?

Top chefs aren't known for their **warm personalities**. Assistants who overcook the pasta by ten seconds usually **struggle** to get out of the kitchen alive. My father was a top chef. We'd had a **stormy relationship** for years, but I decided to **follow in his footsteps** anyway, and train as a chef. It was better than the **dead-end** I'd reached with the job I'd been doing.

After three years I became head chef in a restaurant called The Tortoise. As the boss, I **called the shots**, but if anything went wrong, I was the one **in the firing line**. Experiencing the sweaty kitchens, the egos, the closeness, I learned why my father was the way he was. When I began, I didn't **have my sights set on** anything much – I just wanted a regular job – but soon I realised my career **was taking off**. The rich and famous started to visit the restaurant and eventually I **reached a crossroads**: I could either open my own restaurant or go and work for one of the big ones. Then destiny intervened. My father retired and I got his job.

On my first day, I received a **frosty reception**. No one would talk to me. What made it worse is that I was **feeling under the weather** – I had a cold, and my hands were shaking as I went into the kitchen. I held my breath, stood up in front of everyone and said, 'My name is Leah Kleist. You all know my father. Whether you liked him or hated him, I don't care. He is the past. Now let's get to work.' And we did.

2 Write the metaphors **in bold** next to their meaning.

Describing life as a journey
1 do the same things someone did before you: _____
2 with no progress possible: _____
3 start to become successful: _____
4 a time when you have to decide about your future: _____

Describing character/feelings as weather
5 friendly character: _____
6 with lots of arguing and strong feelings: _____
7 unfriendly welcome: _____
8 ill: _____

Describing business as war
9 fight: _____
10 make the important decisions: _____
11 responsible if something goes wrong: _____
12 have a goal/an objective: _____

3 Complete sentences 1–8 using metaphors from Ex. 2.

1 I went to the doctor because I was feeling a bit _____ the _____.

2 We tried to develop the project, but soon we'd reached a _____ _____.

3 They're always shouting and screaming at each other. They definitely have a _____ _____!

4 I'm the Chief Executive and major decision-maker, so I have to _____ _____ shots.

5 My career began to _____ _____ when I landed a role in a TV series.

6 As the manager, you are _____ the _____ line when things go wrong.

7 She had her sights _____ _____ fame and fortune so she went to Hollywood.

8 Will you follow _____ your mother's _____ or work in a different field?

4 Work in pairs. Tell your partner about:

• something you struggled to do
• a dead-end job you'd hate
• something you have your sights set on
• someone whose footsteps you'd like to follow in
• someone who'd get a frosty reception in your home

5 **a** Create your own metaphors. Write five sentences with the structure below. Use interesting adjectives and nouns. The sentences do not have to be logical.

It is a + adjective + adjective + noun
It is a stunning tropical island.

b Student A turn to page 147. Student B turn to page 149. Take turns to ask your questions. Answer using your metaphors from Ex. 5a.

3 | Communication

Telling stories

1 Read the openings to some pieces of fiction and discuss the questions in pairs/groups.

1 Is there anything unusual about the situation described?

2 Where and when do you think each book is set? Why do you think this?

3 What can you guess about each story? What type of story might it be?

4 Which extracts make you want to read more? Why?

2 **a** In pairs/groups, choose one of the openings and discuss how the story could continue. Decide who will tell each part of the story and practise telling it together.

b Tell your story to another pair/group. Which pair/group has the most interesting/unusual story?

1 Milena boiled things. She was frightened of disease. She would boil other people's knives and forks before using them.
(*The Child Garden* – Geoff Ryman)

2 It was a bright cold day in April, and the clocks were striking thirteen.
(*1984* – George Orwell)

3 Rose Pickles knew something bad was going to happen. Something really bad this time.
(*Cloudstreet* – Tim Winton)

4 I'm often asked what it's like to be married to a genius. The question used to please me ...
(*The Mind-Body Problem* – Rebecca Goldstein)

5 If I am out of my mind, it's all right with me, thought Moses Herzog.
(*Herzog* – Saul Bellow)

6 When he didn't get any answer the second time he knocked, Parker kicked the door in.
(*The Split* – Richard Stark)

7 As Gregor Samsa awoke one morning from uneasy dreams, he found himself transformed in his bed into a gigantic insect.
(*Metamorphosis* – Franz Kafka)

8 Someone must have been telling lies about Joseph K, for without having done anything wrong he was arrested one fine morning.
(*The Trial* – Franz Kafka)

9 All children, except one, grow up.
(*Peter Pan* – J.M. Barrie)

10 It was a wrong number that started it, the telephone ringing three times in the dead of night, and the voice on the other end asking for someone he was not.
(*The New York Trilogy* – Paul Auster)

Narrative tenses review

We often use narrative tenses together in order to make clear the order of events in a story.

Use the Past Simple to talk about completed actions in the past.

We went to Paraguay last year.

The Past Simple can be used for short actions, long actions or repeated actions.

Use the Past Continuous to talk about actions in progress at a particular time in the past.

We were talking about her when she walked in.

We often use the Past Continuous to set the scene in a narrative.

The sun was shining and the children were playing in the garden. Suddenly ...

Use the Past Perfect Simple to talk about completed actions that happened before another action in the past. The Past Perfect Simple is only used when we refer to two actions/moments in the past.

She took out a DVD, but I'd already seen it.

We don't need the Past Perfect when we are describing past events in chronological order.

We ordered the food, ate and paid.

Use the Past Perfect Continuous to talk about actions or situations which continued up to the moment in the past that we are talking about.

Before he gave up, he'd been smoking for years.

The Past Perfect Continuous is often used to show the reasons for a situation.

He was angry because he'd been waiting for ages.

Compound words

Compounds frequently use a hyphen (-) between the words, but there are no definite rules about this.

Often the second word ends in *-ed* or *-ing*.

When the first word of the compound is an adjective, the stress is usually on the second word.

*big**headed**, strong-**willed**, slow-**moving***

When the first word of the compound is a noun, the stress is usually on the first word.

***man**eating shark, **sun**tanned*

Participle clauses/gerunds

Use participle clauses:

as reduced relative clauses. Instead of complete verbs, we use a participle clause:

I recognise the man who is sitting over there. →
I recognise the man sitting over there.

like full adverbial clauses, expressing cause, result, conditions, etc. Adverbial participle clauses sound formal and are more common in writing than speech.

Feeling hungry, he bought a cake. = Because he was feeling hungry, he bought a cake. (cause)

Having + past participle is a special form that shows the cause of a second action/a sequence of actions.

Having run the marathon, he was exhausted. = After running the marathon, he was exhausted.

after many conjunctions and prepositions, e.g. *as, after, before, since, when, once, without, in spite of*. After prepositions, *-ing* forms are called gerunds.

Before leaving, he gave me a present.

He swam in spite of having a sore arm.

as the subject of the sentence. In this case, the *-ing* form is a gerund.

Talking is the best therapy.

The subject of the participle clause is usually the same as the subject in the main clause.

Running around till they were tired, the kids had fun. (the kids ran and the kids had fun)

NOT: ~~Waiting for hours, the day seemed to Tom as if it would never end.~~ (Tom was waiting; the day wasn't)

Key vocabulary

Tales

tell a white lie   spread rumours   a bit of a gossip
make a feeble excuse   conceal/reveal the truth
elaborate hoax   prone to exaggeration
barefaced liar   be taken in   storyteller

Describing books

I couldn't put it down   It's very readable   hooked
It's a page-turner   It was quite moving/gripping
the characters are one-dimensional   a best-seller
based on a true story   avid reader   depict

Compound adjectives

single-minded   self-sufficient   thick-skinned
kind-hearted   stand-offish   career-orientated
level-headed   absent-minded

Humour

farce   puns   cartoons   black humour   surreal
irony   exaggeration   satire

Metaphors

follow in his footsteps   reach a crossroads
a career takes off   a dead-end job   frosty reception
feel under the weather   stormy relationship
warm personality   a struggle   has her sights set on
call the shots   in the firing line

1 Find seven mistakes with narrative tenses and correct them.

In April 2000 journalists at *Esquire* were deciding that life at the magazine was getting a bit boring. So they published an article about FreeWheelz, an Internet company that gave customers free cars which were covered in advertising. The article had claimed that FreeWheelz 'will transform the auto industry more than Henry Ford did.' The company didn't yet become famous but it would 'on 1 April, when FreeWheelz launches on the web for real.' Readers who were seeing the website, which had been created by the author of the article, were impressed. Within days, the site had been receiving over a thousand hits and messages from other entrepreneurs who claimed they had been planning similar businesses. The website contained a questionnaire for potential clients which was including a number of bizarre questions such as 'Does hair loss concern you?' In the following edition, the magazine owned up, explaining that the article had been an April Fools' hoax. The magazine prepared to forget all about it when suddenly an offer for the domain name FreeWheelz came in. The author of the article sold the name for $25,000, splitting the profits with the owners of the magazine. The conclusion? Never trust a strange story which contains the date 1 April.

2 Rewrite the sentences so that they have the same meaning. Use participle clauses with the verb in brackets. Change the form of the verb.

Because we couldn't find our way, we had to turn back. (lose)

Lost, we had to turn back.

Robbie ate all the cherries and then he was sick. (have/eat)

Having eaten all the cherries, Robbie was sick.

1 Life's biggest pleasure is when you do things for other people. (do)
2 Anyone who wishes to take the exam must register in June. (wish)
3 Most of the dead animals that were found after the earthquake were domestic pets. (find)
4 Because she felt sleepy, Luisa went to bed. (feel)
5 When you swim, it is compulsory that you wear a bathing cap. (swim)
6 He had been famous for years, and he finally wanted some peace and quiet. (have/be)
7 As they were banned from exhibiting their paintings in the national exhibition, they decided to set up their own. (ban)
8 David woke up early as usual and looked out of the window. (wake up)

3 Put the underlined letters in the correct order.

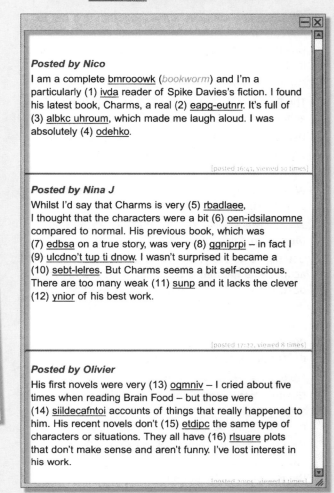

Posted by Nico

I am a complete bmrooowk (*bookworm*) and I'm a particularly (1) ivda reader of Spike Davies's fiction. I found his latest book, Charms, a real (2) eapg-eutnrr. It's full of (3) albkc uhroum, which made me laugh aloud. I was absolutely (4) odehko.

[posted 16:41, viewed 10 times]

Posted by Nina J

Whilst I'd say that Charms is very (5) rbadlaee, I thought that the characters were a bit (6) oen-idsilanomne compared to normal. His previous book, which was (7) edbsa on a true story, was very (8) ggniprpi – in fact I (9) ulcdno't tup ti dnow. I wasn't surprised it became a (10) sebt-lelres. But Charms seems a bit self-conscious. There are too many weak (11) sunp and it lacks the clever (12) ynior of his best work.

[posted 17:22, viewed 8 times]

Posted by Olivier

His first novels were very (13) ogmniv – I cried about five times when reading Brain Food – but those were (14) siildecafntoi accounts of things that really happened to him. His recent novels don't (15) etdipc the same type of characters or situations. They all have (16) rlsuare plots that don't make sense and aren't funny. I've lost interest in his work.

[posted 20:05, viewed 2 times]

4 Complete the dialogues by adding one word.

A: He's the new boss, isn't he?
B: Yes, he the shots.

Yes, he calls the shots.

1 A: How are you?
   B: I'm feeling a bit under weather, actually.
2 A: How are Julia and Antonio?
   B: Well, they seem to have a very stormy.
3 A: In 1988 you became Head of Exports. Is that right?
   B: Yes, that's when my career really took.
4 A: So are you going to become a carpenter too?
   B: No. I really don't want to follow in my father's.
5 A: I don't know whether to get a job or continue with my education.
   B: It seems you've a crossroads in your life.
6 A: So she takes responsibility for all the decisions?
   B: Yes, she's the one in the line.

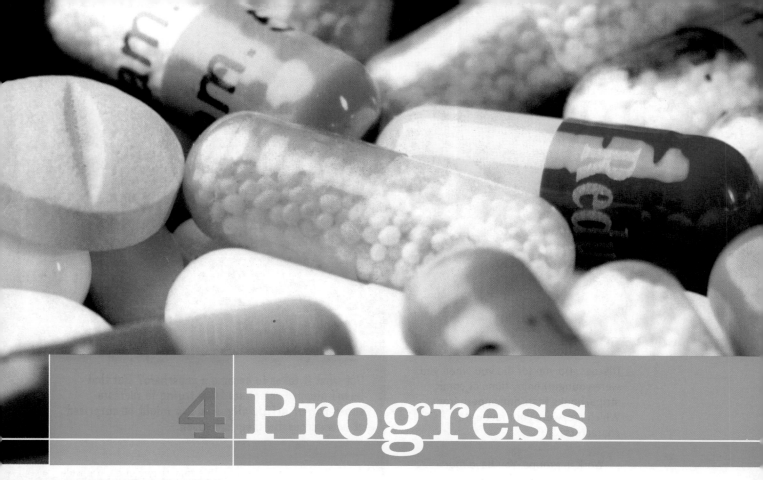

4 Progress

Lead-in

1 Discuss. What types of progress are shown in the photos? What developments have there been recently? What developments might there be in the future?

2 **a** Match the news headlines 1–4 below to a photo.

1 Resistance to antibiotics on the increase
2 New virus destroys global computer systems
3 Human cloning to make spare parts for children
4 Space mission in danger as budget crisis grows

b Match the words/phrases to the news headlines.

> network cell crash a system organ hacker skin tissue
> gene test tube software strain microchip mission
> firewall orbit scan shuttle genetic engineering
> superbug launch analysis

c **4.1** Listen to check your answers and summarise the stories.

3 Check the meaning of the words **in bold** and then answer the questions in pairs.

1 Would you describe yourself as a '**computer nerd**' or a '**technophobe**'?
2 Are you **up-to-date** with the **latest technology**? Are there any new **gadgets** you would like to buy/own?
3 Do you enjoy reading scientific **journals**/watching **documentaries**? Which scientific areas interest you most? Why?

Speaking

1 Discuss. Do you (or did you when you were younger) enjoy films or comic strips/books featuring superheroes? Which are/were your favourite characters?

2 **a** Work in groups. You have four minutes to test your knowledge of superheroes. Write down:

1 the names of four different superheroes

2 the colour of the Incredible Hulk

3 four of Spider-Man's five special powers

4 the name of the planet where Superman was born

5 the name of the actor who played Superman, and who was later paralysed in a tragic accident

6 the name of the film released in 2002, which broke all box-office records on its very first weekend

7 the name of the female character who has super-strength, bullet-proof bracelets and a lasso that makes people tell the truth

b `4.2` Listen and check your answers.

Reading

3 **a** Read the article and tick (✓) next to research which you think is important, write (✗) next to research which is less important and (!) next to information which worries you. Compare your views with other students.

b Read the article about superheroes again and write (?) next to sections where you think text might be missing.

HOW TO BE A

Got what it takes to become a superhero? But that hasn't stopped scientists from trying to recreate super-powers artificially. And you might be surprised at how successful they have been.

Wall climbing

Gecko lizards are so good at this that they can hang upside down from a glass surface by a single toe. Now scientists at Manchester University are developing a material covered with similar nanoscopic hairs that would enable a person to walk on a ceiling or up a wall. One square centimetre of the tape holds one million artificial setae and could support a kilogram of weight. There is every chance that this system could allow people to walk up walls.

Teleportation

Just as superhero Nightcrawler can teleport, scientists in Australia have discovered how to teleport matter for real – albeit on the atomic scale for the time being. The researchers have succeeded in transmitting information about quantum particles across space and then using it to reassemble exact copies of the original particles.

Regeneration

Both Superman and the X-men's Wolverine can regenerate tissue instantly – they can be hit by a bullet and recover in seconds. Doctors at a children's hospital in Boston have pioneered a similar way of helping terminally ill patients to re-grow healthy organs.

Super-strength

No matter how many steroids you take, you don't stand a chance of achieving the strength of the Incredible Hulk. Johns Hopkins University scientists have created Mighty Mouse – a rodent that has been genetically modified so that a protein which limits muscle-growth is blocked. 'They are normal in every respect, except their muscles are two to three times larger than normal,' says molecular biologist Se Jin-Lee. 'They look like Schwarzenegger mice.' Presumably, it'll also help scientists to better understand muscle-wasting diseases.

SUPERHERO

Force field

The Defence Science and Technology Laboratory run by the UK Ministry of Defence has developed a similar force field to protect tanks from rocket-propelled grenades. Once shielded by the force field there is very little chance that the tanks can be destroyed.

Web-shooter

The US army has developed a device for the New York police, which acts like Spider-Man's webshooter. The victim caught in the net stands no chance of escape as the nets come in three varieties: a regular net, one that can give an electric shock – and, most fittingly of all, one that becomes sticky on contact with air. These crime-stopping devices are bound to cause some sticky problems for New York criminals!

X-ray vision

Everyone would like to have Superman's ability to see through walls. The solution could be 'terahertz imaging'. Terahertz radiation lies between the infrared and microwave regions of the spectrum so these low energy rays can penetrate matter just like X-rays but without the harmful effects. Researchers are developing it for defence and medical imaging.

Flying

Superman has the ability to fly without the aid of wings or rockets. The original research was carried out by a Russian researcher working in Finland in 1996, but so far no other researchers have managed to verify his claim. It is doubtful that we will be able to achieve this in the foreseeable future.

Invisibility

The Invisible Woman is part of the Fantastic Four. Now a virtual reality expert in Japan has created a 'see-through' coat, which appears to make the wearer's body disappear. A tiny video camera is then attached to the back of the coat. The image from the back of the coat is projected onto the front of the coat, which makes observers think that they can see through it.

4 Read sentences 1–11 below and put them in the correct place in the article. There is one extra sentence.

1 However, there is a distinct possibility that genetics could help those seeking a Hulk-like physique.

2 But the odds are against the general use of X-rays as they are dangerous, and repeated exposure to them isn't good for your health.

3 It is done by coating the material with microscopic reflectors that work like a cinema screen.

4 The secret lies in the millions of tiny hairs, called setae, which are on the gecko's skin.

5 There is every likelihood that the procedure could eventually be commonly used to grow organs for transplants.

6 The nets are designed to restrain people without causing serious injury and are shot from a kind of stun gun.

7 There is a slim chance that the scientific material obtained during the process would result in further complications.

8 For most of us the answer is a resounding 'no' – things that are part of the day-job for world-savers are beyond the reach of mere mortals.

9 Researchers have looked into the possibility of using spinning discs to defy gravity.

10 Superman's hideaway, the Fortress of Solitude, is protected by a force field.

11 The process hinges upon the weird properties of quantum mechanics, and so it is unlikely that it could be used for macroscopic objects, because of the vast amounts of information involved.

Grammar | future probability

5 Complete the tasks in the Active grammar box.

> ### Active grammar
>
> 1 To talk about future probability we can use modal verbs *will/could/may/might*
>
> 2 Which phrases are used to talk about future probability in a) the text about superheroes and b) the sentences in Ex. 4 on page 49? <u>Underline</u> them and then add them to the table below.
>
> | Sure to happen | It almost definitely will …/ will presumably … |
> |---|---|
> | Likely to happen | The chances are that … There is a strong possibility … It may/might well … |
> | Unlikely to happen | There's a slight/remote possibility that … I doubt whether … It probably won't … |
> | Impossible | You haven't a hope of … It is inconceivable that … |

see Reference page 59

6 **a** Circle the option which is <u>not</u> possible.

1 There is no *chance/option/doubt* that we'll make it to the laboratory on time.
2 It's *hopeless/doubtful/possible* that I'll see you again before I go into hospital.
3 They haven't a *hope/doubt/chance* of finding life on Mars.
4 There is a *remote/chance/slim* possibility that the virus will spread.
5 The experts are *bound/sure/hope* to agree with what you have said.
6 There is every *doubt/likelihood/chance* that Superman will kiss the girl at the end.
7 There is *every likelihood/a distinct possibility/ any chance* that the antibiotics will work.
8 Is there any *chance/hope/doubt* of you getting the results back earlier?

b What is the difference in meaning (if any) between the two correct options?

7 Rewrite the sentences using the prompts **in bold** so that the meaning is the same.

There is no chance that I'm lending her my laptop. **stand**

She doesn't stand a chance of me lending her my laptop.

1 It's highly unlikely that they will make a breakthrough in the near future. **doubtful**
2 It is vaguely possible that we'll be able to travel to Mars by 2050. **inconceivable**
3 I'm sure they'll notice it's missing. **bound**
4 We can't be entirely confident that the family haven't already been informed. **chance**
5 We're being met at the airport so we don't need train tickets. **presumably**
6 Unfortunately, he doesn't stand a chance of getting the job. **hope**
7 China has a good chance of winning the space race. **distinct**
8 There doesn't seem to be much hope that the relationship will improve. **doubt**

Person to person

8 Discuss. What are the chances of the following happening in the next twenty years?

1 We will be able to have holidays in space.
2 There will be a cure for cancer/AIDS.
3 Nuclear energy will have been abolished.
4 Parents will routinely be able to choose the gender, hair, eye and skin colour of their babies.
5 All foods will be genetically modified.

Listening

9 **a** `4.3` Listen to an interview with Stan Lee, the creator of Spider-Man. In what order does he answer the questions below?

1 Will there ever be real superheroes?
2 Why make him a scientist?
3 How did you think of Spider-Man?
4 Are you at all scientific?

b Listen again. What does he say about the things in the box?

> Fantastic Four   a fly   a scientist
> science-fiction   a 'dummy'   diseases
> wars   Mars   genetics

10 Discuss. Do you agree with what Stan Lee says about diseases, going to Mars and genetics? Do you think that 'anything will be possible'?

Vocabulary | arrangements

1 Discuss.

1 How do you keep in touch with your family/ friends?

2 Do you agree with the quotation below? Do you think communications technology has made our lives better or worse?

'Modern communications technology is designed to keep us too busy to actually see anyone.' (*Paul Mendez, psychologist*)

2 Read the emails below. What is Tom trying to do? What happens in the end?

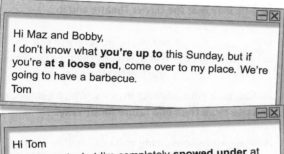

Hi Maz and Bobby,
I don't know what **you're up to** this Sunday, but if you're **at a loose end**, come over to my place. We're going to have a barbecue.
Tom

Hi Tom
Thanks mate, but I'm completely **snowed under** at the moment. I have to write an essay by Monday afternoon, so I'll be working all weekend. I've got nothing **lined up** for the following weekend though, so maybe we can meet then? I'll call you later.
Bobby

Dear Tom,
Like Bobby, I'm a bit **tied up** tomorrow. Unfortunately, I have to go to my great uncle's house for a family lunch. He was ill so we thought it might **fall through**, but it looks as if it's **going ahead**. I really can't **get out of** it because it's the old man's 60th birthday and most of the family will probably be there.
Maz

OK you guys,
I'm **calling off** the barbecue. Judging from the grey sky, it's going to rain all weekend anyway.
Maybe you'll have done your various duties by the end of the evening and we can go for a drink instead! If you want to **wind down**, I'll be in The Hart, a pub on King Street. Gloria and I are meeting there at about 8.30, as long as nothing else **crops up**! Don't forget it closes at 10.30 on Sundays.
OK, time to **put my feet up** and take it easy!
Later,
Tom

3 Read the emails again and match the words/ phrases **in bold** to the definitions below.

1 be engaged in activity
2 arrive unexpectedly (a duty or problem)
3 busy/not free
4 planned/arranged
5 relax (usually at home)
6 avoid doing something
7 cancel
8 extremely busy
9 not happen/take place (a plan)
10 proceed as expected (a plan)
11 bored because you have nothing to do
12 become relaxed

4 Complete the sentences with one word.

1 The match was ruined by rain, and eventually we had to call it.
2 Your feet up. You deserve a break.
3 If you aren't to anything this afternoon, why don't you come over here?
4 She's finished it so she's now a loose end.
5 Another problem has cropped: the printer isn't working.
6 I'm tied all of January, but I'll have some free time in February.
7 We've got a very good new band lined for tonight.
8 I decided to go to the beach in order to wind.
9 Despite the rain, the festival ahead yesterday.
10 She can't come tomorrow because she's absolutely under with work.
11 My mum says I have to clean my room now, and I can't get out it.
12 Their wedding plans fell when she realised she didn't love him.

5 **a** Answer the questions below.

1 What are you up to this evening?
2 When do you usually put your feet up?
3 What do you have lined up for next weekend?
4 What do you do when you're at a loose end?
5 Are there any responsibilities you'd like to get out of?
6 Have any problems cropped up recently at work/school?

b Predict what the answers might be for two other students in the class. Ask them to see if you were correct.

Grammar | future forms review

6 Complete the tasks in the Active grammar box.

Active grammar

1 Read the emails on page 51. Which different verb forms are used for talking about the future?

2 Match the beginning of explanations 1–8 with the correct endings a–h below.

  1 Use the **Present Simple** __e__
    Don't forget it closes at 10.30 on Sundays.

  2 Use **will** _____
    I'll call you later.

  3 Use **will** _____
    Most of the family will probably be there.

  4 Use **be going to** _____
    We're going to have a barbecue.

  5 Use **be going to** _____
    Judging from the grey sky, it's going to rain anyway.

  6 Use the **Present Continuous** _____
    Gloria and I are meeting there at about 8.30.

  7 Use the **Future Continuous** _____
    I'll be working all weekend.

  8 Use the **Future Perfect** _____
    Maybe you'll have done your various duties by the end of the evening.

a) for predictions you make because of present evidence.

b) for something that will be finished before a time in the future.

c) for immediate decisions made at the same time as you speak/write.

d) for something you think, guess or calculate about the future.

e) for fixed timetables, schedules and arrangements.

f) for something that will be in progress during a period of time in the future.

g) for fixed plans or arrangements.

h) for a personal intention or arrangement.

---

see Reference page 59

7 **a** Complete sentences 1–12 using the verb in brackets.

1 She looks terrible. I think she _____ (faint).

2 You've dropped your pen. It's OK, I _____ (pick (it) up).

3 We _____ (get) married in July.

4 Oh no! The train is delayed. We _____ (be) late.

5 Do you think you _____ (retire) by 2030?

6 Sorry, you can't borrow the car tonight. I _____ (use) it.

7 This time next month, we _____ (lie) on a beach in Thailand!

8 What do you think you _____ (do) in ten years' time?

9 She offered to help us at 9.00! That's useless. We _____ (finish) by then!

10 The play is at the Olivier Theatre and it _____ (start) at 7.30.

11 I _____ (write) to you as soon as I can.

12 We can't get there until late. By the time we arrive they _____ (eat) all the food.

b Compare your answers in pairs. Which sentences can use more than one future form? Why?

8 **a** Make questions using *will* (*do*), *will be* (*doing*) or *will have* (*done*).

In a year's time …

1 Do you think you _____ (still study) English?

2 Do you think you _____ (have) the same lifestyle?

3 Do you think you _____ (live) in the same place?

4 Do you think your country _____ (have) a different government?

In ten years' time …

5 Do you think you _____ (change) much?

6 Do you think you _____ (have) the same hobbies?

7 Do you think you _____ (have) the same close friends?

8 Do you think you _____ (see) more of the world?

b **4.4** Listen to the questions. Which words are contracted? Repeat the questions paying attention to contractions.

Person to person

9 Work in pairs. Ask each other the questions from Ex. 8a. Tell the class two things you learned about your partner.

Listening

10 4.5 Listen to two telephone conversations. What is the speakers' relationship? What plans are they trying to make?

11 Read the How to ... box and complete the task.

HOW TO ...

be vague and/or imprecise

We use vague or imprecise expressions when we don't want to (or can't) give details. Listen to the conversations again and complete the expressions in the grid below.

Give imprecise information about how often something happens	once in a blue _____ from time to _____
Give imprecise information about quantity, time and/or numbers	more or_____ _____ of mistakes about _____-ish in an hour _____
Give imprecise information about things you do/have been doing	bits and _____ that kind of _____
Give imprecise answers to direct questions	sort of/_____ of in a _____

12 Put the words in the correct order to make sentences. Start with the <u>underlined</u> word. Don't add punctuation.

1 <u>We</u> go time to to that still time from café.

2 <u>We</u> to before bits various leave pieces going do and we are.

3 <u>I'm</u> pushed weekend time sort this for of.

4 <u>Her</u> job solving thing that kind whenever they crop involves problems up, of.

5 <u>They'll</u> less or here more a for month stay.

6 <u>Because</u> I'm a in busy, I moon so see my sister once only blue.

7 <u>By</u> time loads next new I'll have this of met year, people.

8 <u>We're</u> ish at about hoping meet four- to.

9 <u>I'll</u> at or arriving so ten be.

10 <u>In</u> home a at I prefer on staying nights way, Saturday.

13 a 4.6 Listen to six questions. Write short answers. Try to make your answers imprecise or vague.

b Compare your answers in pairs.

Speaking

14 Work in pairs and play *Twenty Questions*. Follow the instructions in the box below.

Twenty questions

Think of a famous person. Don't tell your partner who it is.

Try to find out who your partner is thinking of. Take turns to ask questions.

You have twenty questions each and you can only ask *yes/no* questions. However, you can add imprecise or vague information to your answers if you like (provided it doesn't make it too easy for your partner to guess who you are thinking of). The first student to guess the identity of the famous person wins.

Student A: Does your person appear on TV?

Student B: Yes, I suppose so. From time to time. Is your person middle-aged?

Student A: Sort of ... he/she is fifty-ish I think.

Vocabulary | special abilities

1 **Discuss.** How old are the children in the photos? What can children usually do by the time they are two years old/ five years old/ten years old?

2 Match the words/phrases in box A to those with a similar meaning in box B.

A	B
1 gifted	a) for the future
2 in the making	b) difficult
3 prodigy	c) completely abnormal
4 adulation	d) extremely talented
5 peers	e) admiration
6 demanding	f) genius
7 freak	g) contemporaries

3 Look at the photos and the words/ phrases in box A above. What do you think the article is about? Make predictions in pairs.

4 Read the text quickly. Were any of your predictions correct?

5 Read the text again and answer the questions.
   1 Why were Son's parents surprised?
   2 What does Son think of his gift?
   3 According to the article, what problems do child prodigies face?
   4 What is 'the big question' about child prodigies?
   5 What answer does the article suggest?

6 Discuss.
   1 Have you heard any stories about other child geniuses?
   2 How do you think society treats them?
   3 What might be the benefits and drawbacks of having a child prodigy in the family?
   4 Do you know any children who have a special gift for something?
   5 Do you think child prodigies are 'born' or 'made'?

HOW TO MAKE YOUR CHILD A GENIUS

When he was nearly three years old, Nguyen Ngoc Truong Son watched his mother and father playing chess in the family's ramshackle home in the Mekong Delta, and, like any toddler, pestered them to let him play, too. Eventually they relented, assuming the pieces would end up strewn around the kitchen. Not for one minute had they imagined that their son would be able to play. To their astonishment, not only did Son know how to set up the chessboard, but he had also learned many of the complex rules of the game. Within a month he was defeating his parents with ease. By the age of four, Son was competing in national tournaments against kids many years older. By age seven, he was winning them. Now twelve, he is Vietnam's youngest champion and a grand master in the making.

Son's parents – teachers with a combined income of less than $100 a month – are at a loss to explain their otherwise ordinary child's talents. 'It's an inborn gift,' says his father. 'You couldn't train an ordinary three-year-old to play like that.' The young prodigy, for his part, doesn't think the question is worth pondering. To him, the strategies and logic of chess comes as naturally as chewing bubble gum. 'I just see things on the board and know what to do,' he says. 'It's just always made sense to me.'

How a child prodigy like Son comes by his talent has never made much sense to scientists. Throughout history, prodigies have been celebrated as objects of envy and adulation. Rarely, however, have they been understood. Often taunted by their peers, hounded by the press, prodded by demanding parents and haunted by expectations of greatness, they are treated as wondrous curiosities. As Maria McCann, a specialist in the education of gifted children, puts it, 'They are our beautiful freaks.'

The question most people want to answer is whether prodigies are born or made. Only recently has science begun to probe the cultural and biological roots of child prodigies. And there are still no definite answers. Studies have shown that raw intelligence, as measured through IQ tests, is very inheritable. But the connection between high intelligence and the behaviour of prodigies is far from absolute. Prodigies master very specific skills. Nowhere can this be more clearly seen than in the case of Indian prodigy, Tathagat Avatar Tulsi. At the age of six, he was able to take any date in history and immediately calculate which day of the week it was. The newspapers nicknamed him 'computer brain'. This type of intelligence cannot be inherited.

One thing the experts are beginning to agree on is that a child's upbringing has a big impact on whether a gift is developed or not. According to Wu Wu-tien, a Taiwanese educationalist, 'Prodigies are half born, half made.' The parents provide stimulating environments: the home is full of books, they read to the child at an early age, and take them to museums and concerts. They do not talk down to their children and they allow them a high degree of independence.

Grammar | inversion

7 Complete the tasks in the Active grammar box.

Active grammar

1 The text on page 54 contains the following examples of inversion. Find two other examples.

1 ***Not for one minute had they imagined*** *that their son would be able to play.*

2 ***Not only did*** *Son* ***know*** *how to set up the chessboard, but he had also learned many of the complex rules of the game.*

3 ***Rarely,*** *however,* ***have*** *they* ***been*** *understood.*

We use inversion to emphasise the adverbial phrase in a sentence and to add variety to a text. Inversion is usually used in more formal texts.

We put a negative or adverbial expression at the start of a sentence (*never, nowhere, not only*, etc.) followed by auxiliary verb + subject.

He plays football and tennis. → *Not only* ***does he play*** *football, but he also plays tennis.*

He arrived and we left immediately. → *No sooner* ***did he arrive*** *than we left.*

We do not use auxiliary verbs when the main verb is the verb *to be* or a modal verb.

He is a great singer and can also play the piano. ***Not only is he*** *a great singer,* ***but*** *he can also play the piano.*

2 Match the rules with the sentences a–d below:

1 We use inversion after phrases that use *not*.

2 We use inversion after negative adverbs which emphasise a time relationship.

3 We use inversion for general emphasis with phrases that use *only*.

4 We use inversion with *no way* in informal speech.

a) ***No way am I*** *going to sing in public!*

b) ***Only if*** *we start to play more intelligently* ***will we*** *win this game.*

c) ***Not since*** *I was a child* ***have I*** *enjoyed myself so much.*

d) ***No sooner*** *had I arrived* ***than*** *I had to go out again.*

---

see Reference page 59

8 **a** Read the pairs of sentences below and tick (✓) the correct option.

1 a) Not since Mozart there has been a greater genius.

 b) Not since Mozart has there been a greater genius.

2 a) Only after the age of three did she begin to show her gift.

 b) Only after the age of three she did begin to show her gift.

3 a) Nowhere do the rules say you can't teach advanced subjects to children.

 b) Nowhere the rules say you can't teach advanced subjects to children.

4 a) Only later did we understand the truth about our gifted child.

 b) Only later we understand the truth about our gifted child.

5 a) Not only did he able to write poetry when he was five years old; he also played the violin well.

 b) Not only was he able to write poetry when he was five years old; he also played the violin well.

6 a) No sooner had we given her a paintbrush than she produced a masterpiece.

 b) No sooner had we given her a paintbrush, she produced a masterpiece.

b **4.7** Listen to the answers. Which words are stressed? Check on page 169.

9 Complete the phrases below and practise saying them in pairs. Remember to pay attention to word stress.

1 No way would I want to …

2 Rarely do I go …

3 Not only can I …, but I can also …

Reading

10 a Work in pairs. Student A: read the text on page 149. Student B: read the text on page 150. Complete the texts then make notes about the following:

- name
- special talent
- what others think of him/her

b Tell your partner about the person in your text.

Listening

11 a You are going to listen to an expert on gifted children describing a strange case. Before listening, read the notes below and the advice in the Lifelong learning box. What information do you need to complete the notes?

<u>People involved</u>

The case involved twins called (1)_____.
Physically they were (2)_____ and wore thick glasses. At school people (3)_____ at them.

<u>Their gifts</u>

They could tell you (4)_____ in the past and future 40,000 years.

They could remember long sequences of (5)_____.

If you asked them about a day in their lives, they could remember (6)_____.

<u>Conclusions about them</u>

Their ability is mathematical and (7)_____.

When asked how they do it, they reply, '(8)_____.'

Lifelong learning

Completing notes – predict!

Think about what type of information is needed (a date, a name, a place, etc.) and use the context to help you guess or predict. It doesn't matter if your guess is wrong; predicting helps us when we listen.

---

b [4.8] Listen and complete the notes.

12 Discuss.

1 In which jobs would the twins' abilities be useful?
2 How else could they use these abilities?
3 If you could have one special mental ability (e.g. memorising numbers or words, having a photographic memory, being able to read super-fast, being able to learn many foreign languages quickly, etc.), what would it be? Why?

Writing

13 a Write a summary of John and Michael's story in thirty words.

b Now cut your summary to twenty words. Which words can you omit? Which words are essential?

4 Vocabulary

Two-part expressions

1 Match the two-part expressions in sentences 1–12 to the definitions a–l below.

1 We are concerned about the breakdown of **law and order** in the country.
2 Here are a few **facts and figures** about the city.
3 I learned most of what I know about computers through **trial and error**.
4 I'm sick of all their petty **rules and regulations**.
5 Apart from the usual **aches and pains** she felt all right.
6 These are **tried and tested** security procedures.
7 Most teenagers would rather be **out and about** with their friends.
8 **By and large**, the new arrangements have worked well.
9 Let's settle this matter **once and for all**.
10 I hear from him every **now and again**.
11 When the doorbell rang he was **ready and waiting**.
12 I'm **sick and tired** of your excuses.

a) testing different methods in order to find which one is the most successful
b) used when making a general statement
c) a situation in which people respect the law and crime is controlled by the police
d) a method which has been used successfully many times
e) official instructions saying how things should be done/what is allowed
f) prepared for what he was going to do
g) angry or bored with something that has been happening for a long time
h) deal with something completely and finally
i) in places where you can meet people
j) the basic details and numbers concerning a situation or subject
k) slight feelings of pain that are not considered serious
l) sometimes

2 Work in groups of three. Close your books and test your partners like this:

A: Trial? (B and C try to answer)
B: and error. Law? (A and C try to answer)
C: and order.

3 Cover Ex. 1 and complete the sentences.

1 The police have a tough job keeping _____ in the run-down parts of the city.
2 The documentary confused me with all those _____.
3 We eventually found the answer by means of _____.
4 I hated being in the army because of all the _____.
5 I must be coming down with flu. I am all _____.
6 If you like the cake, I'll give you my _____ recipe.
7 He won't be at home now. He's always _____.
8 _____, it looks like it has been a good year for sales.
9 We really need to make a decision about this _____.
10 We only see each other every _____.
11 Has Martina arrived yet? Yes, she's _____.
12 I am _____ of always having to do his work for him.

4 **a** Answer the questions in pairs.

1 What do you think of the current state of law and order in your country? Do you think anything should be done about it? If so, what?
2 Is there anything that you are sick and tired of? If so, what could be done to make the situation better?
3 Are there any rules and regulations you have to abide by (at home/school/work)? Do you think they are good/reasonable rules and regulations?
4 Can you think of anything that you learned by trial and error? How long did it take you to learn?
5 What sort of things do you do only now and again? Why?
6 Can you think of a decision you would like to make (or would like someone to make) once and for all?
7 Are there any facts or figures you have read recently which you find interesting and/or surprising?

b Write three questions using the two-part expressions in Ex. 1 and then ask and answer the questions in pairs.

5 Write a short paragraph about law and order in your country (75–100 words). Try to use some of the other two-part expressions in Ex. 1 in your paragraph.

4 Communication

Great steps forward

1 **[4.9]** Listen to four speakers talking about important discoveries/inventions and answer the questions.

 1 Which do they mention and what do they say about them?

 2 Can you think of any other important discoveries/ inventions?

 3 How have they changed our lives and/or made the world a better place?

2 Look at the texts opposite and answer the questions.

 1 Is each area of research valid/likely to succeed/ likely to affect your life?

 2 Would you contribute money to further research in this area?

 3 How could you raise funds to support it?

3 **a** Work in groups to present a case for research funding. Group A: present a case for research into space travel; Group B: present a case for research into how robots can help mankind; Group C: present a case for research into genetic engineering. First, discuss the questions below:

 1 What important discoveries do you think might be made in this area in the future?

 2 What do you think is needed to make this research possible?

 3 How do you think the research should be funded?

 4 How will the research affect people's lives?

 b Decide how you are going to present your case for research and rehearse your arguments. Then present your ideas to the rest of the class. Which group makes the strongest/most convincing case?

Space travel/exploration

NASA spend billions of dollars every year to send professional astronauts to the Moon, Mars and beyond. Now Virgin Galactic is offering to take private citizens into space. They have already collected $6 million in deposits. For $200,000 the paying public will fly seventy miles above the Earth, see the planet's curvature and experience weightlessness for at least six minutes.

Robots

Various domestic robots are available which can do your ironing or mow the lawn, etc. Now, some hospitals in the UK are experimenting with robo-docs so that doctors can 'visit' patients from a distance (another ward, or even specialists from another country). Also, scientists are improving robots for space exploration.

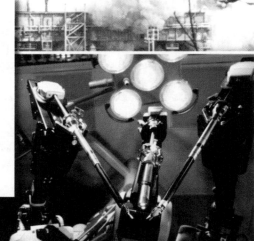

Genetic engineering

Using DNA, scientists can now manipulate the development of life. In 2001 a cloned cat called 'Little Nicky' was sold to a Texan woman for $50,000. Now scientists are researching the use of DNA to predict hereditary illnesses in unborn babies. The scientists could then potentially alter the babies' genes to prevent the illnesses. Many people worry that the techniques will be used commercially, for example to manufacture 'superchildren' with unnatural physical advantages.

Future probability

Use *will* to talk about something that is definite or a very strong probability.

Use *could, may* or *might* to talk about something that is possible but not certain.

There are many other phrases for describing possibility.

Adverbs/adverbial phrases:

it will almost definitely, it almost definitely won't, presumably it will

Verb phrases:

it may well, it might well, I doubt

Adjectives/adjectival phrases:

it's bound to/certain to/sure to/unlikely to

Noun phrases:

the chances are that, there's a strong/slight possibility, you haven't a hope of -ing

Future forms review

For timetables:

Use the Present Simple to talk about timetables.

The plane underlineunderline{departs} at 14.30 from Warsaw.

For decisions, plans and intentions:

Use *will* to talk about a decision made at the time of speaking (including offers and promises).

I don't think I 'll have a coffee, thanks.

Use *going to* to talk about a plan or intention (maybe details haven't been decided yet).

I 'm going to work in finance.

Use the Present Continuous to talk about a future arrangement (details such as time and place have been decided).

I 'm playing tennis at 4.30 with Zara.

For predictions:

Use *will* to make predictions based on what you know/believe. We often use *think, hope, believe*, etc. with *will* in this case.

I think Mike will be a good manager.

Use *going to* to make predictions based on what you can see/hear/think/feel now.

I think I 'm going to be sick.

Use the Future Continuous to talk about something in progress at a definite time in the future.

This time next year I 'll be living in France.

We can use the Future Continuous to ask about someone's plans, especially if we want something or want them to do something.

Will you be working late tonight?

Use the Future Perfect with time phrases with *by*. E.g. *by that time, by this time next week, by the end of February, by the end of the day*, etc.

By June we will have finished the project.

Inversion

We use inversion to emphasise the adverbial phrase in a sentence. Inversion is usually used in more formal or literary texts.

The form is negative adverb + auxiliary verb + subject. Note: the word order is the same as the question form.

Not once did she look up from her book.

We do not use auxiliary verbs when the main verb is the verb *to be* or a modal verb.

Not only is he a great musician, but he can also teach.

Inversion can be used after restrictive words like *never, rarely, little, hardly*, etc.

Never before had he seen such a beautiful vase.

We also use inversion with phrases beginning with *only*. These emphasise the first clause.

Only when I heard her speak did I remember her.

We use *no way* + inversion to show that something is impossible or that the speaker doesn't want to do something. This is informal.

No way would I do a bungee jump!

Key vocabulary

Progress

antibiotics   virus   human cloning   space mission   network   cell   crash a system   organ   hacker   skin tissue   gene   test tube   software   strain   microchip   mission   firewall   orbit   scan   shuttle   genetic engineering   superbug   launch   analysis

Expressions for plans and free time

be up to   at a loose end   snowed under   lined up   tied up   fall through   go ahead   get out of   call off   wind down   crop up   put my feet up

Sounding imprecise

sort of   once in a blue moon   more or less   about eight-ish   from time to time   in a way   kind of   bits and pieces   that kind of thing   etcetera (etc.)   loads   or so

Two-part expressions

law and order   facts and figures   trial and error   rules and regulations   out and about   by and large   tried and tested   once and for all   now and again   ready and waiting   sick and tired

1 Rewrite the sentences in three different ways using the words in brackets. There may be more than one answer.

1 We expect the weather to improve in the coming months. (chance/distinct/well)

2 I doubt if they will succeed in contacting us. (remote/probably/slim)

3 We will almost certainly move house in the spring. (likelihood/chance/bound)

4 I don't believe they will offer him the job. (hope/chance/distinct)

5 The organisers are confident that attendance will be high this year. (presumably/bound/strong)

6 There is a slight chance that Thompson could score a goal. (inconceivable/odds/possibly)

2 Choose the most appropriate words.

1 Max *retires/is retired/will retiring* soon, so we *'ll be looking/look/will be look* for a new manager.

2 Wait a moment. I'm just *coming/will come/will be coming*.

3 By this time next year, he *'s going to be/'ll be/is* at school.

4 Will you *going to see/have seen/be seeing* Jade this week?

5 Don't worry if you haven't finished. I *'m working/'m going to work/work* on it later.

6 I'm sure he *'ll make/makes/will be making* a great recovery, whatever the doctors *say/will say/will be saying*.

3 Choose the correct option.

1 No sooner _____ left the airport than I realised I had picked up the wrong suitcase.
(a) did I (b) had I (c) would I

2 No _____ should you be made to pay the difference.
(a) means (b) cases (c) way

3 Not _____ did they think it would be possible.
(a) for once (b) for one moment (c) for ever

4 On no _____ should I be disturbed during the meeting.
(a) way (b) time (c) account

5 _____ that I am asked such a difficult question.
(a) Not often it is (b) Not is it often (c) It is not often

4 Complete the text with suitable words.

A new problem has arisen in the school. No (1)_____ can teachers afford to lose their temper with pupils at any time. It has been noted recently that some pupils are using their mobile phones to film angry teachers. (2)_____ now (3)_____ we discovered what these videos are being used for. (4)_____ only are the videos sent to friends for amusement, but in some cases teachers' heads have been superimposed on another body to make them look stupid. Little (5)_____ we know that the resulting images had also been posted on Internet sites. (6)_____ no (7)_____ can this behaviour be allowed to continue. In order to curb the problem, all teachers are to ensure that mobile phones carried into the classroom are switched off. (8)_____ before has it (9)_____ so important to exercise patience and maintain high standards at all times.

5 Use the prompts in brackets and the phrases in the box to complete the sentences.

put my feet up   more or less   in a blue moon
time to time   cropped up   fell through   up to
snowed under   bits and pieces   at a loose end

1 I see her once _____. (very occasionally)

2 I have to do a few _____. (things)

3 I'm _____. (have nothing to do)

4 What are you _____ tomorrow? (doing)

5 I've _____ finished. (nearly)

6 A few problems _____ yesterday. (appeared)

7 I still go to that restaurant from _____. (not regularly)

8 I just want to _____. (relax)

9 I am absolutely _____ at the moment. (very busy)

10 The dinner _____. (was cancelled)

6 Complete the text with suitable words.

In the future, there will be a number of new developments in healthcare to add to tried and *tested* procedures. The development of (1)_____ engineering will be important, not only for curing our everyday aches and (2)_____, but for repairing skin (3)_____ damaged in accidents. Another development will be the insertion of (4)_____ into the human body. These tiny devices will carry medical information about the person. Machines will simply (5)_____ the individual to find out his or her genetic history instantly.

Scientists will continue looking for ways to cure common illnesses (6)_____ and for all. New (7)_____ will be discovered, to add to penicillin and others, but unfortunately new (8)_____ will also evolve to attack the body. New rules and (9)_____ will be necessary to stop increasing use of human (10)_____.

Lead-in

1   Discuss. How many ways can you think of to earn a fortune? Which are the easiest/most risky/quickest?

2   Discuss the meaning of the words/phrases **in bold** in sentences 1–8 below. Could any of them be used to describe the photos?

1   She **came into a fortune** when her mother died.
2   They **haggled** to get a good deal.
3   The **stock market** is a little unpredictable at the moment.
4   The employees have asked for a **rise**.
5   The taxes will affect **high-income** families.
6   Turner's paintings are **priceless**.
7   The sales team is **paid on commission**.
8   He's been in a bad way since his business **went bankrupt**.

3   Discuss statements 1–6 in pairs.

1   Art belongs to everyone. Priceless paintings should be available for all to see.
2   It's rude to haggle when you buy something. You should pay the asking price.
3   Paying people on a commission basis makes them work hard.
4   High-income families should pay higher taxes.
5   Gambling on the stock market is a sure way to go bankrupt.
6   The best way to get a rise is to be nice to your boss.

Reading

1 Discuss.

1 Is prison a successful form of punishment?

2 Does it reform or harden criminals?

3 What are the alternatives?

2 **a** Complete phrases 1–8 using the words in the box.

> fraud bouquet hope
> cool funds profit/living
> experience span

1 kept her _____

2 credit card _____

3 limited attention _____

4 hands-on work _____

5 start-up _____

6 bridal _____

7 make a _____

8 glimmer of _____

b Read the text to check your answers. Use the context to work out the meaning of any new phrases.

3 Answer the questions.

1 Does Paula Pryke specialise in traditional floral design? How do you know?

2 What are 'peonies and hyacinths'?

3 Did the ex-convicts have any relevant experience?

4 What is the significance of the name of the shop?

5 What does Paula mean by 'flowers work on so many levels'?

6 Why was the project difficult?

7 Do you think the project was a good idea?

4 Read the text again and a) underline words/phrases related to business and b) Circle words/phrases related to crime. Compare your answers with a partner.

1 Paula Pryke, one of the most innovative florists in the world, is not in the least bit afraid of anything or anyone. So when the team of ex-convicts she trained to become florists for a new television show were at their most difficult – unable to concentrate, fighting like cats and dogs – she kept her cool.

2 What they reminded her of were the days before she became fond of the subtle charms of peonies and hyacinths, when she worked as a teacher in a comprehensive school. 'They couldn't even sit still,' she says of the group. 'Their attention span was very limited indeed. But they did know an awful lot about credit-card fraud.'

3 Pryke gave the group eight days' training at her base in Islington, followed by some hands-on work experience. Now they are, in theory at least, on their own – running a shop called 'A New Leaf' in Islington, London. Television Channel 4 provided the start-up funds, but the business is owned and run by its staff; if they fail to make a profit, they will lose their livelihood.

4 'It's close by,' she says. 'So I'm still in almost daily contact with them. It's me they call when they've got a bridal bouquet to make at 5.30p.m. on a Friday and they're not quite sure how to do it. I keep telling them, 'Whatever you do, please don't take orders for things you can't make!''

5 Pryke heard about the project a year ago. 'It didn't seem a crazy idea at all. I remembered buying my own flowers from Buster Edwards [the train robber who famously had a flower stall outside Waterloo Station]. The wonderful thing about flowers is that they work on so many levels.'

6 Her six students were: Cliff, forty, who has a conviction for grievous bodily harm; Judith, forty, who served two years for cocaine smuggling; Greg, twenty-three, a former burglar; Rob, thirty-six, who has convictions for firearms offences; Kim, forty-six, jailed for intent to supply drugs; and Terrence, twenty-three, also convicted of drugs charges. They were recruited for the series through adverts in cafés, launderettes and snooker halls. But the project was by no means easy. Of the six, two dropped out, and two have been bought out of the business by the remaining pair, Judith and Cliff.

7 'I didn't know what any of them had done wrong,' says Pryke. 'I didn't want to.' So how did they take to the business? 'There were no naturals, but there was one guy where I saw a glimmer of hope. What amazed me was that some people wanted to be on TV, yet still couldn't always be bothered to turn up.

8 'But six people can't really make a living from one shop anyway, so it was obvious that we would end up with only those who really wanted their own shop.' Is A New Leaf the kind of place she would buy a bunch of flowers? 'It's getting there.'

5 Complete the sentences using words/phrases from the text.

1 _____ fraud is an increasingly common problem.

2 People involved in violent crime should _____ long prison sentences.

3 The best thing about _____ your own business is that you can be your own boss.

4 If you lose your job when you're fifty-five, it's hard to know how to make a _____.

5 If you put your CV on the Internet, you might get _____ by a big company.

6 If you are caught with large amounts of illegal drugs, you could be charged with _____ to supply.

Do you agree with the statements above. Why/why not?

Grammar | emphasis

6 Complete the tasks in the Active grammar box.

Active grammar

We can add emphasis by including certain words, for example:

1 *own* – to intensify possessive adjectives.
Find an example in paragraph 8.

2 *very/indeed*
Find an example in paragraph 2.

3 emphasising negatives: *in the least bit/at all*
Find an example in paragraph 1.
Find an example in paragraph 5.

4 adjectives/adverbs to add emphasis: *actually/by no means/even*
Find an example in paragraph 2.
Find an example in paragraph 6.

5 Auxiliary verbs: *do/did*
Find an example in paragraph 2.

We can use cleft sentences (sentences split into two clauses) for emphasis.

Cleft structures include:

The reason why we left the party early is ...

The thing that most annoys me about it is ...

The person who I most admire is ...

6 *It* clauses
It was Simon who asked ...
Find an example in paragraph 4.

7 *What* clauses
What you need is a cup of coffee ...
Find an example in paragraph 7.

---

see Reference page 73

Lifelong learning

Use more emphasis

When speaking, use stress and intonation to emphasise what you want to say. When writing, you may need to add words, change the structure of the sentence or add punctuation.

7 a Rewrite the sentences to add emphasis using the clues **in bold**.

1 He can't complain. It's his fault he lost the money. **own**

2 We're not certain that it isn't the same man committing the crimes. **by**

3 I really miss having enough time to spend with friends. **what**

4 They didn't understand what we wanted. **all**

5 He didn't stop at the red light. He just drove straight through. **even**

6 The costs were very high. **indeed**

7 Sammy always got into trouble. **it**

8 Keith wasn't annoyed when we cancelled the meeting. **least**

b **5.1** Listen to the answers. Mark the main words which are stressed. Practise saying the sentences with the same stress and intonation.

Person to person

8 Discuss the following questions in pairs. Use emphasis where possible.

1 What are the three most important elements of a successful business?

2 Would you consider starting your own business. Why/why not?

3 Who would/wouldn't you choose for a business partner? Why/why not?

Listening

9 **5.2** Listen and complete the notes.

The speaker warns against doing business with (1)_____.

The only way to get rid of a bad business partner legally is to (2)_____.

Successful partnerships will combine two types of people: (3)_____ and (4)_____.

It's a good idea if partners have complementary (5)_____.

One may be good in the area of product design, the other in marketing. If your business is lacking in a particular area, you may need to (6)_____.

Good (7)_____ is essential to ensure that arguments do not interfere with the success of the business.

Ideally, your business partner will be committed to the (8)_____ success of the business.

10 a **5.3** Listen again in sections. As you listen, notice how the speaker uses the following phrases:

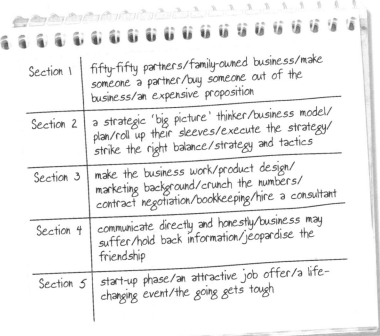

Section 1	fifty-fifty partners/family-owned business/make someone a partner/buy someone out of the business/an expensive proposition
Section 2	a strategic 'big picture' thinker/business model/plan/roll up their sleeves/execute the strategy/strike the right balance/strategy and tactics
Section 3	make the business work/product design/marketing background/crunch the numbers/contract negotiation/bookkeeping/hire a consultant
Section 4	communicate directly and honestly/business may suffer/hold back information/jeopardise the friendship
Section 5	start-up phase/an attractive job offer/a life-changing event/the going gets tough

b Check you understand the meaning of the words/phrases from Ex. 10a. Then reconstruct what the speaker says using the words/phrases and your notes from Ex. 9.

11 Discuss.

1 Do you agree with what the speaker says? Do you know people in successful/unsuccessful partnerships? Why do you think the relationship does/doesn't work?

2 Are you a 'visionary' or an 'operations' person? What skills, experience and qualities would you bring to a business partnership? In which areas are you lacking? Would you work well with the other students in your group?

Grammer | conditional sentences
Can do | discuss financial decisions/regrets

Reading

1 Read the quotes below. Which do you agree/disagree with?

'There's a million ways to make money and a billion ways to lose it.'

'Whoever said money can't buy happiness simply didn't know where to go shopping.'

'Money is only a tool. It will take you wherever you wish, but it will not replace you as the driver.'

2 Work in pairs. Student A: read about William Post on page 151. Student B: read about Leon Spinks on page 65. Make notes about the following as you read:

1 How did he win his money? How much was it?
2 How did he lose his money?
3 What does he do now?
4 What is his relationship like with his family? Why?
5 How does he feel about what has happened/the future?

3 Tell your partner about the person in your text using your notes.

4 **a** Work in pairs. Find words/phrases in the texts which mean the following:

1 take someone to court to get money from them (text A)
2 ask someone continuously to do something (text A)
3 new business activities (text A)
4 declare that you are unable to pay your debts (text A)
5 money you receive from the government when you are unfit to work (text A)
6 treat someone unfairly in order to get what you want (text B)
7 offer to work (usually for no money) (text B)
8 receive a discount (text B)
9 the power to make legal decisions regarding finances (text B)
10 didn't receive any of the money (text B)

b Complete the sentences with a phrase from Ex. 4a.

1 The cover was slightly damaged so I _____ 15 percent _____ the asking price.
2 He's made a lot of money with his new _____ _____.
3 Don't lend them your car! They're just _____ _____ of you.
4 She said she would send a cheque, but I still haven't _____ _____ _____ of the money she owes us.
5 Steve has kindly _____ to help me sort out the office.
6 If you can get a doctor's certificate, you may be eligible for a _____ _____.
7 The business had been failing for years before he _____ _____.
8 My sister is always _____ me for money.

Text B

RICHES TO RAGS

For Leon Spinks it has been a hard fall from glory. The former heavyweight champion, who gained world fame and fortune when he beat Muhammad Ali in 1978, now works as a cleaner at the YMCA in Columbus, US. Now, the only gloves he wears are cleaning gloves and the people he fights are the hangers-on who have taken advantage of him. He cleans the local YMCA for $5.15 an hour on weekends, sometimes unloads trucks at McDonald's, and volunteers to help the homeless. He likes his job at McDonald's. 'I get 50 percent off on Big Macs and everything,' he says.

On a Friday night, Spinks sits at the bar and has a few beers. The public perception of him is that he partied away the nearly $5 million he made from fighting. He denies this. 'That's what people think. I was stupid and I gave [the lawyers] power of attorney.' He says he never saw a penny of the $3.75 million he made from Ali–Spinks 2.

Spinks' luck contrasts to his brother, Michael's, though they were both boxers. The two brothers won gold medals in Montreal and when Michael Spinks beat Holmes in 1985, the Spinks boys became the first brothers to become world heavyweight champs. But whereas Michael Spinks kept his money and bought a $5 million estate in Delaware. Leon lost his. 'Me and my brother are close,' Leon said. But he won't ask him for financial help. 'I'm not into that thing,' he said. 'I can make it myself.'

But Spinks does worry about the future. 'I worry about that all the time,' he acknowledged. 'I want to live comfortably for the rest of my life. I need money. I don't hurt nobody. I do what I can. I still help people as much as I can. I keep doing my best.

If you want to be my friend, be my friend. If not, leave me alone.'

5 Discuss in pairs.

1 Do you know anyone who has won, lost, borrowed or lent large amounts of money?
2 Do you know anyone who is particularly generous, or mean with their money?
3 Do you think it is a good idea to buy lottery tickets? Why/why not?

Grammar | conditional sentences

6 Complete the tasks in the Active grammar box.

Active grammar

1 Check how well you know your conditionals. Put the verb in brackets in the correct tense.

If you go into business with relatives, it <u>tends to</u> (tend to) put a strain on your relationship.

1 If you happen to _____ (see) Tom, could you tell him I need some money?

2 I wish I _____ (not buy) that expensive car, or I might still have some left.

3 She wouldn't have been able to pay her debts if she _____ (not come into) large amounts of money.

4 Supposing Post had been killed, his brother _____ (inherit) some of the winnings.

5 They wouldn't have _____ (be able) to buy the house if it hadn't been for her father.

6 Provided the business ventures _____ (be) successful, he shouldn't have to declare bankruptcy.

7 If you _____ (like) to follow me, I'll show you to your rooms.

8 We'd be rich now if we _____ (not lost) the ticket.

9 _____ (Shall) you have any queries, please do not hesitate to contact me.

10 If only he _____ (stop) pestering me, I'd try to help.

2 Match the phrases in the box to their uses in 1–7 below.

> a) if it hadn't been for ...   b) should you ...
> c) provided (that).../as long as ...   d) if only ...
> e) happen to/should happen to ...   f) supposing ...
> g) if you will/would ...

1 _____ can be used with First Conditional sentences to emphasise that something is unlikely to occur.

2 _____ can be used instead of *if* to show that specific conditions should be met for something to happen.

3 _____ can be used instead of *if* to emphasise the imaginary. This is especially common in everyday speech.

4 _____ is often used to show how a negative result would have occurred without a certain person or event happening.

5 _____ can be used to express a wish or regret.

6 _____ is often used in formal business communication.

7 _____ can be used as a polite form.

---

see Reference page 73

7 Use the prompts in brackets to rewrite the sentences so the meaning stays the same.

I'll renew the contract if the conditions stay the same. (provided)

Provided that the conditions stay the same, I'll renew the contract.

1 Would we get to the bank in time if we left immediately? (supposing)

2 I failed the exam because the last question was so difficult. (if it ... passed the exam).

3 I didn't have my credit card with me so I didn't buy any presents. (I would ...)

4 The business isn't doing well because there is so much competition. (if only ... better).

5 You can call me if you have any problems. (should)

6 Thanks to Dr Hyde I survived the operation. (if it ... might not)

7 They fell out over money and their marriage broke up. (if they ... married now.)

8 In case you arrive late, just ask for me at the desk. (should you ...)

Person to person

8 Discuss in pairs.

1 What would you do if only you had more time?

2 If you happened to win £100, what would you do with it?

3 Supposing you could do any job in the world, what would you do?

4 Is there anything which you wish you had done when you were younger?

5 How might things be different now, if you had made a different decision at some point in your life?

Reading and speaking

9 a Read the text below and <u>underline</u> the correct alternative.

   b Discuss the questions.

   1 What do you think of Andrew Carnegie's ideas?

   2 Do you believe in giving money to charity? Which causes do you/ would you support, and why?

   3 Tragedy often inspires generosity. Would you agree?

   4 What is your greatest extravagance?

   5 Are there any rich/famous people you particularly admire? Why?

   6 Do you know of any other famous philanthropists?

   7 'You cannot buy scientists or poets.' Do you agree? Why/why not?

Andrew Carnegie

GREAT PHILANTHROPISTS

Can you imagine becoming the richest person in the world, and then giving all your money away? That's exactly what Andrew Carnegie did. Carnegie made billions of dollars during his highly successful business career. As a result, when he retired in 1901, at the age of sixty-six, he was the world's richest man. But Carnegie outlined his beliefs about wealth in an essay, 'The Gospel of Wealth'. In the essay, he describes how wealthy men ought to live without (1) *greedy/ charity/money/extravagance*, provide moderately (2) *of/for/on/to* their families, and consider the rest of their wealth as extra money that should be distributed to promote the (3) *welfare/farewell/sickness/richness* and happiness of other people. The 'Gospel of Wealth' was read all over the world, and Carnegie's worthy intentions were praised. Very

wealthy people of that period lived (4) *greatly/lavishly/hugely/cheaply* and spent huge amounts of money on their own personal needs and wishes, but Andrew Carnegie was not one of them. In his lifetime, he gave away more than $350 million or almost 90 percent of his (5) *treasure/ fortune/collection/account* for what he considered to be the improvement of all mankind.

But he wasn't the only generous American of his time. John D. Rockefeller once said, 'Giving away money intelligently is more difficult than making it.' Having given away $530 million to (6) *care/help/charity/ cause*, he should know. Rockefeller's entrepreneurial skills started when he was young. When he was just twelve years old, he lent $50 to a farmer. The following year he got the money back, and (7) *charged/asked/insisted/ paid* interest! But his philanthropic journey was inspired by the tragic death of his three-year-old grandson. When the boy died of scarlet fever, Rockefeller began putting his money (8) *onto/in/into/to* medical research. He (9) *foundation/founded/found/ foundered* the Rockefeller Institute in 1901, and later his doctors became famous for flying around the world providing vaccines for children.

Helping children is a (10) *mission/missive/work/problem* close to the heart of another famous philanthropist, Bill Gates. Gates

not only earns, but also gives away more money than anyone else in the world. The Bill and Melinda Gates Foundation has saved 700,000 children's lives through its health programmes. Gates (11) *puts/spends/ dedicates/creates* billions to fighting diseases like malaria, which are still killers in the developing world. Closer to home, he has set up education programmes and scholarship funds designed to have a major (12) *change/ affect/result/impact* on children growing up in the US.

Bill and Melinda Gates

Whilst we can (13) *inspire/admire/ cope/afford* the generosity and (14) *idea/visual/ambitious/vision* of all these men, perhaps we should leave the last word to Rockefeller's colleague, Raymond Fosdick. He wrote that it's a mistake to think 'that money can create ideas, and that a great (15) *amounts/sum/deal/lot* of money can create better ideas. You cannot buy scientists or poets.'

The Rockefeller Center

Speaking

1 Discuss in pairs. What is important in a job? Make a list of the five most important things for you.

2 Check the meaning of the words/phrases in the box. Did any appear on your list?

> job satisfaction   recognition   good salary
> promotion prospects   travel opportunities
> supportive colleagues/boss   pension plan
> freedom/autonomy   flexible working hours
> professional/personal development
> perks and benefits   working environment
> convenience of location   challenging tasks

3 Complete the How to ... box using the words below.

> about   absolutely   could   main
> do   really

HOW TO ...

express priorities

Saying it's very important	My _____ priority is ...
	The essential thing for me is ...
	This is _____ vital!
	I couldn't _____ without ...
Saying it's not important	I'm not _____ bothered/concerned _____ this.
	This isn't a major priority.
	I _____ do without ...

4 Discuss in pairs. Which of the things in Ex. 2 are priorities and which are not? Try to use some of the expressions in the How to ... box.

Reading

5 Read the article and answer the questions.

1 How does Fortune Magazine get the results for its annual list?

2 What makes the winners special?

3 What is Wegmans' philosophy?

4 Why does a manager say that the company is run by sixteen-year-old cashiers?

TOP COMPANIES

Every year since 1998, Fortune Magazine has published a list of the '100 Best Companies to Work For'. How does the magazine choose the companies? Firstly, it uses a survey. 350 employees answer fifty-seven questions about their company. Secondly, Fortune Magazine looks at important features of companies; for example, pay, benefits, and communication between workers and management. Finally, the magazine compares the results to find its Top 100.

To a certain extent, the results are guesswork, but the companies on the list, by and large, have many things in common: they pay their employees well, they allow workers to make decisions, and they offer a comfortable workplace. Broadly speaking, however, the winners tend to offer something above and beyond the norm. J.M.Smucker, a jam and jelly company, gives its workers free muffins and bagels for breakfast; at Griffin Hospital, employees get free massages; a bank called First Horizon National gives its employees time off to visit their children's classrooms. Wegmans Food Markets sent one worker on a ten-day trip to London, Paris and Italy to learn about cheese. This is not unusual for the New York-based company, which is well-known for the scholarships it gives its employees to further their education. At W.L.Gore, workers decide on their colleagues' salaries. Surprisingly enough, the most important thing for employees is not money. It is freedom to develop ideas. Timberland offers a six-month paid sabbatical for employees who have 'a personal dream that benefits the community'.

Let's not forget that all these companies are businesses whose priority is making money. They have to make a profit. And do they? Seemingly, the answer is a big 'yes'. The number one company on Fortune's 2005 list, Wegmans, makes a fortune. The company, which has a motto, 'Employees first, customers second', is one of the fifty largest private companies in the US, with annual sales of $3.6 billion, according to Forbes magazine. Apparently, being good to your employees is no obstacle to making money.

How much of Wegmans' success is due to the company's policies? 'Up to a point, the success is because of the freedom they give us,' says one employee. 'On the other hand, no company gets rich just by being nice. Wegmans has great marketing strategies and it's well-positioned within the community. I've been here for fifteen years. Looking back, I'd say that the company's innovations for customers, such as the Shoppers' Club electronic discount programme in the 90s, have been just as important as the benefits to staff.'

But the employee benefits are striking. Fundamentally, Wegmans believes in professional development. As well as scholarships, the company gives its employees business opportunities. For years, one employee made delicious cookies for her colleagues. Eventually, she started selling the cookies in Wegmans. 'I just asked the manager,' she says. 'With hindsight, I should have asked earlier. I could have made more money!'

The staff's freedom to make decisions is another thing you won't find everywhere. Essentially, Wegmans wants its workers to do almost anything to keep the customers happy. Believe it or not, an employee once cooked a Thanksgiving turkey in the store for a customer because the woman's turkey, bought in Wegmans, was too big for her oven. One manager says, 'We're a $3 billion company run by sixteen-year-old cashiers.'

Grammar | sentence adverbials

6 Complete the tasks in the Active grammar box.

> ### Active grammar
>
> **1** Read the text on page 68 again. What purpose do the <u>underlined</u> words/phrases serve?
>
> **2** (Circle) the correct option to complete the rules below.
>
> Sentence adverbials show how the sentence fits in with the rest of the text, and frequently go at the <u>beginning/middle/end</u> of a sentence, though they can go in the other positions. Sentence adverbials show the speaker's attitude and feelings and are usually separated from the rest of the sentence by a <u>full stop/comma</u>.
>
> **3** Complete the table using the <u>underlined</u> examples in the text on page 68.
>
> | ADVERBIAL FUNCTIONS | EXAMPLES |
> |---|---|
> | Basic ideas | *fundamentally essentially* |
> | Unexpected points | |
> | Generalisations | |
> | How something appears | |
> | Contrast | |
> | Reflection on the past | |
> | Partial agreement | |
>
> **4** Add any other adverbial phrases that you can think of to the table.

see Reference page 73

see Reference page 73

7 <u>Underline</u> the sentence adverbial which does not fit the context.

We want our workers to be happy. Fundamentally/Essentially/<u>With hindsight</u>, this means helping them to foster a sense of pride in their work.

1 We believe in giving our employees as much autonomy as possible. *Broadly speaking/Apparently/By and large*, we try not to interfere unless really necessary.

2 Our employees don't complain if they have to work at weekends. *On the other hand/Seemingly/However*, they do expect to be paid overtime for this.

3 We believe in second chances, because employees learn from their mistakes. *Believe it or not/Surprisingly enough/Broadly speaking*, our company has never dismissed a worker.

4 Employees like to set their own system *up to a point/apparently/to a certain extent*, but we don't let workers pay themselves huge amounts.

5 Some employees' salaries were getting too high too fast. *Believe it or not/Looking back/With hindsight*, we should have introduced a pay cap earlier.

6 We studied some large companies. It is *apparently/seemingly/surprisingly enough* difficult, but not impossible, to change the whole culture of a company.

Person to person

8 Discuss in pairs.

1 It's a good idea for employees to set their own salaries.

2 Employees shouldn't have to wear uniforms.

3 Employees should be allowed to evaluate their bosses formally.

4 In future, everyone will work flexitime.

5 Working at weekends will become normal for every profession.

Listening

9 Discuss. Do you know any companies with particularly favourable/poor working conditions? What effect do/did they have on the employees and on the company results?

10 a **5.4** Listen to an interview with a company director. What do you think of the conditions he describes?

b Listen again and make notes about the following:

1 Type of business
2 Staff
3 Incentives
4 Salaries
5 Atmosphere
6 Personal involvement

c Compare your answers with a partner.

11 Discuss.

1 What do you think of the ideas introduced at Piranha Recruitment? Would you like to work for the company? Why/why not?

2 If you were the director of a new company, what ideas would you like to introduce to help retain your staff?

Vocabulary | expressing quantity

12 a Complete phrases 1–10 from the listening in Ex. 10a using the words in the box.

> most   many   plenty   majority   awful
> handful   few   much   deal   bit

1 as _____ as (a surprisingly large number)
2 a little _____ more (a little more)
3 a great _____ of energy (a lot of energy)
4 _____ of benefits (lots of benefits)
5 not _____ of an expert (not really an expert)
6 for the _____ part (generally)
7 an _____ lot of time (a surprisingly large amount)
8 the vast _____ (most of)
9 quite a _____ staff (a considerable number)
10 only a _____ of people (very few people)

b **5.5** Listen to check your answers.

c Listen again. Mark the stressed words. Which words are weak? Repeat the phrases.

13 Rewrite the sentences using the words **in bold**.

1 The government spends a lot of money on defence.
The government ... **great**

2 Not as many people turned up to see the race as had been expected.
Surprisingly ... **few**

3 The customers generally appreciate our top-quality service.
For ... **most**

4 It isn't a huge fee if you consider the amount of work involved.
It ... **much**

5 There are more than enough bottles on the rack.
There ... **plenty**

6 Three or four people asked questions at the end.
Only ... **handful**

7 The crowds were huge.
There ... **awful**

8 Most of the workers joined the strike.
The ... **vast**

14 a Complete the sentences below using phrases from Ex. 12.

> I'd like to ...
> this course by ...

> *I'd like to get the most out of this course by doing a little bit more homework.*

1 I think the government wastes ... on ...

4 There are ... women in top management positions because ...

2 ... of people in this country ...

5 I spend ... my time ...

3 ... of road accidents could be avoided if ...

6 There are not ... as there used to be.

b Compare your sentences with a partner.

Writing

15 Choose one of the sentences in Ex. 14a and write a short paragraph (75–100 words) on the topic to present to the class.

1 Read the dialogue below and discuss. What are the two meanings of *fortune*?

A: 'Thanks to my good fortune, I picked the correct lottery numbers.'

B: 'Yes, you won a fortune, didn't you?'

2 Match the phrases **in bold** in A to phrases with a similar meaning in B.

A

1 I could never afford that watch. It **costs a fortune**.

2 He's got six cars and a yacht! You know, he**'s worth a fortune**.

3 If you're careful you **can live on** £150 a week, even in London.

4 I**'m not well off** but I still have a good lifestyle.

5 That shirt only cost me £15. It **was a bargain**.

6 I had a rather expensive holiday. Now I**'m broke**.

7 Great meal! **Shall** we **split the bill**?

8 It's my birthday so I**'m going to treat myself** to a bottle of champagne.

9 That business closed down. The owners **were always in debt**.

B

a) That house was dirt cheap. It's really spacious and it only cost £150,000.

b) I'm not rich, but I get by on my salary.

c) Neither of us have much money so let's go halves.

d) He can't afford a holiday. He's a bit hard up.

e) We're in the red at the moment, but the company's finances will improve in June.

f) I'm glad you like my new car. It cost me an arm and a leg.

g) She's always splashing out on new clothes. Look at her!

h) You should have let him pay! He's rolling in it!

i) I can't go out tonight. I'm skint.

3 Discuss in pairs.

1 Which phrases are generally more colloquial – those in A or B?

2 Are the phrases in A formal or neutral?

3 Do you have similar phrases in your language?

4 Look at the photos above. Which phrases from Ex. 2 could you use to describe them?

5 a Discuss in pairs.

1 In your home town, how much money does a person need to live on per month?

2 When was the last time you treated yourself to something?

3 What would you splash out on if you suddenly got some money unexpectedly?

4 Do you know anyone who has been in debt or skint? What happened?

5 Where's the best place to look for bargains in your opinion?

6 Which businesses in your home town are worth a fortune?

7 Do you usually go halves when you go out with people? Are there ever any occasions when you don't go halves? What does it depend on?

8 Are most students in your country hard up? Why?

b Compare your answers with other students.

1 a **5.6** Listen to two people discussing what they would do if their company suddenly had a fortune ($1,000,000) to spend. What ideas do they have?

   b Compare your answers. How are the speakers' characters different? Listen again to check.

2 Work in groups. What would you suggest if your company/university/school suddenly had a fortune to spend? Which group has the best ideas?

3 Read the profile of Fortune Foods and answer the questions.

   1 What are the company's main strengths?
   2 What are the main problems for employees?

4 Fortune Foods has just received a donation of $2,000,000 from a philanthropic ex-employee! Read the instructions below and decide what the company should do with the money.

   1 Work in two groups (one group represents the employees and the other represents management). Group A (workers) read page 147. Group B (management) read page 149.
   2 Spend some time preparing your arguments and then begin the negotiation.
   3 Discuss. How did the negotiation go? What did you decide? Was everyone happy with the decision?

Company Profile

The company: Fortune Foods

Produces: quality food for parties.

Strengths: the company has an excellent reputation and is growing. The clients are rich businesses.

Problems: workers often stay late at night to finish preparing food. They are stressed. The factory is in a part of the city with bad roads and heavy traffic. It is difficult to drive there.

Financial Situation: Fortune Foods made a profit last year.

Emphasis

Passive constructions can be used to emphasise information at the beginning of a sentence.

The suspect was arrested by police.

Fronting

You can change the order of clauses in a sentence to put a clause at the beginning which would not normally be there.

What she thinks she is doing, I don't know!

Cleft sentences

Sentences introduced with *It is/It was*, or by a clause beginning with *what* can be used to emphasise different parts of the sentence.

It was me who spotted the mistake.

Adding words for emphasis

*She used her **own** ingredients.*

*We were very pleased **indeed**.*

*They aren't **in the least bit** scared.*

*I haven't thought about it **at all**.*

*Some people were **even** asking for discounts.*

*It was **utterly** pointless us being there.*

*I **do** think we should warn them about the delay.*

Conditionals review

To talk about something that is always true, use *if* + Present Simple + Present Simple.

If you <u>go</u> into business with relatives, it <u>tends</u> to put a strain on your relationship.

To talk about a possible real situation in the future, use *if* + present tense + *will* (*might/may/could/should*).

If we <u>find</u> a bank, we <u>could change</u> some money.

To talk about a hypothetical or unlikely situation in the future, use *if* + Past Simple + *would* (*might/may/could/should*).

If they <u>asked</u> me to go back, I <u>wouldn't hesitate</u>.

To talk about a hypothetical past situation, use *if* + Past Perfect + *would have* (*could have/should have/might have*).

If he <u>had taken</u> his phone, I <u>could've called</u> him.

To talk about past regrets, use *if only/I wish* + Past Perfect.

If only I <u>hadn't told</u> him about Johnny.

I <u>wish</u> I'<u>d thought</u> of looking it up on the Internet – it <u>would've saved</u> so much time.

Mixed conditionals

These may express a hypothetical present result of a past action: *if* + Past Perfect + *would/could/may/might/should*.

If we <u>hadn't answered</u> the advertisement, we <u>wouldn't be</u> here now.

Other words/phrases can be used with, or instead of, *if* in conditional sentences, e.g. *provided that, as long as, if only, should you happen to, supposing, if it hadn't been for ...*

Sentence adverbials

These are adverbial phrases which comment on part of a sentence. They can be used to show the speaker's attitude towards a subject, to organise information, rephrase, change the subject, summarise or generalise, etc. They are usually separated from the rest of the sentence by a comma.

Broadly speaking, we all agree.

Common adverbials: *fundamentally, essentially, broadly speaking, however, surprisingly enough, seemingly, apparently, up to a point, on the other hand, looking back, with hindsight, believe it or not*

Key vocabulary

Finance expressions

came into money   haggle   stock market
high-income   rise   priceless   paid on commission
go bankrupt

Money, achievement and charity

volunteer   get money off something   philanthropist
power of attorney   not see a penny of the money
pester someone   business venture   provide for
declare bankruptcy   disability benefit   vision
put money into research   run a foundation

Expressions for saying what is/isn't important

the main priority   the essential thing
absolutely vital   couldn't do without
not bothered/concerned about something

Describing a job

job satisfaction   recognition   perks and benefits
promotion prospects   supportive colleagues/boss
travel opportunities   freedom/autonomy   salary
professional/personal development   pension plan
flexible working hours   convenience of location
working environment   challenging tasks

Money idioms

costs a fortune   worth a fortune   live on
not well off   bargain   broke   split the bill
treat myself to   in debt   dirt cheap   get by on
go halves   hard up   in the red   rolling in it
cost an arm and a leg   splash out on   skint

1 Rewrite the sentences using the correct option in brackets. There may be more than one possibility.

1 He was offered the job, but he didn't accept. (*surprisingly enough/broadly speaking*)

2 They explained how the project would be too difficult to manage and I agree. (*on the other hand/to a certain extent*)

3 They didn't know who I was talking about. Georgia left the company years ago. (*Principally/Apparently*)

4 I decided to leave and change careers. I'm not sure that I made the right decision. (*Essentially/With hindsight*)

5 The new arrangements have worked out well. (*By and large/Primarily*)

6 The new minister was faced with an impossible task. (*however/seemingly*)

2 Circle the clauses which <u>cannot</u> be used to complete the sentences.

1 If he'd planned to give the money back, why a) didn't he contact the police? b) hadn't he contact the police? c) would he contact the police?

2 Supposing you lost your job tomorrow a) what are you going to do? b) what would you do? c) you could call me.

3 He can come with us provided that a) he pays for his own meals. b) he would pay for his accommodation. c) he doesn't drive the car.

4 If you happen to find my bag a) could you call this number? b) just put it on the side. c) I'd be really surprised.

5 If it hadn't been for Mary a) you will still be waiting. b) we would never have found you. c) everything would have been fine.

3 Rewrite the sentences using the words **in bold** for emphasis.

1 We weren't at all surprised to hear that she got the part. **bit**

2 I couldn't believe it when they told me to leave! **what**

3 It was very hot soup. **indeed**

4 I think it is surprisingly warm here. **actually**

5 She makes a lot of her clothes. **own**

6 It is not certain that the game will take place. **means**

7 Rachel had the courage to complain about the service. **it**

8 They have done nothing to put the problem right. **all**

4 Unjumble the words in brackets to complete the sentences.

1 Those charity workers are always _____ me for money. (etsegpirn)

2 Handling the take-over was one of the most _____ tasks of his career. (glanhingcel)

3 The head of department's duty was to _____ the strategy. (cuexete)

4 Increasing sales has to be our main _____. (trioripy)

5 The job has excellent _____ prospects. (morotipon)

6 Come on! Let's _____ out on an expensive hotel. (salhps)

7 I'm sending her some money. She's a bit _____ up at the moment. (drah)

8 Why don't you _____ yourself to something nice? (retat)

9 Within a few months of opening, he had declared _____. (kracynopbut)

10 He doesn't worry about money. He's _____ in it! (ginlorl)

5 Complete the text using the words in the box.

> vision   charity   mind   remarkable   wealthy
> worth   design   fortune   venture   founded

Anita Roddick, who (1)_____ The Body Shop, says she plans to give away her entire £51m (2)_____ to (3)_____. One of the UK's best-known and most (4)_____ entrepreneurs, she started her business (5) _____ in 1976 with her husband. Their strategy, (6) _____ and excellent product (7)_____ meant that the business, selling body scrubs and ethical beauty products, was a fantastic success. Dame Anita was soon (8)_____ a huge fortune. Now she says she finds business life 'boring' and hopes to achieve peace of (9)_____ by sharing her good fortune with those who have not been so lucky. 'The worst thing is greed,' she said. 'I do not know why people who are extraordinarily (10)_____ are not more generous. I don't want to die rich. Money doesn't mean anything to me.'

6 | Power

Lead-in

1   Discuss. What sort of 'power' is represented in the photos? Can you think of any other types of 'power'?

2   **a** Which words collocate with 'power'? Which words collocate with 'powerful'? Write the words in the correct place in the table. Some may go in both columns.

> nuclear   speech   medicine   spending   argument   economic
> reasons   solar   brain   tool   influence   world   political
> people   army   consumer

POWER	POWERFUL
power tool	a *powerful* tool

b Can you add more words to each column?

3   Check you understand the phrases **in bold**. Discuss the questions.
1   Do you think people **have** enough **power over** the decisions that affect their lives?
2   Should more women be **in positions of power**?
3   Can you think of any countries which are growing in **economic power**?
4   In what circumstances should police be given **special powers**?
5   What political changes often occur when a new leader **comes to power**?
6   Who **holds the power** in your family/school/workplace?

Vocabulary | architecture

1 cuss.

1   What is the most impressive building you have ever seen?
2   Do you generally prefer modern or traditional architecture? Give examples.
3   What is the most beautiful/ ugliest building in your town/city? Are there any which you feel should be knocked down or restored?
4   If you had money to invest in your town/city, what would you build?

The Pentagon

The Eiffel Tower

The Forbidden City

2 ! the words in the box to complete the definitions and related example sentences 1–8 below. You may need to change the verb tenses.

> win | gain   impressed   part   by   play
> over | important   be

_____ : *to obtain or achieve something*

1   Radical left-wing parties _____ control of local authorities.
2   We are hoping to _____ a better understanding of the process.

_____ _____: *to get someone's support / friendship by being nice to them*

3   The party worked hard to _____ _____ undecided voters.
4   He took her out to restaurants and the theatre, and she was completely _____ _____.

_____ _____ _____ : *feel admiration and respect for*

5   We _____ very _____ _____ the standard of her work.
6   The chief executive _____ _____ _____ your presentation.

_____ *an* _____ _____ *in: to have a big effect or influence*

7   Diet _____ *an* _____ _____ in helping people live longer.
8   Everyone from the cleaners to the management _____ *an* _____ _____ in this year's financial success.

3 ad the text and check your answers.

Architecture of Power

No one knew better than the Romans how to gain political influence through the use of engineering and architecture. The Romans built roads, bridges, aqueducts, forums, amphitheatres and baths in order to win over the minds of the cultures they were conquering. It's hard not to be impressed by a power which provides you with clean water to wash in, a road to the capital city, a way to travel across previously impassable rivers, and incredible public buildings.

Architecture has played an important part in public life throughout history, whether as homage to an individual, or as a monument to an institution or ideology. Architecture has always been a potent symbol of wealth, status and power. From castles to cathedrals, from the pyramids to skyscrapers, architecture has always served to glorify the ideal of the time. 'Architecture of Power' explores some of the world's most famous architectural buildings and structures to see what we can learn about their history.

The Millenium Dome

Hassan II Mosque

Sydney Harbour Bridge

The Great Pyramid of ancient Egypt

4   Discuss.

1   According to the text, how did the Romans use architecture to increase their power?

2   How has architecture been used through history?

3   Can you think of examples of 'powerful architecture' in your town/city/country?

Listening

5   **a**   Look at the photos and guess which structure:

1   is large enough to house the Eiffel Tower?

2   was built to celebrate a king's 60th birthday?

3   was constructed by 400,000 men?

4   is known as the 'coathanger'?

5   takes twenty minutes to walk around?

6   is one of the largest palaces in the world?

7   was built in 1889?

b   6.1 Listen and check your answers.

6   Listen again and write notes about each building/structure (e.g. size/date built, etc.).

7   Compare your notes. What does the speaker say about each structure?

8   Discuss. Which structures do you think are the most impressive or interesting? Which have you visited/would you like to visit?

Grammar | articles

9   Complete the tasks in the Active grammar box.

Active grammar

1   Write some rules for when we use the definite, the indefinite, or no article.

2   Check your ideas with the Reference on page 87.

3   Find examples of each type in the tapescript on pages 170–171.

4   Choose the correct option to complete the rules below.

Use *a/an/the/no article* to introduce something new/unexpected. It indicates that the reader/listener does not know what we are talking about.

I just bumped into ___ old friend. (This is news)

Use *a/an/the/no article* to indicate 'common ground'. It may refer the reader/listener to shared experience, or general knowledge and the context will be important to establish exactly which noun is being referred to.

I went to see ___ house this morning. (I told you about this house. Shared experience)

Use *a/an/the/no article* to refer to something general.

I enjoy talking to taxi drivers. (taxi drivers in general)

see Reference page 87

10 a In each space put *a/an/the* or leave the space blank.

The Sagrada Familia in (1) _____ Barcelona is one of (2) _____ Gaudí's most impressive works. This enormous church, as yet unfinished, is in some respect (3) _____ summary of everything that Gaudí designed before. (4) _____ architectural style of the Sagrada Familia has been called 'warped Gothic', and it's easy to see why. The contours of (5) _____ stone façade make it look as though the Sagrada Familia is melting in (6) _____ sun, while (7) _____ towers are topped with brightly-coloured mosaics which look like (8) _____ bowls of fruit. Gaudí believed that (9) _____ colour is life, and, knowing that he would not live to see (10) _____ completion of his masterpiece, he left coloured drawings of his vision for future architects to follow.

For nearly thirty years, Gaudí worked on the Sagrada Familia and other projects simultaneously, until 1911, when he decided to devote himself exclusively to (11) _____ church. During (12) _____ last year of his life, Gaudí lived in (13) _____ studio at the Sagrada Familia.

Tragically, in June, 1926, Gaudí was run over by (14) _____ tram. Because he was poorly dressed, he was not recognised and (15) _____ taxi drivers refused to take a 'vagabond' to the hospital (they were later fined by (16) _____ police). Gaudí died five days later, and was buried in the crypt of the building to which he had devoted forty-four years of his life, (17) _____ as yet unfinished Sagrada Familia.

b Work in pairs. Explain the use or non-use of articles in Ex. 10a above.

11 Correct the mistakes. There may be more than one mistake in each sentence.

1 She really enjoys the sport, and plays the tennis a lot.
2 If the Mr Atkinson phones, can you tell him I'm in meeting.
3 There is a cold weather, especially in north.
4 Go down the Forest Street, and turn right into Sundale Avenue.
5 The violent crime is definitely on increase.
6 I went to one restaurant there years ago.
7 The life in London is getting more and more expensive.
8 Katia is ideal candidate for job. She has a great deal of the experience.
9 Maurice has a flu and won't be coming back to work for all the week.
10 It's without doubt best hotel in an area.

Person to person

12 a Think of three more important buildings/structures. What do you know about them? Make notes.

b Compare your ideas with a partner. Decide which are the three most important buildings/structures and explain your reasons to the class.

13 Use the tapescript on pages 170–171 to complete the How to ... box.

HOW TO ...	**describe important architecture**	
Use superlatives	The Great Pyramid is _____/ probably the most ...,	
	It is _____ _____ Australia's best known, and most photographed ...	
	It is _____ to be/It is the largest/ tallest ...	
Use fronting for dramatic effect	_____ on 31 December 1999, the Millennium Dome ...	
	_____ to house the body of a pharaoh, the base of the Great Pyramid ...	
	Fondly known as the 'coathanger', Sydney Harbour Bridge ...	
Provide details (size/ description, etc.)	It is built from metal/stones ...	
	The base is ...	
	_____/Covering an area of more than ... metres squared	
	It is over 1km round, and 50m high.	
	It _____ ... of ground floor space.	
	Standing 134m high/above ...	
Describe reason for building/ purpose	It was built to _____ the anniversary .../as a memorial for .../ in order to .../in honour of ...	
	Built to house .../as office space ...	

Writing

14 a Work in pairs/groups. Choose two important buildings/structures that you know about. If possible, do some research to find out more information about them.

b Write short texts about the buildings/structures you have chosen using phrases in the How to ... box as appropriate.

c Read your texts to other students. Which buildings/structures do you think have been most influential? Why?

Grammar	whatever, whoever, whenever
Can do	take notes from fluent connected speech

Listening

1 a Discuss.

1 What gadgets are the people in the photos using? Why do you think they are so popular with teenagers?

2 Where do you think big companies go to find out how teenagers use technology?

3 What do you think the next big technological development will be?

b Listen to find out if your answers are correct.

2 a Complete the notes in pairs.

1 Microsoft began the trend for ...

2 Kids drive technology because ...

3 Kids want technology that can be ...

4 Text messaging caught on because ...

5 Teenagers influenced the ThinkPad because ...

6 Collaborative computing will be useful because ...

7 Converse trainers sent their market researchers to ...

b Listen again to check.

Vocabulary | fashions and fads

3 a Match the phrasal verbs in bold in 1–8 to the definitions a–h below.

1 Using teenagers really to find out what's **in** and what isn't, what the market wants ...

2 ... anywhere they thought trends might **kick off**.

3 They experiment and they automatically **home in on** the new.

4 Anything bigger than a few inches **is out**.

5 Text messaging **caught on** because kids wanted to pass notes to each other during class.

6 ... all of these things **came about** because of the needs of kids.

7 And what's **coming up** on the horizon?

8 ... if you want to **keep up with** the latest style of trainers, who do you ask?

a) start

b) know the most recent developments

c) focus/direct their attention towards something

d) is going to happen in the near future

e) is popular at the moment

f) became popular and stylish

g) is unpopular at the moment

h) happened

b Which two phrasal verbs in Ex. 3a are exact opposites? Are they formal or informal? Which has a literal meaning connected with football?

4 Correct the mistakes in the text (they are all connected with phrasal verbs).

A new trend is catching off. Budding basketball star, Mark Walker, can shoot the ball into the basket eighteen times in a row. On his website, which is sponsored by Reebok, he faces the camera and says, 'I am the future of basketball. I am Reebok.' Mark Walker is three years old. Big business has always homed in at talented youth – the phenomenon really kicked up with Michael Jordan – but now it appears that talent isn't necessary. Horton Chesleigh is even younger than Mark Walker, and he is already associated with a brand. His parents, Sean and Deanna, agreed to name him after a character from a Ruffles potato crisps ad. How did this situation go about? The food company agreed to donate $50,000 towards little Horton's education. So, will personal branding become popular? Will we be seeing branded kids walking the streets? Maybe. Jim Nelson had the orange, blue and black logo of an Internet company tattooed on the back of his shaved head. In return for showing the tattoo for the next five years, he gets $7,000. Who knows what's coming off next? Kids called Coke and Big Mac?

5 Discuss.

1 What's the best way to keep up with developments in your job or hobby?

2 Are there any interesting events coming up in your life?

3 What trends have caught on recently in music, food, etc. where you live?

4 How do global trends come about? Can you think of any examples?

5 Think of one piece of technology/clothing that used to be 'in' but is now 'out'.

Speaking

6 Look at the photos and discuss.

1 How old are the people?
2 What are they doing?
3 Can you think of any problems associated with their behaviour?
4 How would you deal with these problems?

Listening

7 **a** Work in groups. Do you think that teenagers (aged 15–17) should be allowed to do the following:

1 watch however much TV they want?
2 stay up late whenever they want?
3 decorate their room in whatever way they want?
4 go wherever they want at night?
5 socialise with whoever they want?
6 wear whatever they want?

b **6.3** Listen to two parents and two teenagers discussing various issues. Which questions from Ex. 7a do they answer?

Conversation 1: _____
Conversation 2: _____
Conversation 3: _____
Conversation 4: _____

c What were their opinions? Listen again to check.

Grammar | whatever, whoever, whenever

8 Complete the tasks in the Active grammar box.

Active grammar

'Teenagers shouldn't be allowed to watch however much TV they want.'

'Teenagers should be able to socialise with whoever they want.'

1 Underline the correct answer. *Whenever, whoever, whatever*, etc. (a) are conjunctions that join two clauses together. (b) mean the same as *if*.

We use *whenever, whatever, whoever*, etc. when 'it doesn't make any difference *when/what/who*, etc.' or when we don't have to be specific. They also mean 'we don't know the exact details of *when/what/who*, etc.'

What/who/when is a little different to *whatever/whoever/whenever*. Compare the example sentences below:

a) *Stop what you are doing now!*
b) *Stop whatever you are doing now!*
c) *Whatever you are doing, stop it now!*

NOT: ~~*What you are doing, stop it now!*~~

2 Which sentence(s) mean(s) 'I know what you are doing and I want you to stop'?
3 Which sentence(s) mean(s) 'I don't care what you are doing, but I want you to stop'?

Watch out! *However* is also a conjunction that means *but* or *on the other hand*.

We often use *however* with an adjective or adverb. It means *even if* ...

However brilliant you are, eventually you'll meet someone more brilliant.

However hard he works, he'll never get promoted.

see Reference page 87

9 Complete these sentences with *whenever/ however/whatever/whoever/wherever*.

1 _____ you do, don't lose these keys!

2 Send me an email _____ you have time.

3 Carry your documents with you _____ you go.

4 _____ is at the door, tell them I'm busy.

5 _____ you travel – train, car or bus – it will take you at least three hours.

10 Complete the second sentence so that it means the same as the first. Use *whenever/however/ whatever*, etc. Use three words in each space.

1 If it's the last thing you do, make sure you turn off the power.

_____, don't forget to turn off the power.

2 Even if you're a good swimmer, Thorpe is better than you.

_____ are at swimming, Thorpe is better.

3 Call me if you feel down.

_____ down, give me a call.

4 It doesn't matter where we go; they always follow us.

_____, they're always close behind.

5 I'll see her as soon as I can.

_____, I'll see her.

6 It doesn't matter who we employ; he'll have to be a genius.

_____, he'll have to work miracles.

7 No matter how you fix this photocopier, it keeps breaking down.

_____ the photocopier, it always breaks again.

8 Those children can do anything, and it turns out successful.

_____ do, they make a success of it.

11 a `6.4` Listen to the answers. Which syllable is stressed in *whatever, however*, etc?

b Repeat the sentences.

Mohammed Ali

Nelson Mandela

Diana, Princess of Wales

Reading

1 a Read the definition of *charisma* below. Can you think of any famous charismatic people? Do you think the people in the photos are charismatic? In what ways?

> **charisma** /kəˈrɪzmə/ *n*
> [U] the natural ability to attract and influence other people

b Discuss.

1 Who is the most charismatic person you know? In what ways are they charismatic?

2 Are there any dangers connected with being charismatic?

3 Is charisma something you can learn or do you have to be born with it?

2 Read the text and choose the best title.

1 Five Ways to Learn Charisma

2 How to Be a Great Leader

3 The Mystery of Charisma

1 According to Joan Collins, some people 'eat you up with their eyes. I don't know whether it's magic or a trick, but it's the best act I've ever seen.' For example, Mohammed Ali has loads of it. It's questionable whether any of the British Royal family has it, *although* Diana, Princess of Wales, tried to develop it. Charisma. *Hard as we try* to understand it, the formula remains elusive. All we can do is watch the masters at work and learn from them.

2 Colleen Dawson's grandson was in the same class as Nelson Mandela's grandson. **During** one parents' night, the adults were sat talking to the teachers. The evening was progressing as usual, **at which point** Mandela suddenly walked in. 'Normally we would have asked about homework and other silly details,' says Dawson, 'but no one spoke. So he just started talking in a quiet authoritative way about the important job of teaching.' **While** the parents and teachers in the room were struck dumb with reverence, **on finding** himself suddenly the centre of attention, Mandela found common ground for everyone present — education. Mandela's charisma shone through.

3 *Even though* charisma is usually associated with politicians, businesspeople and artists, Richard Feynman proved that people in other fields can have it. **You had no sooner begun** a conversation with Feynman than you'd be struck by his attitude toward the subject. *Despite* the fact that Feynman's field was theoretical physics — not exactly a crowd-pleaser — he had such enthusiasm for the mysteries of the universe that he infected everyone within earshot. The Nobel Prize-winning scientist was a larger-than-life figure, and very charismatic. One ex-student recalls, '**He'd hardly started** his lecture when you'd notice the whole audience on the edge of their seat.'

4 Most of the great leaders in history possessed a star quality that drew others to them and helped them gain power and success. Churchill, Napoleon and Martin Luther King had a magnetism which is easier to identify with than to explain. Broadcaster and confidence tutor Jeremy Milnes says, 'There are some people who are just naturally charismatic. But I believe that there are techniques and skills which can be learned and practised.' Milnes says that, *much as* charisma can be learned, it can't be faked. 'Whatever skills and techniques you have are rooted in your own personality.' His thoughts are echoed by other experts in the field, who estimate that charisma is 50 percent innate and 50 percent trained.

3 Answer the questions.

1 Does the writer believe there's a simple way to become charismatic?

2 What did Mandela discuss? Why?

3 Does the writer believe charismatic people are associated with particular professions?

4 Why did people want to listen to Feynman?

5 Why does Milnes think there's hope for normal, uncharismatic people?

4 Discuss. What do you think the following words/expressions from the text mean? Use the context or a dictionary to help you if necessary.

the formula remains elusive (paragraph 1), *struck dumb with reverence* (para 2), *a crowd-pleaser* (para 3), *he infected everyone within earshot* (para 3), *a larger-than-life figure* (para 3), *on the edge of their seat* (para 3), *star quality* (para 4) *innate* (para 4)

Grammar | link words of time and contrast

5 Complete the tasks in the Active grammar box.

Active grammar

There are many words/phrases we use to link ideas in sentences.

Time clauses

1 There are six time clauses **in bold** in the text. Put them in the correct place in the table. The first one has been done for you.

It happened soon after another thing	It happens at the same time as something else	It comes at the end of a long, continuous sequence of action. It often introduces a moment of change in the sequence OR the result of this sequence.
on finding ...		

2 Add the words/phrases **in bold** below to the table.

when   whilst   by which time

Contrast clauses

3 There are five expressions of contrast *in italics*. Put them in the correct place in the table.

Expressions that are always followed by a clause (with a verb)	Can be followed by a noun phrase or *-ing* form	Expressions that use adjective/adverb + *as* + subject + verb to emphasise the contrast

4 Add the words/phrases *in italics* below to the table.

in spite of   while   difficult as it was

see Reference page 87

6 Complete the texts using the words/phrases from the boxes. Some of the phrases can't be used.

Two Charismatic Women

> despite   much as
> by which time   on being
> when   although   during
> hardly had she begun
> hard as she tried

(1) _____ King William IV died in 1837, his daughter Victoria became Queen of England, (2) _____ she was just eighteen years old. (3) _____ her reign when she married Albert, and together they had nine children. When he died, Victoria wore black for the rest of her life and was hardly seen again in public. (4) _____ this, she is remembered as a successful leader. (5) _____ her reign, Britain's Empire grew extremely strong, and British society changed in many ways. She died in 1901, (6) _____ she had reigned for sixty-three years.

> despite   hard as
> he had no sooner
> even though   when
> by which time   much
> on getting the job

Until he was six, John Smith lived on a farm with his grandmother. (7) _____ his family's poverty, he had access to books, and he read and preached in church. He got his lucky break (8) _____, aged seventeen, he was offered a job at a radio station, (9) _____ he lacked experience. His talk show later became very populor and is watched by over 20 million people a day. (10) _____ as he enjoyed her TV success, John's real ambition was to act, and in 1985 he starred in a film which brought him a lot of fame.

Vocabulary | personal characteristics

Meryl Streep

Pelé

Bruce Lee

7 Match the adjectives 1–8 to the words/phrases in a–h below that have the opposite meaning. Check the meaning of any phrases you do not understand.

1 charismatic
2 inspirational
3 dignified
4 aloof
5 idealistic
6 tireless
7 trustworthy
8 resolute

a) 'She's a bit **lacking in drive and energy**.'
b) 'He **wavers in the face of problems**.'
c) 'He's very **approachable**. He always has time to talk to people.'
d) 'He's **corrupt**.'
e) 'She is rather **nondescript**.'
f) 'She's very **down-to-earth** and practical.'
g) 'She's **not very inspiring**.'
h) 'She **lacks** *gravitas*.'

8 a ⬛ 6.5 Listen to the way the words/expressions above are pronounced. Mark the stress.

b Listen again. How do we pronounce *gn* in *sign*? How do we pronounce *gn* in *dignified*? How do we pronounce *ch* in *much*? How do we pronounce *ch* in *charismatic*?

9 Discuss.
1 What do you know about the people in the photos? Which adjectives would you use to describe them?
2 Can you think of any other famous people who could be described using the adjectives or the phrases above?
3 Which qualities are important for (a) a politician, (b) a teacher, (c) an actor, (d) a businessperson?

Writing

10 a Read the autobiographical statement in the Writing bank on page 163 and do the exercises.

b Read the text below and follow the instructions.

SCHOLARSHIP AWARD – $5,000

Piaget Educational Consultants is offering a scholarship award to study for one year at a university in Australia. The winner will be given lodging, tuition and $5,000 spending money. Write an autobiographical statement (150–200 words) describing your character and your relationships with colleagues/teachers/professors. Mention one colleague/teacher/professor who has influenced you. Send your statement to Piaget Educational Consultants, PO Box 45993, Perth, Australia by 5th May.

1 **a** Look at the pictures and make a story.

1

2

3
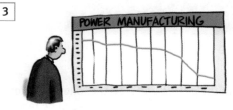

4

5

b Read the text. Were your stories the same or different? How?

Mr Power's story

1 For ten years, I owned a manufacturing company, but I really **had my hands full** with it. I never had time to enjoy myself. So I sold the company and retired. But after a few years, I heard that the company needed a new Chief Executive. Bored with retirement, I decided to reapply for my old job. I got it, and I found the job easy. After all, I **was an old hand** at it.

2 Back in my old job, I thought: 'This is great. I've **landed on my feet** again.' But soon I **was rushed off my feet**. There was too much to do and no time for golf or even to visit my holiday home in Monaco. What's more, the company's results were down.

3 We had a meeting, at which **it all came to a head**. The shareholders said, 'You're wasting company money on your expensive cars and yachts.' 'Rubbish!' I replied. 'I've **got a good head for business**, and I know what we can and can't afford.'

4 'I only **have** the company's **interests at heart**,' I told them. But they said that if results didn't improve, I'd be out. And my **heart** really **sank** when they demanded that I return my sixth Ferrari and sell the house in Barbados that I'd felt was necessary to keep senior executives (me) happy.

5 Unfortunately, results didn't get better, so we had another meeting. 'You have to **face the music**,' said one of the shareholders. 'Your time as Chief Executive has been a disaster.' I'm sure they were about to fire me when I decided to **save face**. I resigned. Now I'm retired again. Here I am in my beachfront home in Brazil.

2 Match the idioms **in bold** in the text to the phrases with a similar meaning.

Paragraph 1: Hands
a) have a lot of difficult tasks to do
b) very experienced at doing something

Paragraph 2: Feet
c) be extremely busy
d) get into a good situation because you're lucky

Paragraph 3: Head
e) be naturally good at commercial matters
f) reach such a bad situation that something has to be done

Paragraph 4: Heart
g) to want what is best for someone or something
h) suddenly feel very disappointed

Paragraph 5: Face
i) avoid losing the respect of other people
j) take responsibility for something bad

3 Discuss.
1 Do you have a good head for business?
2 Are you rushed off your feet at work/school?
3 Are you an old hand at anything? If so, what?
4 Are you the type of person who always lands on your feet?
5 When was the last time your heart sank?
6 Do you have your hands full at home/school/work?
7 Can you think of a time when you wanted to save face? Did you succeed?
8 When was the last time you had to (or told someone else to) face the music?

Who's the leader?

1   Look at the picture and read the following information about the passengers: One of these people is a spy, one is a criminal, one used to be famous, one will be famous, one is a doctor, one is a lawyer, one has a dark secret, one is a journalist and one is a soldier. Who is who? Guess the identity of the different people and label the picture.

2   Imagine you are one of the people. Write a short profile of him/her by completing the phrases below.

My name is

I work as a

I am

I believe in

My strengths are

My weaknesses are

I will always

3   Imagine that the plane crashes. Everyone survives and you all wake up on a desert island. You decide to start a new community. Your character wants to be the leader. Think about the following questions.

1   What ideas do you have to run the community? What is your manifesto?

2   How will you persuade the others that you should be leader?

3   What experiences do you have that will be useful?

4   What are your beliefs?

4   Work in groups. Take it in turns to present your manifesto and argue your case for becoming the leader of the new community.

5   Elect a leader and explain your choice to other groups.

Articles

Definite article

Classes: *The arctic fox is known to inhabit the area.*

National Groups: *The French are unhappy about the new policy.*

Other groups: *The Green Party has staged a protest.*

Unique objects: *The sun was setting on the horizon.*

Titles: *The President has yet to make the decision.*

Musical instruments: *She learned to play the harp.*

Geographical names: rivers *(the Seine)*, oceans *(the Pacific)*, compass points *(the North)*, collective countries *(the UK)*, mountain ranges *(the Alps)*.
NOT: lakes *(the Lake Erie)*, single mountains *(the Mount Everest)*, continents *(the Asia)*, countries *(the Germany)*

Shared knowledge or experience: *We'll meet them in the café.* (the café by our work – shared knowledge)

Indefinite article

Jobs: *Martha is a dentist.*

Measuring: *It costs £150 a week.* (per week)

Introducing something new: *There's been an accident!*

No article (Zero article)

Names: *Tom Hanks is my favourite actor.*

Streets: *They live on Harvard Street.*

General countable plurals: *I love cats.* NOT: *I love the cats.*

Whatever, whoever, whenever

Whenever, however, whatever, etc. are conjunctions. They join two clauses together. We use them when it doesn't make any difference *when/what/who*, etc. or we don't have to be specific, OR we don't know the exact details of *when/what/who*, etc.

*Come **whenever** you can.* (It doesn't matter exactly when you come)

What/who/when are a little different to *whatever/ whoever/whenever.* Compare:

*Repeat **what** you just said!* ✓

*Repeat **whatever** you just said!* ✓

***Whatever** you just said, repeat it!* ✓

NOT: *What you just said, repeat it!* ✗

***Whoever** you saw was probably the criminal.* ✓

NOT: *Who you saw was probably the criminal.* ✗

However has two meanings. Compare:

***However** you go, whether by train or car, it takes a day.*

*It takes two days by car. **However,** if you go by train, it takes only a day.*

The second *however* contrasts two statements.

Link words of time and contrast

There are many words/expressions which allow us to link our ideas and narratives in different ways. To link:

things happening at the same time use *while, whilst, when, as.*

As the plane took off, she felt free.

things that happen when other longer actions are finishing/have finished use *by which time* or *at which point.*

*I reached the end, **by which time** I was tired.*

things that happen immediately after the previous action use *hardly + when, on + -ing* form, *no sooner + than.*

***On hearing** of the crash, he ran straight to the hospital.*

things that contrast with previous information use *though, although* and *even though* + verb phrase.

***Although** he's short, he's good at basketball.*

We can also use *despite* and *in spite of* + noun phrase or *-ing* form.

***In spite of** my poor exam results, I still managed to get a good job.*

We can use adjective/adverb + *as/though* + subject + verb to add emphasis to the contrast. Typical examples are *much as* (*I like*), *hard though* (*we tried*).

***Much as I love** television, even I can't watch for more than three or four hours a day.*

Key vocabulary

Power

nuclear   speech   medicine   spending   argument   economic reasons   solar   brain   tool   influence   world   political   people   army   consumer   power over (decisions)   in positions of power   economic and political power   give special powers to   power-hungry   come to power   hold the power

Phrasal verbs

be in   be out   kick off   home in on   catch on   come about   come up   keep up with

Describing people in positions of power

charismatic   inspirational   dignified   aloof   idealistic   tireless   trustworthy   resolute   nondescript   waver in the face of problems   approachable   corrupt   down-to-earth   inspiring   (lacking in) drive and energy   (lacks) gravitas

Idioms

have your hands full   be an old hand (at something)   land on your feet   be rushed off your feet   it all comes to a head   have a good head for business   have (someone's) interests at heart   your heart sinks   face the music   save face

1 Complete the text with articles where necessary and change the punctuation accordingly.

> ## The Shanghai World Financial Centre
>
> This 492m high building consists of two elements that correspond to Chinese concept of earth as square and sky as circle. Hole in top also has practical use – to relieve pressure of wind on building. Glassy tower is being built just blocks away from 420m Jinmao Tower in district of Shanghai that has been designated Asian centre for international banking. Tower's lower levels will be used for offices, and its upper levels for hotel, art museum and restaurants.

2 Complete the dialogues with *whatever, whoever, whenever*, etc. The same word can be used more than once.

1 A: Why do you like Italy?
   B: Because _____ you go in Italy, you can find amazing architecture.
2 A: What's so different about that school?
   B: There are no compulsory subjects. You can study _____ you want.
3 A: We can buy the black one or the blue one. Which would you like?
   B: _____ you prefer. I don't mind.
4 A: What time shall I come to your house?
   B: Come _____ you can make it.
5 A: How will you manage to get time off work?
   B: It'll be OK – they're quite flexible. I'll talk to _____ is on duty.
6 A: Will it be quicker if we take the bus or the train?
   B: _____ you travel, it takes over two hours.

3 Choose a verb and particles from each box to complete the sentences. Change the verb tense where necessary.

> come   be   home   catch   keep   kick

> in x 2   up   on x 2   off   about   with

1 We _____ _____ _____ the latest developments by reading magazines.
2 The new series _____ _____ just three weeks ago; its first episode was a great success.
3 I don't think that new type of phone will ever _____ _____. It's too ugly.
4 I've lost touch with the music scene. I've no idea what _____ _____ any more.
5 This extraordinary situation _____ _____ because our marketing men had a great idea.
6 Hi-tech companies are increasingly _____ _____ _____ teenagers as their number one consumer.

4 Make idioms from the words in the box and complete the sentences.

> head   hands   feet   a   your   have
> came   full   my   land   on   to

1 The problem had been developing for a long time, when it finally ...
2 Sorry, I can't help you tonight because I ...
3 So you found a great job and a nice house! You're so lucky! You always ...

> hand   face   heart   feet   an   off
> at   old   rushed   her   interests   save

4 I knew all the rules of the game already because I was ...
5 She's too busy to attend the meeting. She's ...
6 I want you to do really well. I only have your ...
7 It was an embarrassing situation but, by being honest about it, they managed to ...

> face   head   heart   a   the   his
> sank   business   music   for   good

8 I thought he would make a good managing director, because he has ...
9 When he saw that he'd failed the exam, ...
10 She committed the crime, and now that she's been caught, she has to ...

5 Find and delete any unnecessary words in the text.

1 An hour with the Body Earth Power Group was
2 enough for me. No sooner but had Carin Brook
3 entered than everyone became silent. Much as I
4 tried to keep my mind open — and despite of the
5 fact that I have been known to do a bit of tree-
6 hugging myself — I couldn't help thinking that
7 this was going to be a waste of time. Brook, even
8 and though she is tiny, had a charismatic presence.
9 We started stretching in order to 'feel the Earth's
10 rhythm', but it didn't last long. I'd hardly but lifted
11 my hands up when she told us all to sit down, close
12 our eyes and 're-visualise ourselves from above'.
13 Hard as though I tried, I just couldn't imagine what
14 the top of my head looked like, and in the spite of
15 her promptings to 'relax', the hard floor was getting
16 very uncomfortable. Thankfully 4.00p.m. came, by
17 which the time I was desperate for a nice soft chair
18 and a cup of tea.

7 Nature

Lead-in

1   Discuss. Where are the animals in the photos? Are they being used by people? If so, how? Do you approve of the way they are being used? Why/why not?

2   Put the words into the correct column in the table below.

> mammal   fur trade   carnivore   tame   natural habitat   stalk
> animal rights   breed (v)   breed (n)   hibernate   sanctuary
> nature reserve   endangered   reptile   animal testing   exotic
> rare   cage   lay eggs   nest   predator   over-hunting/fishing

3   Work in groups.

1 Types of animal (noun)	2 Describes animals (adjective)	3 Where animals live	4 Things animals do	5 Animal issues

1   Think of examples of the types of animal in column 1.
2   What types of animals live in the places in column 3? Do you have these in your country?
3   Which animals do the things in column 4?
4   What do you know about the issues in column 5? How do you feel about them? What solutions are there?

Reading

1 **a** Match 1–6 to a–f.

A	B
1 natural	a) the human eye
2 carried to	b) lives
3 animal	c) safety
4 rescue	d) disaster
5 save	e) instincts
6 invisible to	f) team

b The expressions in Ex. 1a are from the text. What do you think the text is about?

c Read and check. Were your predictions correct?

2 Answer the questions.

1 What was strange about the elephants' and the flamingos' behaviour?

2 What do animals typically do before natural disasters occur?

3 How do we know what the sharks did before Hurricane Charlie?

4 What specific ability allows animals to predict natural disasters?

5 Why can't people predict natural disasters, according to Rupesh Kaneira? What other reason does the text give?

6 What are the similarities and differences between the 'rescue dogs' and the 'rescue rats'?

7 How do rescue teams know that the rat has found someone?

8 In what particular conditions would a rat be much better than a robot in a rescue situation?

3 Discuss.

1 What differences between humans and animals does the article describe?

2 Do you believe in a 'sixth sense' or 'animal instincts'?

3 The text says that, when disasters occur, we hope to use animals in two ways. What are these ways? Are they ethical?

4 Do you think the ideas for using animals will be successful? What problems might there be?

How watching animals will save us

During the tsunami disaster of 2004, over 300,000 people died. No one has counted the number of animals killed, but we know that it wasn't many. All over the region, before the disaster struck, animals were behaving strangely.

Shortly before the tsunami, in Khaolak, Thailand, twelve elephants that were giving tourists rides became agitated. They suddenly left their usual habitat, carrying four surprised Japanese tourists to safety. On the eastern coast of India, flamingos, which should have been breeding at that time of year, suddenly flew to higher ground. Of the two thousand wild pigs that inhabit an Indian nature reserve, only one was found dead after the tsunami.

The idea that animals are able to predict disasters is nothing new. In fact, it has been well-documented over the years. Twelve hours before Hurricane Charlie hit Florida in 2004, fourteen electronically tagged sharks left their natural habitat and stayed in deeper waters for two weeks. The sharks, which were being observed by US biologists, had never done this before. They escaped the hurricane. In the winter of 1975 in Haicheng, China, snakes which would normally have been hibernating were seen on the ground. Days later there was an earthquake which measured 7.3 on the Richter Scale.

Unlike human beings, wild animals perceive a great deal of information about the world around them. Their senses are sharper and they can feel even the smallest changes in the environment. In other words, they see natural warnings that are invisible to the human eye. Ancient people probably had similar 'animal instincts', which they needed to survive, but these have been lost to us as modern technology leads us further away from the dangers that nature poses.

The real question is, can we use the reactions of animals to save ourselves from natural disasters? Animal behaviour expert, Rupesh Kaneira, believes we have no choice. 'The technology which we rely on isn't always perfect, and in poorer countries it isn't even available. Animals know the environment better than any of us. When they run for their lives, we must follow.'

And how rats will rescue us ...

In the earthquake capitals of the world – Japan, Los Angeles, Turkey – rats will soon be Man's new best friend.

In the aftermath of an earthquake, rescue teams send in dogs which are trained to smell people. No one knows how many lives they have saved, but there are, of course, drawbacks: dogs are big and they can't get into small spaces. Now a new research project is using a smaller animal to save lives: the rat.

How does it work? Firstly, the rat is trained to smell people. When this happens, the rat's brain gives off a signal, similar to what happens when a dog smells a bomb. So, the trained rats are sent into the wreckage. On their back is a very small radio, which is connected to the rat's brain. The rescuers, at a safe distance, monitor the radio signals. When the rat's brain activity jumps, the rescuers know that someone is alive.

Of course there are already robots which can do this job, one of which looks and moves like a snake, but rats are better because they can smell more efficiently than robots, whose noses don't work well when there are other smells around. Rats also crawl efficiently in destroyed buildings – something which robots are not as good at – and they don't need electricity. What's more, rats have a survival instinct: they get out when it isn't safe.

Grammar | relative clauses

4 Complete the tasks in the Active grammar box.

Active grammar

1 Read sentences a–g below and <u>underline</u> the relative clauses.

2 Which sentences (a–g) contain defining relative clauses (essential information)? What type of information is described in the other relative clauses?

3 In which type of relative clause (defining or non-defining) can we use *that* instead of *who* or *which*?

4 When do we use commas with relative clauses?

5 Which clause contains a dependent preposition? Where does the dependent preposition go in the relative clause? Find another example in the final paragraph. Where can the preposition go in formal English?

6 Find a sentence in the final paragraph of the text that contains the structure '_____ of which'? What other words sometimes come before *of which*? E.g. *all of which ...*

a) *... twelve elephants that were giving tourists rides became agitated.*

b) *... flamingos, which should have been breeding at that time of year, suddenly flew to higher ground.*

c) *The sharks, which were being observed by US biologists, had never done this before.*

d) *Of the two thousand wild pigs that inhabit an Indian nature reserve, only one was found dead.*

e) *... there are already robots which can do this job.*

f) *... rats are better because they can smell more efficiently than robots, whose noses don't work well ...*

g) *The technology which we rely on ...*

---

5 Do the sentences below have the same meaning? If not, how are they different? Which are wrong?

1 a) Monkeys whose DNA is similar to humans are often used in research into the brain.

   b) Monkeys, whose DNA is similar to humans, are often used in research into the brain.

2 a) Guide dogs were first used by soldiers who had been blinded during World War One.

   b) Guide dogs were first used by soldiers, who had been blinded during World War One.

3 a) Seals, whose blubber is used for fuel and food, are hunted by Inuits.

   b) Inuits hunt seals whose blubber is used for fuel and food.

4 a) The tiger shark is one of the few members of that species that attacks people.

   b) Most sharks are not dangerous, but one exception is the tiger shark, which attacks people.

5 a) The funnel spider's web, which is extremely fine, was used to cover wounds.

   b) The funnel spider's web, that is extremely fine, was used to cover wounds.

6 a) There are 100,000 types of mollusc (snail, oyster, octopus, etc.), all of which have to be moist to stay alive.

   b) There are 100,000 types of mollusc (snail, oyster, octopus, etc.), of all which have to be moist to stay alive.

7 a) Homing pigeons are able to return, weeks later, to the place which they came from.

   b) Homing pigeons are able to return, weeks later, to the place from which they came.

Person to person

6 **a** Put the phrases in the box into the right sentences below. Add commas where necessary.

> which take animals from their natural habitat which is done only for sport and not for food about which there has been much debate in the fashion industry   which is being destroyed

1 Should hunting be allowed?

2 Should zoos be banned?

3 Should the Amazon Rainforest be protected against industry? If so, how?

4 Should the use of fur for clothing be banned?

b Discuss the questions in pairs. Think of arguments for and against each issue.

see Reference page 101

Listening

7 **7.1** Listen to two people giving explanations about how to do something. Mark the sentences true (T), false (F) or doesn't say (?).

1 You need to make some plans before you even buy your rabbits.
2 Rabbits eat almost any type of food.
3 You should be vaccinated.
4 You should have at least two rabbits in a hutch.
5 Lots of people choose their dog because it looks cute.
6 The speaker thinks it's a bad idea to keep a cat outside.
7 The owner's lifestyle is an important consideration in choosing the breed of cat.
8 The speaker knows a lot of cat-owners.

b Listen again to check.

Pronunciation

8 **a** How is *to* pronounced in these clauses?

1 The first thing you need to do.
2 So you need to plan well.
3 You have to make sure they like the food they're given.
4 It's best to get it from a farmer.

b **7.2** Listen to check.

c **7.3** Identify the weak prepositions in the following clauses. How are they pronounced? Listen and check.

1 Some people, for example, just go for the cutest cat they can find.
2 The first thing you've got to do is to ask yourself a number of questions.
3 ... the next thing is to think about what type of cat.
4 ... if you spend most of your time at home watching TV, get a less active cat.

9 Complete the How to ... box by putting the words in the box into the correct place.

> easy   without   step   any   doesn't
> first   it   be   piece   the

HOW TO ...

explain procedures

Prefacing with a general statement	It can _____ a bit tricky at _____. It's pretty straightforward. It's really _____./It's a _____ of cake.
Sequencing	Firstly .../_____ first thing you've got to do is ... Then/Secondly, .../The next _____ is to + infinitive ... Once you do/'ve done this ... Finally,
Addressing the listener	You do this .../Do this ... One does this (formal/usually written English)
Conditions/ what can go wrong	_____ doing this, it won't work. if it _____ work, you should ...
Checking it's understood	OK?/Got _____?/_____ questions?

10 **a** Complete paragraphs 1–3.

1 It's really easy. You can do it by _____ the _____ into the _____. The next step is to _____. Once you've done this, all you need to do is _____. Any questions?

2 It's pretty straightforward. What you have to do is _____. Without doing this the _____ can't _____. Then you _____, and finally the _____ should work perfectly. If it doesn't, _____! OK?

3 It can be a little bit tricky the first time. You put the _____ in the _____ and then you _____. If it doesn't _____, then it means you need to _____. Got it?

b Read your paragraph to other students.

Writing

11 A friend is going to stay in your house while you go on holiday. Write three notes for them explaining how to use your washing machine, feed your pet, water your plants, etc.

David Hewson

Speaking

1 Discuss. What's the hottest place you have been to? What problems could you have visiting a very hot place? Think about animals, accommodation, health, etc.

2 Work in pairs. Imagine you are taking a trip in the desert for a month. What would you take with you? Choose five things from the box below and compare your ideas with other students.

> candle and matches   mobile phone
> sleeping bag   tent   mirror   laptop
> compass   map   hat   gun   umbrella

Listening

3 a **7.4** Listen to the first part of David Hewson's story. Answer the questions.

1 What does David need from the bureaucrat's office?

2 What is the bureaucrat's attitude to David's trip? How do we know?

3 The bureaucrat has a sense of humour. What does he say that shows this?

b Discuss. What will the journey be like? What do you think the Danakil Depression, the world's hottest place, looks like? How do you think David will feel when he arrives?

c **7.5** Listen to the second part of the story. Were your predictions correct?

4 Discuss in pairs/groups.

1 Why do you think David wanted to make this journey? What was his motivation?

2 Why do explorers go to extreme places?

3 Why do you think David is disappointed with the Danakil Depression?

4 How would you feel if you were him? Would you like to go there? Why/why not?

5 'It is better to travel than to arrive.' Do you agree with this proverb?

Vocabulary | descriptive language

5 **a** Listen to the story on page 93 again and match 1–7 to a–g to make common collocations.

A	B
1 spectacular	a) level
2 permanent	b) town
3 tourist	c) settlement
4 below sea	d) landscape
5 active	e) land
6 ghost	f) volcano
7 inhospitable	g) site

b Which of the collocations could be used to describe the photos below?

6 Complete the sentences with collocations from Ex. 5a.

1 The world's most popular _____ is the area around the Eiffel Tower, Paris.

2 Mount Etna in Sicily, Italy, is the world's most _____.

3 Antarctica is the only continent on which there is no _____. It is too cold!

4 The Dead Sea is the lowest point on Earth. It is 418 metres _____.

5 Walhalla, Australia, is a rare example of a _____ that came back to life. Originally a gold mining town, it was abandoned when the gold ran out, but is now popular with tourists.

6 The Atacama Desert, Chile, is an _____. Few people can survive its dry climate.

7 Some of the world's most _____ can be found in Cappodochia, Turkey.

7 **a** Read the tapescripts on page 172. Which words does the speaker use to give emotional impact?

b Read the tapescripts again. What things/people do the words in the box describe?

Verbs	drone zig-zag loom crumble trespass
Adjectives	warped vibrant hunched drenched parched

'Drone' describes the noise of a fan.

c Work in pairs. Try to define the words. Check with your teacher or by using a dictionary.

'Drone' means make a dull, low, continuous sound.

d Now think of other things you can talk about using the adjectives.

Vibrant – 'the colours were vibrant', 'Barcelona has vibrant nightlife', 'She has a vibrant character.'

Lifelong learning

Read on!

Reading literature helps develop your vocabulary. Writers often use unusual images and metaphors. These creative uses of language can extend your understanding of English.

Grammar | verb patterns 2

8 Complete the tasks in the Active grammar box.

Active grammar

Some verbs can be followed by the infinitive or *-ing* form. Sometimes the meaning changes.

Look at the following sentences and answer questions 1–6.

Mean

1 Which verb phrase means (a) intended (b) involved?

Going to the Danakil Depression <u>means walking</u> into hell on Earth.

David <u>meant to write</u> a book after his trips.

Remember

2 Which verb phrase describes (a) a responsibility or something that you need to do (b) a memory of the past?

He <u>remembers experiencing</u> a feeling of emptiness when he arrived.

They tell you … to <u>remember to drink</u> even when you're not thirsty.

Regret

3 Which verb phrase means (a) a feeling of sadness about something in the past (b) a formal apology?

I <u>regret to inform you</u> that your application for a visa has been turned down.

I didn't <u>regret going</u> to the Danakil Depression.

Stop

4 Which verb phrase means (a) paused in order to do something (b) completely finished something?

We <u>stopped to visit</u> a ghost town.

David <u>stopped looking</u> for vegetation and wildlife once he realised nothing survived in the Danakil Depression.

Try

5 Which verb phrase describes (a) an experiment to see what will happen (as a solution to a problem) (b) an effort to do something difficult?

They had <u>tried to build</u> a railway.

He <u>tried drinking</u> more water but he still felt absolutely terrible.

Go on

6 Which verb phrase means (a) continued an action (b) did something after finishing something else?

They waved and <u>went on riding</u>.

David Hewson <u>went on to write</u> a book about his experiences.

---

see Reference page 101

9 Using patterns from the Active grammar box add two words to sentences 1–12.

1 I don't remember photo, but it has turned out really well, one of my best!

2 After six hours of driving, we have a break by the roadside.

3 We visit the cathedral, but it was closed that day.

4 Even after I told her to be quiet, she went loudly.

5 She regrets so early this morning. Now she's really tired.

6 Getting fit means smoking and drinking completely. You'll also have to go to the gym.

7 I didn't mean the window. I lost control of the ball!

8 I remembered traveller's cheques this time. Last time, I forgot and I lost all my money.

9 She used to send letters regularly, but she to me last year. We're not in touch any more.

10 After leaving Oxford with a law degree, she to become a famous lawyer.

11 We regret you that you have not been accepted by the college.

12 If you have problems sleeping, you should hot milk before you go to bed.

Person to person

10 a Choose the correct option.

1 For me, a holiday means *to lie/lying* around on a beach.

2 I can remember *to go/going* on a long journey when I was a child.

3 I try *spending/to spend* time in places of natural beauty whenever I can.

4 I'll never stop *travelling/to travel* even when I'm old.

5 I admire people like David, who go on *to explore/exploring* places even in difficult conditions.

6 I've never regretted *to go/going* anywhere because you can always learn something from different places and cultures.

b Are the sentences true or false for you? Compare your views with a partner.

Listening

1 Discuss. Can you think of any jobs that involve animals? What skills do you think are required?

2 a **7.6** Listen and complete the summary.

Sharon Edwards is (1) _____ at Heathrow Airport. She
(2) _____ the animals that pass through. The biggest
animal they ever had was a (3)_____.
No individual who works there knows about all of the
(4)_____. They have a (5)_____ and the (6)_____
to help them if they need more information. The most
common animals they deal with are (7) _____. Children
even sometimes try to (8)_____ their pets in their
pocket. There are no (9)_____ between 1a.m. and 4 a.m.
When working at night, Sharon (10)_____ the lights.

b Listen again to check.

c Discuss. How does Sharon feel about her job? What qualities do you think are necessary for a job like this? Would you like Sharon's job? Why/why not?

Reading

3 Read the text and choose the best option.

1 The animals are marketed as if they are *useful around the home/dangerous/toys*.

2 The writer is concerned about *all animals/rare animals/the effects of animals on children*.

3 The IFAW was surprised *at the size of the illegal market for wild animals/to find endangered species for sale/at the way the traders treat the animals*.

4 After buying the animal, many people *abandon it/can't look after it/treat it like a doll*.

5 'Monkey moms' are the people who *buy the animals on the Internet/sell the animals on the Internet/hunt the animals*.

6 The online animal trade is one cause of *economic problems in poor countries/violent crime/illegal hunting*.

4 Discuss.

1 Should people have wild animals as pets? Give reasons.

2 What can the IFAW do to stop the illegal trade? Is it possible to stop illegal Internet sales in general?

ANIMALS ONLINE

[1] They are marketed as the perfect birthday present for children, or a classy addition to the image-conscious suburban home. But the products being sold over the Internet are not soft toys or unusual knick-knacks, but potentially dangerous live animals from the world's most endangered species.

[2] Gorillas, tigers and chimps can be bought and sold for as little as a few hundred dollars, despite international bans on their sale. The illegal online trade in rare and exotic wildlife is now worth billions of dollars, according to a report by the IFAW (the International Fund for Animal Welfare). Indeed, IFAW researchers discovered well over 9,000 live animals and products made from endangered species for sale on Internet auction sites, in chat rooms and on the small ads pages. The scale of the trade is astonishing.

[3] So what exactly would it cost and what would you have to do to buy a wild animal? The researchers say you wouldn't have to do a great deal. Want a gorilla in your living room? It's yours for $9,000. Just go to London and pick it up as if it were a kitten, no questions asked. What about proof that you can look after and house it adequately? None needed. Although gorillas require space and very specialised care, the IFAW found a British-based website selling a seven-year-old gorilla in January 2005. For those with a little more headroom, giraffes can also be bought. Got-PetsOnline.com offered a 'sweet natured' two-year-old giraffe for $15,000.

[4] However, it is monkeys that make up a large majority of Internet sales, and experts are particularly concerned at the way they are marketed and traded on the net. A number of websites describe them as if they are little more than large hairy dolls. These websites offer 'accessories' such as nappies, feeding bottles and clothes to go with the monkey. The traders even have a 'cute' name for themselves: 'monkey moms'. They call the animals themselves 'monkids'. Virtually none of these websites explain how to look after the animals.

[5] When the IFAW undercover investigators contacted some of the US traders, they were told it would be possible to export them to the UK – a blatant breach of EU law. There is also concern that demand for monkeys and chimps is fuelling the illegal trapping and trading of wild species. Where there were approximately two million chimpanzees in the wild a century ago, there are as few as 150,000 left, and one research project says that by 2020 there will be a maximum of 100,000.

[6] Phyllis Campbell-McRae, director of IFAW UK, says, 'Trade on the Internet is easy, cheap and anonymous. Criminal gangs are taking advantage of the opportunities provided by the Web. The result is a cyber black market where the future of the world's rarest animals is being traded away. Our message to online shoppers is simple – buying wildlife online is as damaging as killing it yourself.'

Grammar | *as ... as* and describing quantity

5 Complete the tasks in the Active grammar box.

Active grammar

1 *as* + adjective + *as* (1) means two things are equal OR (2) it's a way of showing surprise about a statement.

Find three examples in the text (paragraphs 2, 5 and 6). Which meaning does *as* + adjective + *as* have in these cases?

2 Other ways of describing quantity.

Look at the phrases below and find their opposites in the text. Write them in the space provided.

As much as → _____ (paragraph 2)

Well under → _____ (para 2)

Not very much → _____ (para 3)

A tiny minority → _____ (para 4)

Virtually all → _____ (para 4)

Precisely → _____ (para 5)

As many as → _____ (para 5)

A minimum → _____ (para 5)

3 Which eight phrases are often followed by *of*?

4 Which ten phrases use numbers, e.g. *as much as 20*?

5 Which four phrases <u>can't</u> be used with countable nouns?

---

see Reference page 101

Pronunciation

6 a `7.7` Listen to how *as* is pronounced in *as much as*, *as big as*, etc.

b `7.8` Now answer the questions that you hear, using '*I'm as*' + the prompts.

blind/bat – I'm as blind as a bat.

1 free/bird   **2** strong/ox   **3** quiet/mouse

c Say them again fast!

7 a Put the words in order. Start and finish with the <u>underlined</u> words.

1 <u>Pet rabbits</u> approximately usually minority for small eight years, but live a <u>live longer</u>.

2 <u>Hamsters</u> many birth to as offspring can as give twenty <u>at a time</u>.

3 <u>The</u> to able majority domestic repeat of parrots are vast <u>human speech</u>.

4 <u>The life</u> as housefly of two is short as a <u>days</u>.

5 <u>Koalas</u> lives their virtually of spend all asleep: <u>eighteen hours per day</u>.

6 <u>Horses</u> deal die live twenty–twenty-five, but at can around a great usually <u>longer</u>.

7 <u>Tortoises</u> years, to well longer a over 100 live deal can great <u>than humans</u>.

8 <u>Dogs remain</u> of a minimum maximum fifty-three days and pregnant for a of <u>seventy-one</u>.

b Do you think the sentences are true or false? Look on page 149 to find out.

Person to person

8 a Discuss.

1 Do you own a pet? What type of animal is it?

2 Did you use to have a pet? What type of animal was it? How long did you own it?

3 Are you allergic to animals? Which ones?

4 Would you ever consider buying an animal on the Internet? In what circumstances?

b Report back to the class. Try to use some of the phrases from the Active grammar box.

Virtually all of us have owned a dog or cat at some point!

Vocabulary | buying and selling

9 **a** Match 1–10 to an expression with a similar meaning in a–j.

1 It's in excellent condition
2 It's the latest model
3 It's second-hand
4 It's available now
5 It's hand-crafted
6 It's brand new
7 It features ...
8 It has some wear and tear
9 It's unique
10 It comes in a wide range of (colours/sizes)

a) It's one of a kind
b) It's used
c) It's on the market
d) It's not in perfect condition (it's been used a lot)
e) You can choose from a selection of ...
f) It's made by hand
g) It's still in its packaging
h) It's as good as new
i) It includes ...
j) It's state of the art

b Work in A/B pairs. Look at the expressions again for a few minutes. Student A closes the book and Student B says one of the phrases. Student A says a phrase with a similar meaning.

Speaking

10 Discuss. Which phrases could you use to describe the things in the photos? What animals were used to make these things?

11 Work in pairs. Take a possession from your bag. Think of a way to make it sound wonderful and 'sell' it to your partner. Try to use some of the expressions in Ex. 9.

Writing

12 **a** Read the extracts from ads on sellit.com, an Internet auction site. Find five spelling mistakes and five preposition mistakes.

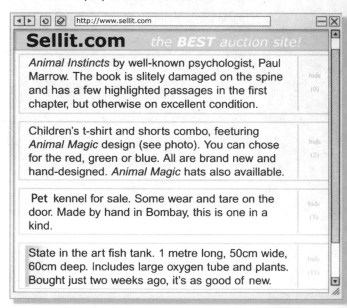

Sellit.com *the BEST auction site!*

Animal Instincts by well-known psychologist, Paul Marrow. The book is slitely damaged on the spine and has a few highlighted passages in the first chapter, but otherwise on excellent condition.
bids (0)

Children's t-shirt and shorts combo, feeturing *Animal Magic* design (see photo). You can chose for the red, green or blue. All are brand new and hand-designed. *Animal Magic* hats also availlable.
bids (2)

Pet kennel for sale. Some wear and tare on the door. Made by hand in Bombay, this is one in a kind.
bids (3)

State in the art fish tank. 1 metre long, 50cm wide, 60cm deep. Includes large oxygen tube and plants. Bought just two weeks ago, it's as good of new.
bids (11)

b Choose a possession that you would like to sell (e.g. furniture, books, toys, clothes, etc.) and write an ad for sellit.com (of 30–40 words) describing the object, price and conditions of sale, etc.

c Work in groups. Show your ads to each other. Ask and answer questions about the different items and try to find something you would like to buy.

d Tell the class about the item you decided to buy and explain why you chose it.

Suffixes

1 Find the words in sentences 1–7 below that need a suffix. Add the suffix (you may need to omit some letters from the original word).

Humans use more and more land to plant crops and extend cities. This <u>signs</u> a great threat to the habitat of a number of species. <u>Answer: signifies</u>

1 Elephants are hunted for their ivory tusks. This highly profit business is illegal.

2 There are only about 400 gorillas left in central Africa. The destroy of their forest habitat has led to this situation.

3 Jaguars are hunted illegal for their fur, which is used for coats, handbags and shoes.

4 The disappear of dinosaurs is a great mystery. Some people believe it happened because of a dramatic climate change.

5 Giant pandas are depend on the greenery in their habitat. As this gets eroded, they struggle to survive.

6 We need to emphasis responsible care of the environment in order to preserve natural resources.

7 In the short term, people hunt animals for their beautiful fur. It is only after – when these animals become extinct – that we regret it.

2 What type of words did you create by using the suffixes? Find two nouns, two adjectives, two adverbs and two verbs.

Lifelong learning

Break it up!

When you come across very long words that you don't understand, try breaking them up. Look for prefixes and suffixes that can help you to guess the meaning. Example: *non-refundable*. What does *non-* mean? What type of word usually ends in *-able*? What is a *refund*? Where might you see the word *non-refundable*?

3 Work in groups. Add one example for each suffix in tables 1–4 below using the words in the boxes.

1 Forming abstract nouns

> tend   sad   global   retire

SUFFIX	EXAMPLES
-cy	redundancy, accuracy, _____
-ation/-isation	nationalisation, compilation, _____
-ment	enjoyment, harassment, _____
-ness	kindness, emptiness, _____

2 Forming nouns – types of people

> motivate   psychology   door   enter

SUFFIX	EXAMPLES
-er/-ar/-or	baker, burglar, aviator, _____
-ant/-ent	assistant, opponent, _____
-ist	biologist, pianist, _____
-man/-woman/-person	spokesman, businesswoman, chairperson, _____

3 Forming verbs

> broad   satire   tolerance   test

SUFFIX	EXAMPLES
-ate	motivate, captivate, _____
-ise/-ize	characterise, idealise, _____
-ify	simplify, clarify, _____
-en	lighten, enliven, _____

4 Forming adjectives

> phenomenon   hope   Poland   permanence

SUFFIX	EXAMPLES
-al/-ical	manual, practical, _____
-ant/-ent/-ient	tolerant, urgent, _____
-ful	tearful, respectful, _____
-ish	selfish, childish, _____

4 Do the crossword on page 151.

Fact file
Paradise island has 50 square kilometres of land which can be developed.
The land has some hilly areas and a little forest.
The land and climate are good for growing vegetables, fruit, etc.
There is a lot of wildlife on the island.
There are two natural springs on the land. This is very good for people's health.
The island nearby is becoming more popular with tourists.

1   Look at the photo and read the notes about Paradise island.

2   Work in pairs/groups. Paradise island belongs to you. Make a list of all the things you could do with the land. Compare your ideas with other students.

3   **7.9** Listen to two people discussing what they could do with the land. Were their ideas the same as/similar to yours?

4   Work in groups. Student A read and memorise the role on page 146. Student B read and memorise the role on page 149. Student C read and memorise the role on page 150.

5   Discuss what to do with the land. You must agree to do something with it (but if you can't agree on one thing, you can combine some of your ideas).

6   Report back to the class. What did you decide to do with the land?

Relative clauses

Defining relative clauses make it clear who/what we are referring to. They cannot be omitted from the sentence.

*That's the town **where** I lived ten years ago.*

That can replace *who* or *which*.

*They're playing the song **which** Jenny wrote* = *They're playing the song that Jenny wrote.*

If the relative pronoun is the object of the clause, it can be omitted.

*John ate the cake (**that/which**) we bought yesterday.*

Don't use commas before the relative pronoun.

Whose can refer to people or things.

*I saw the man **whose** wife won the prize.*

Non-defining relative clauses give extra information. This information can be omitted.

I went climbing at the weekend, <u>which was fun</u>.

That cannot replace *who* or *which*.

The relative pronoun cannot be omitted.

Use a comma before and after non-defining relative clauses unless they end the sentence.

Relative clauses with verb + dependent preposition usually have the preposition at the end of the clause.

That's the company (<u>which</u>) I worked <u>for</u>.

But in formal English, we can put the preposition at the beginning of the clause.

That's the company <u>for which</u> I worked.

A common pattern is (*one/some/all/either/neither*, etc.) ... *of which/whom*. This pattern is slightly formal.

I saw two women, <u>neither of whom</u> was wearing a red woollen coat.

Verb patterns 2

Some verbs can be followed by the infinitive or *-ing* form. Sometimes the meaning changes.

*Abstinence **means** not eating forbidden foods* = involves

*I **didn't mean** to break the door.* = didn't intend

*She **dreads** going to the dentist.* = strongly dislikes

*I **dread** to imagine the mess.* = don't want to (because I imagine it will be terrible)

Some verbs of perception (*hear, watch, feel, observe*, etc.) don't change their meaning when followed by different verb forms. BUT compare:

a) *I <u>saw the camel eat</u> the leaves.*

b) *I <u>saw the camel eating</u> the leaves.*

Sentence (a) describes a finished action. Sentence (b) describes an action that may be unfinished.

As ... as and describing quantity

We use *as ... as* to say that two things are similar in some way.

We can use *as ... as* with adjectives, adverbs, *much* and *many*.

I'm <u>as strong as</u> an ox.

He sang <u>as sweetly as</u> an angel.

The motorbike costs <u>as much as</u> a car.

We can put a clause after the second *as*.

She doesn't talk to me <u>as much as she used to</u>.

We often put *possible, ever* or *usual* after the second *as*.

I got here as quickly <u>as possible</u>.

You're looking as beautiful <u>as ever</u>.

The programme wasn't as interesting <u>as usual</u>.

We can use *as ... as* to show that something is surprising.

The meal cost <u>as much as</u> $400 per person!

Key vocabulary

Animals and their environment

mammal   fur trade   carnivore   tame   stalk
natural habitat   animal rights   breed   hibernate
sanctuary   nature reserve   endangered   reptile
animal testing   rare   exotic   cage   predator
lay eggs   nest   over-hunting/fishing

Collocations

carried to safety   animal instincts   natural disaster
invisible to the human eye   rescue team   save lives
tourist site   permanent settlement   ghost town
spectacular landscape   below sea level
active volcano   inhospitable land

Descriptive language

drone   zig-zag   loom   crumble   trespass
warped   drenched   parched   hunched   vibrant

Describing goods for sale

It's in excellent condition   It's as good as new
It's the latest model   It's state of the art
It's second-hand   It's used   It's available now
It's on the market   It's hand-crafted   It's brand new
It's made by hand   It's still in its packaging
It features   It includes   It has some wear and tear
It's not in perfect condition (it's been used a lot)
It's unique   It's one of a kind
It comes in a wide range of (colours/sizes)
You can choose from a selection of ...

1 Complete the text by putting the phrases in the box in the correct places.

> which trains   when they   that will
> who spend   who trained   who work
> which has

One great problem for prison inmates, most of their time locked up, is how to develop self-esteem and find a purpose to their days. One idea, been piloted at a prison in Washington, US, is to get the inmates to train dogs eventually help disabled people. The project has been a great success. The relationship between the inmates and the warders at the prison has improved considerably. Many of the inmates, leave the prison, go on to work with animals.

In another scheme, Pilot Dogs, a company dogs for the blind in Ohio, US, put five dogs into the hands of prison inmates, the dogs successfully.

2 Rewrite the sentences using *of which/whom* and the words in the box below.

> one   some   all   none   either   neither

I left messages for Dave and Lena. They didn't return my calls.

I left messages for Dave and Lena, neither of whom returned my calls.

1 I tried on ten pairs of shoes. Just a single pair fitted me perfectly.

2 She called her classmates. Nobody had done the homework.

3 We found two good candidates. Both of them could have done the job.

4 We test-drove six cars. Every one of them cost over $20,000.

5 Sixteen people came camping with us in 2006. A group of them returned the following year.

6 I worked with the two children. They didn't speak any English.

3 Circle the correct option.

1 I meant *to say/saying* something to you earlier, but now I've forgotten what it was.

2 She's such a crazy dresser. I hate *to think/thinking* what she's wearing tonight!

3 I always dread *to speak/speaking* to the boss – she's so scary!

4 He remembered *to lock/locking* the door this time. Last time, we got robbed!

5 We regret *to tell/telling* you that your application has been unsuccessful.

6 Sorry, I can't stop *to talk/talking*! I'm late!

7 She tried *to drink/drinking* hot chocolate before bedtime, but she still couldn't sleep.

8 Despite a difficult start, he went on *to become/becoming* the world's greatest athlete.

4 Use the words below to complete the sentences.

> approximately   none   as   much   well
> large   maximum   virtually   precisely   deal

1 Apparently you can buy a leopard for _____ little as $10,000 on the net.

2 A _____ majority of the public voted to keep the old currency – nearly 90 percent.

3 Sorry, but there's not a great _____ we can do about your problem.

4 There are _____ six thousand people in the hall, but we don't know the exact number.

5 I spent _____ all my money on the entrance fee. I only have £1 left for food.

6 We will meet at _____ six o'clock. Don't be late.

7 This lift holds a _____ of eight people.

8 He's huge! He must be _____ over two metres tall.

9 You can earn as _____ as $200,000 a year, if you work hard enough.

10 Virtually _____ of the team had ever played there before.

5 Add four missing words to each advertisement.

http://www.sellit.com

Eco-car for sale, in excellent. This state the art vehicle runs on water-power, and is latest model. There is some wear tear on the seat. Ring Jerry for further details.

http://www.town-classifieds.co.uk

Cat boxes for sale. Perfect for large or small cats. Plenty of space and beautiful decoration (see photo). You can choose from a selection styles and a wide of colours. These wooden boxes were made hand, and painted individually. They are of a kind. £20 per box.

http://www.4sale.com/

Animal Magic books on market, as good new. Just $2.50 per book. Buy the books in a set of 4 and receive a generous discount. The books are perfect condition (some of them are still their packaging).

8 Issues

Lead-in

1 Discuss. What is happening in the photos? Which issues are represented? Do you think they are important? Why/why not?

2 a Make nouns from the words/phrases below.

1 biotechnological   6 immigrant

2 poor   7 identity thief

3 democratic   8 space explorer

4 globalise   9 pollute

5 global warm

3 Which nouns are associated with the words/phrases in the box (there may be more than one answer)?

> unemployment   depletion of the ozone layer   identity (ID) cards
> cloning   the right to vote   freedom of speech   giant corporations
> cost and safety issues   multiculturalism

4 Discuss.

1 Which issues have been in the news recently? What do you think of them? Do any of them affect you personally? Which issues are the most/least important in your opinion?

2 Do you think the problems associated with these issues are exaggerated in the media? Are any of the problems underestimated?

3 Which issues will become more important in the future? Why?

Speaking

1 **a** Match sentences 1–6 to the photos above.

1 **It does more harm than good.** It pollutes the environment and uses too much oil.

2 **It's a waste of space.** Most of it is either repeats or ads, and it ruins your eyes.

3 **It's overrated.** You can't trust the information because anyone can publish things on it.

4 **They're a killer.** They're used in wars, robberies and other crimes.

5 **They've been disastrous for humanity.** The gas from these destroys the ozone layer.

6 **We can do without them.** No one really needs to have conversations every five minutes.

b Read sentences a–f below. Which sentences refer to the issues in 1–6 above?

a) **It's underrated.** It lets us find information quickly by using search sites and also keep in touch with current affairs.

b) **We can't do without it.** It's essential for talking to people while you're on the move.

c) **It's indispensable.** It gives us up-to-date images and news, films and all kinds of programmes.

d) **It's been a force for good.** It means we have more freedom to visit other places.

e) **They're a lifesaver.** They protect us from danger and allow us to hunt more easily.

f) **They've had big benefits for humanity.** They make daily activities, such as putting on deodorant and repelling insects, easier.

c Work in pairs. Check you understand the meaning of the expressions **in bold** and then discuss the issues. Student A gives an opinion on one of the issues and Student B responds:

A: In my view ...

B: On the other hand ...

d Discuss. Can you think of anything that you wish had never been invented? Why? What would you replace it/them with (if anything)?

Reading

2 **a** Discuss. Are the statements true (T) or false (F)?

1 It takes hundreds of years to produce oil.

2 There is enough oil on Earth for about fifty more years.

3 Most of our rubbish is either buried underground or thrown into the sea.

4 Internet fraud is the fastest-growing criminal activity.

5 We can predict the illnesses that people will have by studying their genes.

b Read the text on page 105 and check your answers.

3 Underline the correct answer to complete sentences 1–6.

1 The writers of the text say (a) the bicycle is the greatest invention (b) they are more interested in things that haven't been invented yet.

2 According to the text, (a) a teenager suggested a way to produce oil (b) solar power might provide a source of energy to replace oil.

3 The text says (a) there is too much rubbish for the space available (b) the rubbish is poisoning the environment.

4 Two inventors are trying to find ways to (a) use our rubbish productively (b) reduce rubbish.

5 Protection against ID theft will involve (a) microchips in every object we own (b) technology 'reading' the human body.

6 The main invention in medicine will be (a) a way to predict the illnesses a person is vulnerable to (b) a pill that will enable people to live forever.

4 Discuss. What do you think of the text? Does it have any good ideas? How many examples of irony/humour can you find in it?

FUTURE INVENTIONS

The editors of Future World Magazine look at the inventions we will need for a brighter future.

1 Everyone has their favourite invention. Some of us even make lists of them. One survey recently named the toilet as the world's greatest ever invention. Another survey, which asked for Britain's greatest invention, named the bicycle, which received twice as many votes as the World Wide Web. That's the past, but what about the future? What inventions will shape our lives? J.B.S. Haldane, a British scientist and not one of life's optimists, once made his prediction for the future. He said that whatever hadn't happened would happen and no one would be safe from it. Whether you agree or not, one thing is beyond doubt: human beings need to invent a few things pretty quickly. Here is our own list:

2 Number one is a new source of power. Oil is running out. A teenager, in a recent letter to a newspaper, wrote that it would take over a hundred years to produce fresh oil. He was wrong by a few million years. Once our oil is gone, it's gone forever. We have about fifty years' worth left, less if rates of industrialisation accelerate. A hundred million new cars will need lots of oil. At a recent conference about the world's future, scientist Hilary Craft said we had already found the answer: solar power. She said we could expect enormous mirrors in the sky that would reflect sunlight and provide the world's electricity. We wait with bated breath.

3 Number two on our list is a waste processor. Throughout most of history we just threw the rubbish out the back door. If the jungle didn't swallow it, wild animals would get it. Once the jungles disappeared, we started burying our waste underground or chucking it into the sea. Now we're running out of space. If we want to avoid choking the Earth, we'd better find a way to recycle more effectively. According to inventor Ray Kurzweill, tiny self-replicating microscopic robots will convert rubbish into new sources of energy. Another inventor, Clara Petrovic, said she was working on a prototype that would convert waste into bricks and other building material.

4 Number three on our list is biological ID. Criminal investigator Alexis Smithson said that in the past thieves had always taken objects. Now they steal your identity. ID theft is the fastest-growing type of crime. So how will we stop it? You can expect to have tiny microchips injected into your body; scanners will read your genetic information to check your ID. Or worse, you may need to provide skin cells whenever you go shopping. Imagine scratching yourself at the checkout every time you buy the groceries. Supermarkets will never be the same.

5 Finally, medicine. In the past, a cold killed you. In 1347–50 the Black Death killed half of Europe's population. Now we are examining people's genes for signs of future illness. Find the disease early enough and you can prevent it. Glen Hiemstra of Futurist.com recently claimed that somewhere on planet Earth there is a young child who will be the first person to live forever. If that happens we'll need another invention: a new pensions system.

Grammar | reporting verbs

5 Complete the tasks in the Active grammar box.

Active grammar

1 Find one example of reported speech in each paragraph of the text. What actual words did they say? What happens to the verb tenses when we report speech?

2 Sometimes, instead of repeating the verb and shifting the tense, we use a reporting verb. Which example from the text <u>doesn't</u> shift the tenses back and uses a reporting verb?

3 Often we use a reporting verb to *paraphrase* the meaning:

1 *'Let's go home.'* → She <u>thinks</u> we should leave.

2 *'Why don't we discuss it with everyone?'* → He <u>suggested</u> that we talk it through with everyone.

3 *'It was my mistake.'* → He <u>admitted</u> that it was his fault.

Find pairs of reporting verbs with similar meanings in the box. Are there any differences in meaning/formality?

A	B
admit	maintain
remember	imply
tell	presume
answer	respond
suggest	confess
threaten	recollect
insist	inform
assume	warn

see Reference page 115

6 Delete the option which is not possible.

1 I <u>warned/informed/threatened</u> them that ID theft was common.

2 He <u>suggested that they discuss/suggested discussing/implied discussing</u> immigration at the meeting.

3 She <u>insisted/maintained/informed</u> that technology would solve the problem.

4 He <u>admitted/told/confessed</u> that he knew nothing about developments in biotechnology.

5 I don't <u>remember visiting/recollect visiting/remember to visit</u> the lab when I was a child.

6 We must <u>tell/inform/suggest</u> the audience about the research into global warming.

7 Work in pairs. Report the two dialogues below using the correct verbs from each box. Leave the main (non-reporting) verbs in the same tenses if possible. In one sentence you need to change a positive adjective to a negative.

Dialogue 1

~~admit~~ suggest remember confess warn

Mike: 'I never recycle anything because I'm too lazy.'

Mike admitted that he never recycles anything because he's too lazy.

Sarah: 'If we don't start recycling, the consequences will be serious for the planet.'

David: 'So why don't we start a recycling group in the community?'

Sarah: 'Wait a minute. There's one already.'

Mike: 'Er, there was. I started one, but then it became really hard work, so we stopped.'

Dialogue 2

respond threaten imply assume

David: 'No one drives if they can walk these days, do they?'

Mike: 'What? I drive everywhere.'

Sarah: 'Do you think that's good for the environment?'

Mike: 'If you two don't shut up about the environment, I'll kick you out of my flat.'

Speaking and listening

8 Look at the pictures. Can you guess what these new inventions are/do?

9 [8.1] Listen to seven people answering the question: 'Which new invention would you most like to see?' Match the number of the speaker to the pictures.

10 a Do you think the following questions are true (T) or false (F)?

1 Speaker 1 probably hates housework.
2 Speaker 2 wants to go back in history in order to see different civilisations.
3 Speaker 3 is fed up with the terrible weather.
4 Speaker 4 probably doesn't like cooking.
5 Speaker 5 might be a student.
6 Speaker 6 wants a machine that will instantly move his body to another place.
7 Speaker 7 probably doesn't enjoy getting up in the morning.

b Listen again and check.

11 Read the expressions in the How to ... box and delete any unnecessary words. Read the tapescript on page 173 to check.

stall for time (when you're asked a difficult question)

That's a such good question.

That's one tricky.

That's for a difficult question.

Let me to see.

I'd have to think really about that.

Well come, ...

12 a Discuss in pairs. Try to use the expression from the How to ... box.

1 Which of the inventions in Ex. 9 do you think is/are a good idea? Why?
2 What other invention(s) do you think might help the world?
3 What other invention(s) do you think might help you at work or at home?
4 What invention couldn't you do without?
5 Are there any modern inventions that are overrated?

b Work with another partner. Report your original partner's opinions.

Listening

1 Look at the photos and discuss.

1 What type of people do you think Thomas and Elise are?

2 What are they like?

3 What do they do?

4 Where do they live?

5 What do you think are their most valued possessions?

2 ⬛8.2 Listen to Thomas and Elise talking about their work/life habits. How do their opinions and lifestyles differ?

3 **a** Choose the best answer.

1 What made Thomas change his lifestyle?
   (a) He received an important email.
   (b) He couldn't enjoy Rome because he was obsessed with work.
   (c) He went to the coast and became fond of the sea.

2 Why does he think people carry technology around with them?
   (a) Because they wish they were in the office.
   (b) Because it helps them feel less stressed.
   (c) Because they are worried they will miss important pieces of information.

3 What has Thomas learned from living by the sea?
   (a) That human actions and money aren't so important.
   (b) That you can't make much money there.
   (c) That he should have left his city job much earlier.

4 What do Elise's friends think of her working life?
   (a) They think it's making her ill.
   (b) They think she's too competitive.
   (c) They think Elise never has enough time.

5 Why does Elise carry around so much technology?
   (a) Because she doesn't have an office.
   (b) Because she travels a lot and doesn't want an office.
   (c) Because she travels a lot and the technology gives her confidence.

6 What does she believe about her future?
   (a) She won't do the same job for more than three and a half years.
   (b) She will never have a completely relaxing lifestyle. She doesn't want one.
   (c) Her lifestyle will probably get worse, especially her health, so she will slow down.

b Listen again to check.

Vocabulary | lifestyles

4 **a** Listen again and read the tapescript on page 173. What do you think these idiomatic expressions mean?

a) tearing my hair out
b) crashed out
c) the be-all and end-all
d) security blanket
e) burn out
f) the buzz

b Match expressions a–f to the phrases 1–6 below.

1 the excitement
2 be too exhausted to continue a long-term action (usually a job)
3 lay down, exhausted
4 something that makes you feel safe/confident
5 the most important thing
6 getting into a panic because of frustration

5 Discuss.

1 Do you agree that 'the world is one stressed-out place'? What are the main causes of this stress?

2 What do you think are the symptoms of 'running out of time syndrome'? Do you – or does anyone you know – suffer from these?

3 Do you think people in your country/industry/profession work hard compared with others? Do a lot of people burn out?

Grammar | continuous aspect

6 Complete the tasks in the Active grammar box.

Active grammar

1 The sentences/phrases below are from the tapescript on page 173. Find an example of a) Present Continuous, b) Past Continuous, c) Present Perfect Continuous, d) Past Perfect Continuous e) Future Continuous f) gerund after a preposition.

   1 *I'd been having dinner with a client all evening.*

   2 *I was tearing my hair out trying to get access to a computer.*

   3 *After leaving my job, I moved to the coast.*

   4 *The waves will be rolling in every morning long after we're gone.*

   5 *I've been working in an investment company for about four years.*

   6 *In fact, the statistics are getting worse – I think it's under three years now.*

2 We can use continuous tenses to describe activities. Match the sentences 1–6 from Ex. 1 to the uses a–d below.

   (a) Actions that are background events (possibly finished) before another event (*sentences 1, 2 and __*).

   (b) Actions that are temporary/incomplete or we want to stress the duration (usually a long time) (*sentence __*).

   (c) Actions that are repeated (*sentence __*).

   (d) Actions that are in the process of changing (*sentence __*).

3 We can also use continuous forms (especially the Past Continuous) to sound more tentative and less direct in suggestions, offers, inquiries, etc. Can you think of any examples?

4 'Stative' verbs are not usually used in the continuous. Write four common stative verbs for each category below:

   Verbs of personal feeling: *like*, ____, ____, ____, ____

   Verbs of thought: *know*, ____, ____, ____, ____

   Verbs of the senses: *appear*, ____, ____, ____, ____

---

see Reference page 115

7 **a** Change the verb forms into the continuous. Does this change the meaning? If so, how?

1 I've read that book.
2 He gets bored.
3 I'll work till about 8.00 tonight.
4 She hit me.
5 The first chapter is written.
6 What music do you listen to?
7 He had lost his hair.
8 The coach leaves at 11.00.

b Are the responses 1–8 below to the simple or continuous form of the sentences in Ex. 7a? Could they be replies to both? The first two have been done for you.

1 Was it good? = *reply to 'I've read that book'* (simple form)

2 Why don't you take him to the park? = *reply to 'He's getting bored'* (continuous form)

3 What are your plans after that?

4 How long did this go on for?

5 How long did it take?

6 It's the first time I've heard it. I don't know the name of the singer.

7 I know. I thought he looked completely different totally bald.

8 Can you ask the driver to make it 11.30? The tour party needs a bit more time to see the palace.

8 Use the verbs in the box to complete the text below. Change the verb tense where necessary. Use the continuous if both the simple and the continuous are possible.

> urge   go back   grow   work   begin   drive
> seem   advocate   ponder   quote

At the beginning of last month I looked out of my window and saw the telltale signs: increased traffic, early-morning crowds, glum faces. Yes, that's right, the children (1)_____ to school and parents (2)_____ a new work year. And I asked myself an old question: do we have the work/life balance right?

A new generation of economists (3)_____ the century-long assumption of economics: that men and women are motivated by more – more profit, more possessions, more work. Is the hectic pace of life what we really want? (4)_____ fourteen-hour days long into our old age? And will it make us happy?

The number of people in mid-career who (5)_____ ready to abandon the desperate climb up the corporate ladder (6)_____. And now, several journalists and social commentators (7)_____ us to go slower and enjoy life.

Tom Hodgkinson, in *How to Be Idle*, says that prominent literary figures (8)_____ the idle life for centuries. He (9)_____ Bertrand Russell, Samuel Johnson and others. Carl Honoré's *In Praise of Slow* also suggests that slowing down may be the best way, and he provides a telling anecdote. He recalls a time recently when he (10)_____ extremely fast in Italy because he was late for a Slow Food meal. The irony of it!

Speaking

9 Read the profile of Dana Kolansky. Is she an idler or a striver?

<u>Profile of Dana Kolansky</u>
Dana is a shop assistant and part-time anthropology student.
Before getting a job as a shop assistant, she had been working in a restaurant.
After finishing work she usually goes jogging.
At the moment she's reading a book on anthropology.
In the last few days she has been studying for an exam.
Recently she's been learning German as a hobby.
This weekend she'll be working on a paper for her MA, playing squash with a friend and going to a birthday party with her brother.

10 a Look at the profile outline below. What questions will you need to ask to complete it?

Profile of _____ (name)
_____ is a _____.
Before -ing _____, _____ had been _____.
After finishing work/her daily studies _____ usually _____.
At the moment _____ is reading _____.
In the last few days _____ has been _____-ing _____.
Recently _____ has been -ing _____.
This weekend _____ will be -ing _____.

b Interview your partner. Is he/she an idler or a striver? Choose one or two pieces of information to tell the class about your partner.

Reading

1 Discuss. What is happening in the photos? Have you ever been in any situations like these? What happened? How did you resolve the problem?

2 **a** Read the two bulletins (A and B) from advice.com. What advice can you think of?

b Read the advice (1–4) to Silvana/Jake's problems below. Was your advice similar? Do you agree with the suggestions?

http://www.advice.com

ADVICE.COM

A My friend's kids are too spoilt!

My closest school friend has two healthy, normal children aged seven and nine. The trouble is, they are incredibly spoilt. Every time they come round, they jump on furniture and break things. They even set the kitchen on fire once. When I try to say something to my friend, she gives me dirty looks and says, 'That's kids for you!' What really irritates me is the fact that my friend just can't see it. I don't know what to do.

Silvana

B Too much exaggeration?!

I got a job recently in a very good company. During the application process I exaggerated a few details on my CV. The thing is, I really wanted the job. I knew I could do it, and felt that adding a few things to my CV would give me a better chance. Recently, a colleague of mine who had done the same thing got caught. He had said he had experience in certain areas, but he didn't. They fired him. What really worries me is that my company is now promising to check up on all the employees. I am seriously nervous, even though I am doing a good job and my boss likes me. What should I do?

Jake

1

Dear Silvana,

When our friends have children, it often creates a barrier because the dynamic changes. What you need to do is to put yourself in your friend's shoes. She's used to their behaviour. You're not. She deals with them every day. You don't. She likes them unconditionally. You like them as long as they're as quiet and well-behaved as china dolls. The fact remains that you need to find a solution. One thing you could try is giving the children rewards for good behaviour: a bar of chocolate if they keep their feet off the furniture. This way, it emphasises positive behaviour. What might also work is having some games available for the children. Most bad behaviour is because of boredom, so maybe there's not enough for the children to do in your house. Good luck!

Faisal P

2

Dear Jake,

I can understand why you fooled the company (you wanted the job). Why you insist on fooling yourself I really don't know. You didn't 'exaggerate'. You didn't 'abbreviate the truth'. You didn't even 'add a few things' to your CV. You lied. There are no other words for it. The first thing you must do is admit it to yourself. The second thing you must do is go straight to your boss, explain exactly what you did and why you did it. The truth is, if your boss values you and your work, you may get away with it.

Penelope

3

Dear Silvana,

There's not much you can do. They're her kids, not yours. But you don't have to put up with that kind of behaviour in your house. Why don't you arrange to visit them in her house? That way, if the kids start acting up, you can go at any time. And try to see your friend without the kids, in a restaurant once a month, or arrange something special just for the two of you. The point is, she was your friend before the kids, and she can still be your friend now.

Gertrude Jarvis

4

Dear Jake,

The fact of the matter is that 19 percent of all job applicants claim skills they don't have, 28 percent exaggerate the pay from their former jobs, and millions of people claim to have had experiences like working in the rainforest on 'community projects' that no one can verify. Don't worry about it. Look at it from the company's point of view. Do they really want to go to the trouble of firing you and finding a replacement when they don't really need to? What they really care about isn't the morals or ethics of you embellishing your CV – it's your ability to do the job. That's why your mate got fired. Relax, man! You're safe.

Anthony

Grammar | fronting

3 Complete the tasks in the Active grammar box.

Active grammar

Sometimes we move the object, verb or adverb to the front of the sentence (before the subject) and add *what* (or another question word), so that *The fact that my friend just can't see it really irritates me ...* becomes ***What really irritates me is*** *the fact that my friend just can't see it ...* (text 1)

1 Rewrite this sentence.

'I really don't know why you insist on fooling yourself.'

Check the answer in text 2.

This rephrasing of sentences is called **fronting**.

We do it:

(1) to emphasise the subject (e.g. *the fact that my friend just can't see it*).

(2) sometimes to provide a clear link with the previous sentence: *She told us to go quickly.* <u>*This we did*</u>.

2 Find other examples in texts 1, 3 and 4.

We often use **fronting phrases** (*the trouble is ...*/*the question is ...*/*the fact of the matter is*/*the fact remains that ...*) to emphasise the importance of what we are going to say:

'The trouble is, they are incredibly spoilt.' (bulletin A)

'The thing is, I really wanted the job.' (bulletin B)

3 Find other examples of **fronting phrases** in texts 1–4.

see Reference page 115

4 Change the sentences so that the meaning stays the same. Start with the <u>underlined</u> word.

1 Their bad behaviour bothers me. <u>What</u>

2 I'm not sure how long he hoped to get away with this lie. <u>How</u>

3 I don't know how she manages with those kids. <u>How</u>

4 She didn't discipline them. That was the problem. <u>The</u>

5 My colleague lost his job. This worries me. <u>What</u>

6 They wanted to check up on me, but I really didn't know why. <u>Why</u>

Person to person

5 **a** Work in threes. Student A turn to page 147, Student B to page 149, Student C to page 150. Read the problem or think of another problem.

b Explain your problems to each other and give advice. Try to use fronting expressions.

Listening

6 **a** What can go wrong with everyday machines? Do you have any recent experiences of machines going wrong?

b **8.3** Listen to three people complaining about problems with machines. What machine are they talking about in each case and what's the problem?

7 **a** Read the How to ... box. Are the expressions followed by a gerund, an infinitive with *to* or an infinitive without *to*?

HOW TO ...

describe problems

It keeps _____.

I can't get it to _____.

It's always _____.

I don't know how to make it _____.

I'm having problems _____.

This ... seems _____.

It won't _____.

b Listen to check. Complete the expressions.

c Work in pairs. Imagine there is a problem with an item of technology in your home. Describe it to a partner (without mentioning the name of the item) using phrases from the How to ... box. Your partner has to guess what you are talking about and come up with a solution if possible!

Vocabulary | cause and effect

8 **a** Work in pairs. Put a word in each space to complete the statements. Then match the problems (1–4) to each piece of advice (a–d).

1 My father had a great _____ on me, and I've always followed in his footsteps, but now nothing I do is good enough for him. He criticises me all the time.

2 My obsessive work ethic has _____ in a number of problems. I can't sleep or relax and I get terrible headaches.

3 I dropped out of university. The _____ of my actions is that my parents won't talk to me now.

4 Most of my problems stem _____ my laziness. I just can't get motivated to do anything.

a) Overwork _____ rise to many health problems, such as those you mention. You need to get some balance back in your life. Take some time out every day and take up a relaxing hobby.

b) Personal happiness has its _____ in our achievements. Even if you do something small every day, you will feel happier and more motivated to do more. Take that first step.

c) A child's uncertain future is a major _____ of worry for parents. They probably can't understand why you have dropped out. Try explaining the whole story from beginning to end.

d) You should try to _____ about small changes in your relationship with him. Explain that you are an adult now and you need to find your own path in life.

b Check your answers by looking at the sentences below.

Nouns

Work is a **major source** of stress.

Unemployment is a **cause** of worry.

The argument **has its origins in** family history.

The government's decision **has far-reaching implications/ consequences**.

The **result** is in no doubt.

The rivalry has its **roots** in an old argument.

Teachers are an important **influence** on children.

Verbs

Success **breeds** confidence.

Bad decisions will **bring about** their downfall.

The new law **gave rise to** much protest.

Clashes between rival fans **result in** violence.

The media **influences** a lot of people.

His insecurity **stems from** his childhood.

c <u>Underline</u> any words/expressions you don't normally use.

9 Finish the sentences so they are true for you. Compare your answers with other students.

1 _____ influenced me a lot, because _____.

2 _____ is sometimes a source of stress to me.

3 _____ resulted in me learning English.

4 My family's roots are in _____.

5 _____ has serious implications for my future.

6 I hope to have an influence on _____.

Writing

10 **a** Read the essay in the Writing bank on page 164 and do the exercises.

b Think of a problem/issue, e.g. stress, bad neighbours, unemployment, unhealthy lifestyles, annoying emails, pollution, etc. Make notes about the causes of the problem/issue, the effects it has had on you/others and try to come up with some solutions.

c Write an essay of 200–250 words about the problem/issue.

1 Work in pairs. Choose the correct word/phrase *in italics*. Then put the words **in bold** into the tables.

1 There have been a number of claims (1) *with regard to/regarding/to be precise* the Internet. It is a great tool for information-sharing, and some search engines, (2) *notably/namely/in terms of* Google, are now household names.

~~regarding~~, in terms of (+ noun), notably, namely, in particular, with regard to, to be precise

INTRODUCING A TOPIC	BEING SPECIFIC
regarding	

2 Originally the Internet was used mainly by academics. (3) *Nevertheless,/However,/Furthermore,* criminals recognised its usefulness immediately. The Internet crosses international boundaries. (4) *What's more,/However,/Furthermore,* it allows anonymity.

furthermore, nevertheless, however, what's more, and yet (no comma), in addition, on the other hand,

CONTRAST	SAYING MORE

3 It is necessary to (5) *hint at/highlight/underline* some of the problems: besides massive fraud and other scams, the music industry's sales have suffered because of piracy using Internet technology. We can't be sure but reasonable estimates would (6) *suggest/focus on/hint at* further losses in the near future.

highlight, hint (at), imply, point out, emphasise, infer, stress, underline, focus on, suggest

VERBS OF DIRECT FOCUS	VERBS THAT FOCUS INDIRECTLY

4 If we try to (7) *evaluate/appraise/generate* the Internet's effect on the world, it is possible to (8) *assess/formulate/construct* a thesis that gives a balanced view: the Internet has great benefits because it is free and open, and great drawbacks in that it makes crime simpler.

generate, assess, construct, evaluate, appraise, formulate

VERBS FOR JUDGING	VERBS WHICH MEAN 'CREATE'

5 (9) *To sum up,/In conclusion,/In chronological order,* the Internet has become a tool for good and bad deeds, just like all other technology.

to sum up, for X days/hours running, in order of + (age, importance, etc.), in alphabetical/ chronological order, in conclusion

ARRANGING DATA	FINISHING

2 Read the text. Choose the correct alternative.

There are many differences between academic writing and literary writing. In academic writing every point contributes towards the thesis. (1) <u>Furthermore,/Regarding</u> the purpose of academic writing is usually to inform rather than entertain. (2) <u>Namely/In terms of</u> style, academic writing is more complex and longer, more abstract words are used. (3) <u>Nevertheless/On the other hand</u>, fiction (4) tends to <u>emphasise/infer</u> the things that happen. Another difference is that academic writing is explicit about how parts of the text relate; everything is signalled, whereas writers of fiction leave 'gaps' where things are (5) <u>implied/stressed</u> but not (6) <u>inferred/pointed out</u> overtly. These gaps allow readers to use their imagination. A further difference is that academic writers have responsibility; (7) <u>with regard to/in particular</u>, they must provide evidence for their claims. Writers of fiction, (8) <u>and yet/however</u>, are free to (9) <u>construct/appraise</u> fictitious worlds.

3 Work in pairs. Ask and answer the questions using the words/expressions in this lesson.

1 Will you need to read or write academic texts in English now or in the future?

2 Are there any academic texts which you found particularly memorable or useful?

3 Is formal English easier or more difficult for you to understand than spoken English? Why?

1 **a** Read the statements a–k. Can any of them be used to describe the photos above?

   a) Travel is the greatest form of education.

   b) Marriage is beneficial to mental and physical health and it never gets old-fashioned.

   c) Money can't make you happy.

   d) The dominance of any one culture is bad for the world.

   e) Modern technology has not made the world a better place.

   f) Rich countries should always give money to poor countries.

   g) Space exploration is a waste of money.

   h) As you become older, you become wiser.

   i) Nature gives us the best things in life.

   j) Childhood is the happiest time of life.

   k) For some crimes, the death penalty is appropriate.

   b Read the statements from Ex. 1a again and give them a number from 1–5 (1 = disagree completely, 5 = agree completely).

   c Choose five topics which you would like to discuss.

2 Work in groups. Compare the topics you have chosen but do NOT give your opinions about the issues yet. Decide which five you will discuss.

3 When you have agreed on the topics you are going to discuss, compare the numbers you gave for each statement and exchange opinions.

4 Report back to the rest of the class: which issues did you talk about and what were the main views/opinions on each?

Reporting verbs

Reporting verbs show the function of the original piece of speech.

'You can't leave the office before 6.00.' → She <u>informed</u> him that he couldn't leave the office before 6.00.

Reporting verbs use different patterns. The majority use a verb + (*that*) clause. Other examples are:

Verb + *that* clause: *accept, recollect, respond, imply, insist, presume, maintain, suggest, answer, confess, remember, conclude, state, boast, repeat*

Verb + object + *to* + infinitive: *persuade, remind, tell, advise, urge, warn, expect, force, invite, order*

Verb + object + *that* clause: *inform, advise, remind, tell, warn*

Verb + *to* + infinitive: *agree, refuse, propose, decide*

Verb + *-ing*: *deny, regret, suggest, mention*

Verb + object + preposition + *-ing*: *blame* (someone) *for, congratulate* (someone) *on, thank* (someone) *for*

Continuous aspect

We use continuous tenses to talk about:

background actions that are in progress at the moment we describe:

When I woke up, <u>it was raining</u>.

actions that are temporary or incomplete:

She<u>'s working</u> for me at the moment.

actions that are repeated:

I<u>'ve been training</u> every day for the last month.

actions in the process of change:

Costs <u>are rising</u>.

Sometimes we use the Past Continuous to sound more tentative and less direct.

I <u>was wondering</u> if you could help me.

'Stative' verbs are not usually used in the continuous. Some common stative verbs are:

Verbs of personal feeling: *like, hate, want, prefer, dislike, wish*

Verbs of thought: *know, believe, imagine, mean, realise, understand, doubt, feel* (have an opinion)

Verbs of the senses: *hear, sound, appear, taste, see, smell, resemble, seem*

Verbs of fixed situations: *depend on, contain, belong to, own, involve, include, possess*

Some stative verbs have a progressive form but the meaning may be a little different.

I <u>feel</u> he deserves the prize. (belief) *I<u>'m feeling</u> sick.* (sense)

I <u>see</u> your point. (understand) *I<u>'m seeing</u> the boss tomorrow.* (plan to meet)

Fronting

In informal English, we sometimes begin a sentence with the complement (object, verb, adjective or adverb). This gives the complement more emphasis.

Intelligent she may be, but kind she isn't!

We sometimes use *what* or another question word.

*I don't know **what** she's doing here!* → ***What** she's doing here I don't know!*

*I'll never understand **why** you went there!* → ***Why** you went there I'll never understand!*

We can use fronting to provide a link to information already mentioned.

Her first book was bad. <u>Much better was her second</u>.

We can front verbs and adjectives with *as* and *though*.

<u>Tired though I was</u>, I didn't stop running.

There are a number of common 'fronting phrases' which show the importance of what follows.

The trouble is, *he's so lazy.*

The question is, *can we get her to join us?*

The fact of the matter is, *you're not good enough.*

The fact remains *that we still have no definite date.*

Key vocabulary

Issues

biotechnology   censorship   poverty   democracy globalisation   global warming   immigration identity theft   space exploration   multiculturalism unemployment   depletion of the ozone layer cloning   the right to vote   freedom of speech giant corporations   cost and safety issues ID cards   pollution

Expressions for good/bad inventions

It does more harm than good   It's a waste of space It's overrated   It's a killer   We can do without it It's been disastrous for humanity   It's underrated It's had big benefits for humanity   It's indispensable It's been a force for good   It's a lifesaver We can't do without it

Cause and effect

a major source of (stress)   a cause of   the result far-reaching implications/consequences   breeds has its roots in   an influence on   bring about give rise to   result in   influence (v)   stem from

Academic English

in terms of + noun   notably   in particular with regard to   furthermore   nevertheless and yet (no comma)   in addition   on the other hand imply   emphasise   infer   stress   generate   assess formulate   for X days/hours running   to sum up in alphabetical/chronological order

1 Find seven mistakes and correct them.

'We propose to adopt a new measurement of people's lives. Recently it was explained us that the kingdom of Bhutan measures its citizens' wellbeing by Gross National Happiness instead of Gross National Product. The country encourages people think about quality of life, not just money. In many countries tourism is blamed for destroy the local culture. While the Bhutanese are not accusing anyone of deliberately harm the environment, in Bhutan, tourism is strictly limited.

We suggest to adopt this same idea. We urge people to considering spiritual wealth, as well as money. This approach is guaranteed to opening our eyes to a better way of life.'

2 Complete the questions.

1 _____ (think) of doing a PhD?
Yes, I was. It seemed like a good idea, but I didn't have enough money.

2 _____ (wear) those clothes?
Because I'm supposed to be at a birthday party in ten minutes.

3 _____ (go) when I saw you this afternoon?
To the bank. But it was closed by the time I got there.

4 _____ (play) basketball?
For about ten years. But I only play once a week nowadays.

5 _____ (live) there long before they kicked him out?
Yes, he had. Nearly twenty years. That's why he was so upset.

6 _____ (not/understand) the task?
Because I hadn't been listening when you gave the instructions.

7 _____ (stay) since you left the hostel?
In my sister's flat, but I'll only stay there until I find my own place.

8 _____ (see) what I mean?
Not exactly. Can you explain it again?

3 Put the words in the box in the correct place in the texts.

would   problem   is   matter   what   why   surprises

My family is going to visit my mother-in-law next week. The is, we can't stand her cooking! I want to be culturally sensitive – she is from another country – but the fact of the is that the kids and I just can't eat her meals. Quite we're going to do I have no idea.
Marlene

What me is her cultural insensitivity. The thing, she has to adapt to you, too. Why not take her out to nice restaurants because that's what daughters-in-law do in your country?
Veronica

You're complaining about this I really don't know. All over the world, people are starving. You're lucky enough to have food, so just pretend you like it. If you're desperate, one idea be to train the kids to say 'Mmm, delicious'.
Ayodele

4 Complete the sentences.

1 Carl Honoré had a great _____ on the Slow Life Movement. Many people followed his ideas.

2 The modern work ethic has _____ in more stressful lifestyles. It does more _____ than good.

3 Twenty-two percent of UK citizens suffer from work-related stress. The _____ of this are very serious.

4 Stress at work _____ rise to absenteeism, which is disastrous _____ business.

5 Honoré wants to _____ about a great revolution in lifestyles. His work is a _____ for good.

6 Many people's sense of satisfaction stems _____ their job. Most of us _____ do without work.

7 Violence, job insecurity and overwork are the major _____ of worry in the US.

8 Honoré's philosophy has its _____ in the lifestyles of our ancestors, who didn't work so hard.

5 Some lines in the text below have one extra incorrect word. Write the extra word in the space. Tick (✓) if there is no extra word.

With a regard to the type of language used by academics in their _____
publications, there are a number of tendencies that we wish to point _____
out. Firstly, we must emphasise to the lack of clarity in much academic _____
writing. Of the 400 papers evaluated, over 300–317 really to be precise _____
were considered 'difficult' in their terms of sentence and paragraph _____
construction. What's the more, the writers tend to use deliberately obscure _____
vocabulary. Whilst this study focused up on scientific writing, we believe _____
that its findings can be widely applied. Nevertheless, we must also _____
underline the fact that there is some outstanding writing, too. To sum them up, _____
we need to consider a number of factors. In an order of importance ... _____

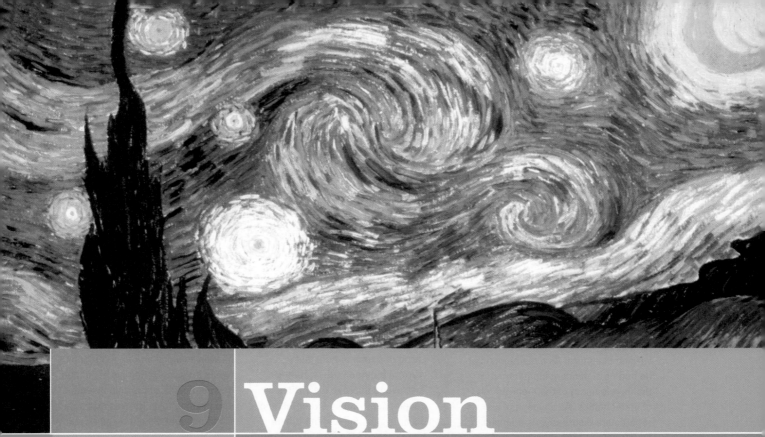

9 Vision

Lead-in

1 Look at the photos and discuss. Which of the arts are represented in the photos? Can you think of any other examples of 'visual' arts? Which do you prefer and why?

2 **a** Do the words and phrases **in bold** refer to books/film/theatre/art/architecture? There may be more than one answer.

1 It was a **spectacular/dreadful/appalling performance**.
2 The **scenery** was **breathtaking/disappointing/stunning**.
3 It's an **absolute masterpiece/not one of his best/his finest piece**.
4 The acting was **stereotyped/poor/over the top**.
5 It's a **fantastic/difficult/heavy read**.
6 The style is **contemporary/traditional/gothic**.
7 The special effects were **astonishing/incredible/awful**.
8 He is famous for his **landscapes/portraits/sculptures**.

b Which phrases above might refer to the photos?

3 Discuss in pairs. How often do you go to the theatre/visit an art gallery/go to a museum or other building of interest/see a classic or blockbuster film/read a novel? Talk about paintings/buildings/films/novels, etc. that you like/dislike, using vocabulary from Ex. 2.

My favourite painting is Picasso's Guernica. *I think it's an absolute masterpiece.*

I didn't really enjoy King Kong. *In my opinion, the special effects were rather disappointing.*

KEIRA KNIGHTLEY

PRIDE & PREJUDICE
'SIMPLY AND ABSOLUTELY GLORIOUS'

Leonardo da Vinci

Reading

1 Discuss. What do the people in the pictures have in common? What do you know about their lives, areas of special interest and achievements?

2 Read the texts to check/find out more information.

Leonardo da Vinci

As a painter, his legacy of works is indisputably less extensive than other master painters. As an anatomist, he failed to publish his research. As a sculptor, he left us not a single verified sculpture. As a mathematician, he had no significant input into **the development of** the theories of mathematics. As a scientist, his records are disorderly. As a musician, he left little record of his music. As an architect, he left no notable buildings for us to visit. And yet he is popularly held as one of the most important figures of the Italian Renaissance. In the words of Sigmund Freud, 'Leonardo da Vinci was like a man who awoke too early in the darkness, while the others were all still asleep.'

Most people recognise the Mona Lisa or The Last Supper as examples of this artist's extraordinary capabilities. However, he was not just an artistic genius, but he was also a genius **in the fields of** architecture, engineering and science. His sketchbooks, with notes often written in mirror form, were full of **ideas for** his inventions. Some were improvements to existing machines, others were new and **ranged from** a primitive tank to a human-powered flying machine. These books were to stun the world when they were discovered centuries after his death.

The Yellow Emperor

The first sovereign of civilised China, Huang Ti, or the Yellow Emperor as he became known, is now recognised as the common ancestor of the Chinese people. Living **in a time of** constant warfare between tribes, Huang Ti strove to improve the virtues of people, pacifying by strengthening his army and unifying the tribes. He introduced **the idea of** military discipline, invented the compass to improve his military strategy, and used carts in warfare.

Once he had established peace, he created civilised systems for his people. Among the many inventions **attributed to** him are the calendar, mathematics (he invented numbers and a system for measuring length and weight), music (he invented the flute using bamboo), writing (he invented Chinese characters), boats, carts, bows and arrows, etc.

His scientific interests also led him to author 'The Inner Book of Simple Questions of the Yellow Emperor', the founding classic of Chinese medicine. His Queen is also **famous for** having been the first to raise silkworms to make clothes with silk.

Sir Isaac Newton

Newton **made** fundamental **contributions to** every area of scientific and mathematical concern to his generation. Born in a rural English village on Christmas Day, 1642, he was so small no one thought he would survive. During his childhood he spent much of his time inventing and building toys. He was distracted at school, and did not do particularly well. So his mother, unwilling to pay for his education, brought him home to look after the sheep. However, he was always so busy building gadgets that the sheep would often escape. Eventually his uncle persuaded his mother to send him to Cambridge University, where he became so **immersed in** his studies, he often forgot to eat or sleep.

When Cambridge was closed for two years, due to the plague, Newton went home to **work on** his ideas. He absorbed himself in mathematics and began developing a mathematical theory that would later become calculus. It is a popular belief that **on one occasion** he was sitting under an apple tree when an apple fell on his head, and that this helped him to understand the laws of gravity. It is now thought that perhaps he invented this story in later life in order to exemplify how he **drew** his **inspiration from** everyday events.

3 Read the texts again and answer the questions. Who:
1 made important contributions to the field of mathematics?
2 wrote his notes and ideas in a type of code?
3 had ideas for military artillery?
4 had a mother who did not want to pay for his education?
5 wanted people to have a better quality of life?
6 was interested in medical science?

4 Discuss. Which of the above people achieved the most in your opinion? Which would you most like to have met? Why?

The Yellow Emperor Sir Isaac Newton

Grammar | dependent prepositions

5 Complete the tasks in the Active grammar box.

Active grammar

1 Look at the examples of dependent prepositions **in bold** in the texts. Write the correct prepositions in the table.

verb + preposition	range __ ... (to ...) work __ ... attribute __ ...
verb + object + preposition	draw inspiration __ ... made contributions __ ...
noun + preposition	in the fields __ ... ideas __ / __ ... the development __ ...
adjective + preposition	(be) famous __ ... (be) immersed __ ...
prepositional phrases (beginning with a preposition)	in a time __ ... __ one occasion ...

2 Look at the phrases below. Add them to the correct columns in the table.

hope for ... make observations about ... succeed in ... devote your life to ... improve on ... (be) obsessed with ... a solution to ... admiration for ... specialise in ... the quality of ... of all time ... in later life ... in recognition of ...

3 Find expressions in the table which mean the following:

a) spend your life trying to do something

b) thought to have been achieved/ accomplished by someone

c) be worried about something all the time

d) be completely involved in something

e) do/make something better

f) feeling of great respect/liking for something/someone

---

see Reference page 129

6 **Choose the correct alternative to complete the text. What is the name of this visionary scientist?**

Widely regarded as the greatest scientist of the 20th Century, or even (1) *of/all/in* all time, this man devoted his life (2) *in/on/to* science. He made major contributions (3) *from/to/for* the development of quantum mechanics, statistical mechanics and cosmology, and in recognition (4) *for/of/about* his work, he was awarded the Nobel Prize for Physics in 1921.

In 1905, while working alone in a patent laboratory, obsessed (5) *in/with/from* relativity, he eventually succeeded (6) *to/in/with* finding a solution (7) *to/at/of* a problem he had been working (8) *in/for/on*. He developed his own theory of relativity, which disproved things that Newton had previously established. Later in the same year he made further observations (9) *in/about/for* the universe and how it is made up, and improved (10) *on/to/with* his own theories until he developed the theory which he became famous (11) *of/about/for*, $E=mc^2$. (12) *In/At/To* later life, he realised both the positive and negative implications of his work as nuclear energy and atomic bombs were developed.

7 **Match 1–8 to a–h and complete the sentences with a preposition from the Active grammar box.**

1 Newton spent his time back at home absorbed

2 Einstein had great admiration

3 The Yellow Emperor succeeded

4 Leonardo da Vinci made observations

5 Newton specialised

6 Mozart was famous

7 At one time, Van Gogh was obsessed

8 Shakespeare made a major contribution

a) ___ the work of Newton.

b) ___ his work.

c) ___ world literature.

d) ___ being able to re-create a piece of music after hearing it only once.

e) ___ the field of mathematics.

f) ___ nature in his sketchbooks.

g) ___ bringing people to civilised life.

h) ___ painting sunflowers.

Person to person

8 Work in pairs. Think of other famous 'visionaries' or inspirational people. Ask and answer questions about them using the phrases in the Active grammar box.

Listening

9 Discuss. Who is the man in the cartoon? What is happening? When do you think geniuses make their greatest discoveries?

10 a [9.1] Listen to a radio interview. Make notes under the following headings.

> 1 Discoveries made outside the laboratory.
>
> 2 The psychology of high achievers.
>
> 3 Can only creative people be geniuses?

b Compare your ideas with a partner. Listen again to complete your notes.

11 Discuss in pairs.

1 Did you find any of the information in the interview surprising?

2 Have you experienced finding the solution to a problem by 'sleeping on it'?

3 Do you pursue any 'creative' hobbies or interests? Did you in the past?

4 What do you do to take your mind off a problem?

12 Read the words/phrases in the box below. Do they express certainty or uncertainty? Write them in the correct column in the How to ... box.

> without a doubt   it's not 100 percent certain
> undeniably   questionable   unquestionably
> irrefutable   debatable   it's not clear-cut

HOW TO ...

describe certainty/uncertainty

certainty	uncertainty
indisputable	

13 Underline the correct alternative.

1 It's *debatable/without a doubt* whether Leonardo da Vinci was a genius.

2 It's *not 100 percent certain/undeniably* what or who killed Mozart.

3 The impact of Einstein's theories are *without a doubt/irrefutable*.

4 The Yellow Emperor was *not clear-cut/unquestionably* a great leader.

5 It's *not clear-cut/irrefutable* why Leonardo wrote in mirror form.

6 Mozart was *not 100 percent certain/irrefutably* exceptionally gifted.

7 The story about Newton's discovery under the apple tree is *questionable/without a doubt*.

8 The novel is *not clear-cut/indisputably* his greatest work.

Speaking

14 Discuss in groups. Do you agree/disagree with the statements? Explain your views using phrases from the How to ... box.

1 Mozart is the most talented musician ever to have lived.

2 Einstein should have kept quiet about his discovery when he realised the implications for nuclear weapons.

3 Being a 'genius' generally implies being at least a little mad. Van Gogh would never have achieved the same recognition if he hadn't suffered a psychological breakdown.

4 Given time and the right encouragement, anyone can become a genius.

9.2 I know what I like

Grammer discourse markers
Can do use colloquial expressions to explain your tastes

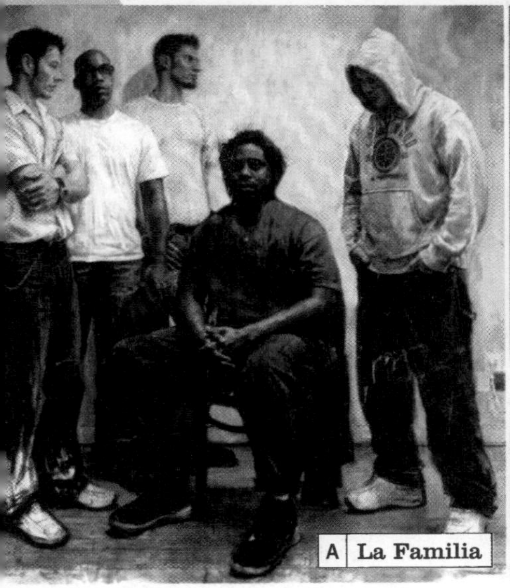
A La Familia

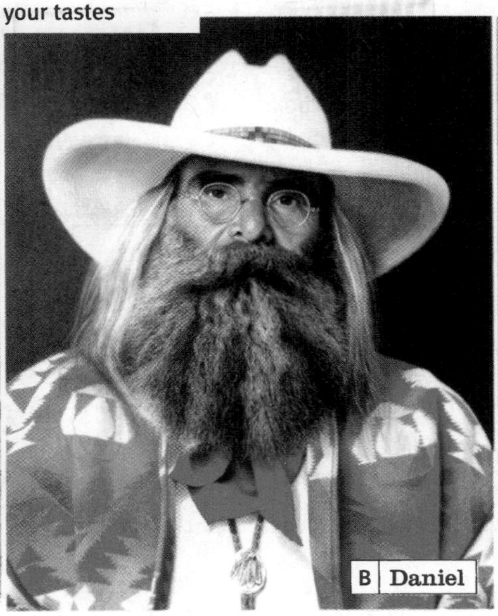
B Daniel

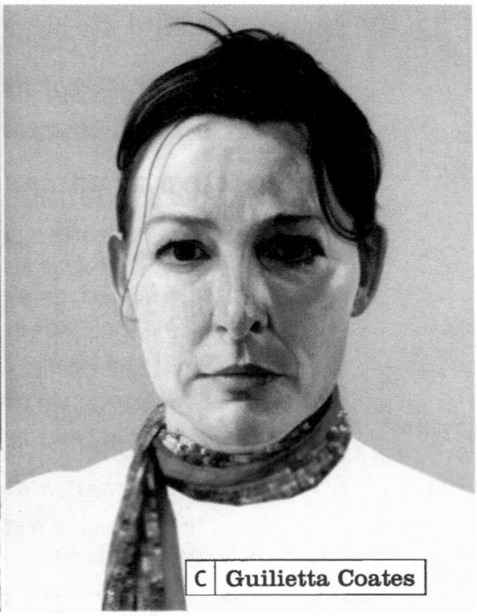
C Guilietta Coates

Speaking and vocabulary

1 Discuss. What sort of art do you like/not like?

2 **a** Work in pairs. Check you understand the meaning of the words **in bold**.

1 This is an **abstract** painting by Mondrian.
2 This painting is really **striking**. It stands out.
3 I don't like **avant-garde** art. I can't understand it.
4 Don't you find her work really calm and **tranquil**?
5 I like **colourful** art, like Matisse's work.
6 That painting is rather **plain**, isn't it?

a) So you prefer more **traditional** stuff?
b) I prefer **monochrome** images.
c) No way! I think her work is very **disturbing**.
d) Oh, I think that one's a bit **dull**. It's not my type of thing at all.
e) I think it's **stunning**. I noticed it at once!
f) He also did a lot of **figurative** work, didn't he?

b Match sentences 1–6 with their opposites in a–f. Which of the words **in bold** are used to show personal opinions? Which describe facts?

3 **a** Check the meaning of the sentences in the box below. Put them in the correct place in the How to ... box.

It's really not my taste. It's not my cup of tea.
I'm really into her work. I'm a big fan of his stuff.
He's one of my all-time favourites.
I can't relate to this type of thing.

HOW TO ...

say what you like/dislike

Saying what you like	*I've always admired her work.*
Saying what you don't like	*It's not my (kind of) thing at all.*

b 9.2 Listen and check. Mark the stress.

c Work in pairs. Tell your partner about a painting/photograph you like (or don't like).

Listening

4 **a** Look at the pictures above and read the text. Which picture do you like best/least? Which do you think should win the competition?

Every year, at the National Portrait Gallery in London, there is a competition for the best portrait. The winner is decided democratically: everyone who visits the exhibition can vote for their favourite portrait. The prize is £25,000.

b 9.3 Listen and answer the questions. Which pictures are they talking about in each conversation? Which words/phrases helped you decide? Which picture do they think should win?

1: _____ 2: _____ 3: _____

c 9.4 Listen and answer the questions. Which picture actually won? What does the speaker think of the winner?

Grammar | discourse markers

5 Complete the tasks in the Active grammar box.

Active grammar

1 Discourse markers are words/expressions which help us to organise what we are saying/writing. They also show our attitude to the subject. Look at the following phrases from the tapescript and put the words **in bold** in the correct place in the table.

... **as I was saying**, it really does look like a photo ...

... the expression on her face **is kind of** intense ...

... **it sort of** looks like a photo ...

... **to be honest**, it's not really my taste ...

... **to tell you the truth**, I still wouldn't want it hanging on my bedroom wall.

focusing on the main topic	returning to the main point (what was said before didn't matter)	returning to a previous line of discussion
introducing a strong opinion or criticism	softening an opinion or criticism	making additional (often contrasting) points

2 Discourse markers can be used for a variety of other purposes. Look at the phrases **in bold** below and add them to the table.

anyway, what I was going to say was ... more or less ... frankly, ... at any rate ... mind you ... as a matter of fact ... as far as ... is concerned, ... in fact ... anyway ... as for ... as regards/ regarding ...

see Reference page 129

6 Complete the statements below with one word.

1 Be honest, Salvador Dali's work isn't really my cup of tea.

2 Caravaggio had a very difficult life. Anyway, I was going to say was he is my favourite artist.

3 I like those old Renaissance paintings. To tell you truth, I don't like modern art at all.

4 Nek Chand must be one of the world's greatest artists. Any rate, he's the best in India!

5 I think the Mona Lisa is overrated. As matter of fact, I don't think it's Leonardo's best painting.

6 As far as modern sculpture is, Henry Moore is undoubtedly the greatest.

7 Georgia O'Keefe's paintings of flowers are kind interesting. I like the colours she uses.

8 I was saying, Lee Krasner's art was overshadowed by that of her husband, Jackson Pollock.

7 Underline the best option.

1 A: *To be honest/As far as it's concerned/ Regarding*, I don't like Impressionism much.

   B: Neither do I. *As for it/What I was going to say/At any rate*, I think it's been overexposed.

2 A: Pollock's technique of dripping paint onto canvas was *as for/ anyway/kind of* strange.

   B: I agree. *More or less,/ Mind you,/As regards* his work did revolutionise modern art.

3 A: I like performance art. *Sort of/Regarding/As a matter of fact*, David Blaine's my hero.

   B: David Blaine? The magician? *Anyway, what I was going to say was/ Frankly,/As I was saying*, I think he's crazy!

4 A: I like Spanish art. *Kind of/In fact/As for* Picasso, I think he was the greatest of all time.

   B: Well, yes, he *more or less/as regards/to tell you the truth* invented modern art.

5 A: *As far as it's concerned/ Regarding/Anyway* photography, Cindy Sherman is currently the most famous artist.

   B: Really? *In fact/As I was saying/To tell you the truth*, I've never heard of her.

Person to person

8 Discuss in pairs.

1 Do you ever go to art exhibitions? If so, what was the last one you went to? Did you like it?

2 Do you have a favourite artist? Why do you like his/ her work?

Reading and vocabulary

9 **a** Look at the cartoon. What is happening?

  b Read the text and answer the questions.

  1 Why was the painting so badly protected?
  2 What type of people are art thieves, according to Charley Hill?
  3 What are Vermeers and Gainsboroughs, and what happened to them?
  4 What did Hill have to do to find *The Scream*?
  5 Who is Stephane Breitwieser and why is he unusual among art thieves?

10 Discuss.

  1 Would you like Charley Hill's job? Why/why not?
  2 Do you think Hill's book sounds interesting?
  3 What type of person do you think Stephane Breitwieser might be?
  4 What type of people collect art? Do you think it would be an enjoyable hobby?

11 **a** Answer the questions.

  1 What does *thug* (line 11) mean?
  2 What words come before *thugs* in the text? How does the text describe the people who steal paintings? How does this help us guess the meaning of *thug*?
  3 Does *thug* have other words in its 'family'?
  4 How can you find out how to pronounce *thug*? What does the dictionary entry below tell us about the pronunciation?

> **thug** /θʌg/ *n* [C] a violent man: *He was beaten up by a gang of young thugs.*

  b Answer the same questions for the following words/phrases: *mastermind* (line 10), *aesthetes* (line 9), *hideout* (line 11), *track down* (line 13), *stuffed* (line 17), *crack a case* (line 26), *haul* (line 43)

Lifelong learning

Guess first

Use contextual clues to help you with difficult vocabulary. Which words surround the unknown word? What is the general meaning of this part of the text? Can you guess from similar words in the same family or similar words in your own language? If you can't guess, and the word seems important, use a good dictionary.

Now you see it ...

¹ No wonder the man in Munch's *The Scream* is screaming. He keeps getting stolen. The famous painting went missing in 1994 and again ten years later, both times from museums in Norway.
⁵ Apparently, security was extremely poor. Officials thought the painting was so famous that it wouldn't be stolen. Wrong.

The world of art theft is not, as one might presume, populated with stylish **aesthetes**,
¹⁰ **masterminding** their operations from tax-free **hideouts**. Art thieves are **thugs**, according to a new book by Charley Hill. Hill was an undercover policeman whose job was to **track down** stolen paintings. He says that the people who steal
¹⁵ paintings were usually stealing wheels from cars a few years earlier. He describes priceless Vermeers being **stuffed** into the back of cars, Gainsboroughs being passed around by drug dealers with dirty hands and a particularly nasty end to one of Henry
²⁰ Moore's huge sculptures. The bronze, *King and Queen*, a masterpiece by Moore, was too heavy for the thieves to move, so they took out a chainsaw and cut off the heads, thinking those might be worth something.
²⁵ Hill's is an adventure story fit for any James Bond fans. In 1986 he **cracked a case** in which eleven valuable paintings had been stolen from Russborough House near Dublin. In order to rescue *The Scream*, Hill posed as a buyer for the J. Paul
³⁰ Getty Museum in LA: bow tie, big suit, even bigger Mercedes. He also had to learn everything about the painting, or should we say paintings: there are four versions of *The Scream*. He even memorised the patterns of wax droplets left on one version of the
³⁵ painting when Munch blew out a candle one night.

The artworks usually turn up, sometimes many years later, though the police don't always catch the thief. Even rarer is when a gentleman thief – one who steals art for personal pleasure only – is caught.
⁴⁰ In 2003, a waiter, Stephane Breitwieser from Switzerland, thirty-two, was found guilty of stealing sixty-nine artworks from museums since 1995. He told the court he did it for the love of art. His **haul** was worth over $1 billion – not bad for a waiter.

Writing

1   **a**   Choose one of the photos. How does it make you feel? What does it remind you of? What do you think is happening? Imagine that you are in the scene. Write a short paragraph about what you are feeling/doing.

     b   Read your paragraph to the rest of the class. Were your impressions similar or different?

Speaking

2   Work in pairs. Look at the words/phrases in the box below. Which words relate to cameras (C) and which relate to photos (P)?

> flash   features   blurred
> holiday snaps   close-up
> out of focus   disposable
> foreground   accessories
> tripod   digital

3   Discuss in pairs.

   1   Have you got a camera? How often do you use it?

   2   What do you think makes a good photo? Can you think of any tips for taking better photos?

   3   What's the best way of recording holidays and memories: taking photos/ writing about them/buying postcards/shooting videos/other ways?

   4   Can you think of any advantages/disadvantages to each method?

Reading

4   Work in pairs. Student A: read the text on page 146. Student B: read the text on page 148. As you read, note what the text says about:

   1   the best time to do it

   2   stories

   3   the local culture

   4   learning from professionals

5   Tell your partner about the main ideas in your text, and your answers to Ex. 4.

6 Discuss.

1 What do you think of the advice in your text? Was it interesting/obvious/surprising, etc?

2 Are the texts for amateurs or people who want to make a living doing these things?

3 Which sounds easier – being a photographer or being a travel writer?

4 Would you like to be a travel writer or a photographer? Why/why not?

5 Do you know of any famous photographers or travel writers? What do you think of their work?

Grammar | unreal past

7 Complete the tasks in the Active grammar box.

Active grammar

Wish/If only

If only I'd taken a better picture.

1 Find more examples of these forms in the introductions to your texts.

2 What verb tense follows *wish/if* only to talk about (a) the present? (b) the past?

It's high time/It's about time

3 Find examples of these forms in text 1 introduction and text 2 section 1.

4 Does *It's high time/It's about time* mean (a) something should be happening now, but it isn't OR (b) something is happening on time?

5 What tense follows *It's high time/It's about time*?

Would rather/Would sooner

6 Find examples of these forms in text 1 section 5 and text 2 section 2.

7 What verb form follows *would sooner/would rather* if the person speaking and the subject are (a) the same? (b) different?

I would rather go. (The person speaking and her subject is *I*).

I would sooner they left. (The person speaking is *I*, but the subject is *they*).

What if/Suppose (or supposing)

Suppose you had taken that job as a photographer? Would you be happier now?

8 Find more examples of these forms in text 1 section 1 and text 2 section 3.

9 What verb tense follows *what if/suppose* to talk about an imaginary situation in the (a) present? (b) past? (c) future?

---

see Reference page 129

8 Correct the mistakes in the sentences (where necessary).

1 What if you'll get ill when you go abroad?

2 It's about time you go to bed.

3 This scenery is so beautiful. If only I brought my camera.

4 Suppose you woke up earlier yesterday. Would you have seen the sun rise?

5 They'd rather we didn't use flash photography in the museum.

6 It's high time we went on a photography course.

7 I wish I can speak the language better. I'd ask them about their lives.

8 I'd sooner you wouldn't write that down, please.

9 Complete the second sentence so that it conveys a similar idea to the first. The base form of the verb you need is in brackets.

1 We should start our journals. (begin)
It's high _____ writing our journals.

2 What if you had the chance to become a travel journalist? (offer)
Suppose someone _____ a job as a travel journalist?

3 Please stop taking photos! (take)
We'd rather _____ photos inside the building.

4 I should have sent in my story for the travel writing competition. (enter)
If only _____ the competition, I might have won!

5 I'd like to be able to take good photos. (be)
I wish _____ good photographer.

6 We should select the photos for my new travel book together. (choose)
I'd sooner _____ photos together.

7 You should finish writing that article soon. (complete)
It's about _____ that article.

8 I'm nervous about my camera jamming at the vital moment. (jam)
What if _____ at the vital moment?

Person to person

10 a Complete the sentences so they are true for you.

It's high time I ...   It's about time ...

I wish ...   If only ...

I'd sooner ... than   Suppose ...

b Compare your sentences with other students.

Speaking

11 a Use the words in the box below to complete the sentences in the How to ... Box.

> I'd   way   unlikely   suppose   to   doing   wouldn't

<table>
<tr><td rowspan="7">HOW TO ...</td><td colspan="2">respond to hypothetical questions</td></tr>
<tr><td>... positively</td><td>It's highly likely _____ agree.
I would probably agree _____ that.
I would consider _____ that.
I _____ I might do that.</td></tr>
<tr><td>... negatively</td><td>I probably _____ accept.
It's _____ I'd be able to do that.
There's no _____ I would do that.</td></tr>
</table>

b **9.5** Listen and check.

12 a Work in pairs. Think about the situations below and discuss. Extend the discussion for as long as possible.

A *What if you were alone in the house and it suddenly caught fire?*

B *I'd try to save my photos.*

A *Why? Wouldn't you rather save something valuable?*

B *No! I'd sooner save the photos because they represent lots of happy memories.*

1 Suppose you were offered a job as a travel writer in the Caribbean, but it meant you would have to live on a tiny island for two years?

2 What if you were offered a free place on a photography course or a free place on a creative writing course, but you couldn't do both?

3 Suppose you could write great novels or paint great pictures or sing brilliantly. Which would you choose?

4 What if a Time Machine was invented which meant you could travel to any one period in the past? Which would you choose?

5 Suppose you opened your bag and there was a surprise gift in it. What would you like it to be?

6 What if you could be Leonardo da Vinci, Albert Einstein or Mozart for one day? Who would you be?

7 Suppose a film director asked to make a film about your life? Would you accept? Who would you like to act as you?

8 Suppose you could interview one famous person for a magazine. Who would it be?

9 What if you had been born a different nationality? Which would you like to be?

10 What if someone asked you to participate in a reality TV show?

b Think of two more hypothetical questions to ask your partner. Start your questions with *What if ...*/*Suppose ...*?

Writing

13 Work in pairs. Choose one of the situations in Ex. 13. Imagine that it really happened. Write the story in about 150 words.

9 | Vocabulary

Confusing words

1 a Read the text and discuss. What new job was created and why? Who got the job?

A few years ago, a committee at my university department held a (1) *reunion/meeting* to discuss a new post for a 'visionary' thinker. A number of the professors were (2) *sympathetic/friendly* to this idea, because, like me, they felt that our educational goals were far too (3) *sensitive/sensible* and boring; no one took risks any more because everyone wanted to (4) *fit into/suit* the current way of thinking. We also felt it would be a great (5) *possibility/opportunity* for an original thinker to come and (6) *prove/test* his or her ideas to see if they (7) *at the moment/actually* worked, while getting paid.

We hired a freelancer to do the (8) *propaganda/advertising*, and this is where we got a big surprise. The freelancer, a lady called Anousha Jalal, came up with a brilliant campaign to advertise the (9) *vacancy/vacation*. It really was a (10) *classic/classical* piece of advertising copy. In fact, her work was so imaginative and interesting that we asked her to (11) *assist/attend* an interview for the job. She wasn't sure if she wanted it, but (12) *in the end/at the end*, after lots of phone calls and emails, she had an interview and got the job.

b Underline the correct alternatives in the text.

2 Read the text again. Find the words to match the following definitions:

1 a) when a group of people come together to discuss important issues _____
   b) when people come together a long time after they last saw each other _____
2 a) willing to support someone's ideas or actions _____
   b) willing to be nice to other people (help and talk to them) _____
3 a) does what is correct and doesn't take chances _____
   b) easily offended/someone who considers the feelings of others _____
4 a) be appropriate/feels right _____
   b) belong in a category _____
5 a) something that might happen in theory _____
   b) a real chance to do something _____
6 a) use/check something to find out if it's successful _____
   b) find evidence that something is true _____

7 a) in reality/in truth _____
   b) now _____
8 a) false information that an organisation gives to the public to influence them _____
   b) publicity for a product/service _____
9 a) holiday (US English) _____
   b) something is available (job/room in a motel) _____
10 a) a style of music _____
   b) a timeless masterpiece _____
11 a) help _____
   b) go to an event _____
12 a) after a period of time (and maybe after discussion/debate) _____
   b) the last part of something (a book, a film, year, etc.). It is often followed by *of* _____

3 Complete the sentences with an appropriate word/phrase from Ex. 2.

1 There's a _____ for a manager at that company. It's the type of job that would _____ you.
2 We would be grateful if you could _____ us in setting up the class's twentieth anniversary _____.
3 Going to the Mozart Conference will be a great _____ to learn more about _____ music.
4 _____ of the book, the hero decides to be _____; he forgets his crazy dream of being a billionaire.
5 There were high hopes for the 'Wonder Drug'. _____ end, scientists _____ that it didn't work.
6 Joan's not studying _____, but there's a _____ that she'll do a PhD next year.
7 I found it difficult to _____ that class; the other students weren't _____ at all.
8 The huge signs promoting government policies were just _____: none of it was _____ true.

4 Choose a few of the confusing words that you had problems with. Write your own sentences using the words.

5 Discuss in pairs.

1 Are there any confusing words in your own language? Are they confusing for native speakers or only for foreigners?
2 Do you know any strategies for dealing with confusing words?
3 Which words in English are confusing for speakers of your language?

Business venture

1 a **9.6** Listen to someone describing how two popular products were developed. Are the statements true (T) or false (F)?

1 Clarence Birdseye was the first person to put food in salt water to freeze it.

2 The equipment for his experiments was cheap.

3 Birdseye sold the first modern freezer for 22 million dollars.

4 Chester Carlson's job was to invent a machine to make copies.

5 Carlson found his work difficult because of his own health problems.

6 The first commercial photocopier was made over twenty years after Carlson had first invented the machine.

b Listen again to check.

2 Discuss.

1 Why do you think it took so long for the photocopier to get funding?

2 Would you describe frozen food as an 'original' idea?

3 Can you think of any other popular products that are based on earlier inventions?

3 Work in pairs. You are planning a new business venture and need to persuade the rest of the class to invest in your idea. Choose one of the following (or come up with an idea of your own) and plan how you are going to 'sell' it to the rest of the class:

A NEW PRODUCT
You have invented a jacket that can change colour and _____. Made of the latest hi-tech material, and with a range of ten colours, the jacket takes five seconds to change colour. It also has special _____. ...

A NEW SERVICE
Doitforyou.com offers to help you with _____. Users pay a fixed monthly fee and can use the service as often as they wish. Additional benefits include _____. ...

A NEW COURSE
You are setting up a new course which teaches people how to _____. What is special about the course is that everyone who participates _____. ...

A NEW FILM
It is 2100. The world has become _____. Only one person can save the planet because he/she has the key to the secret _____. The problem is that there is a terrible _____ who doesn't want the world to be saved. ...

4 a Write the name of the product/service/course or film and a short summary of the main ideas behind it/its main benefits, etc.

b Take it in turns to present your proposals to the rest of the class. Ask and answer questions about each proposal.

5 Discuss. Which proposals are the most interesting? Which would you invest in?

Dependent prepositions

Sometimes prepositions have general meanings (see Unit 10 Vocabulary): *go under, under the thumb*

Sometimes verbs are followed by a preposition: *ask for, contribute to, range from ... (to ...), suffer from*

The verb and preposition are sometimes separated by the object: *remind someone of, distinguish someone from, receive training from ... /in ...*

Sometimes nouns are followed by prepositions. These are sometimes described as collocations: *relationship with, insurance against, in the fields of*

Sometimes adjectives are followed by a preposition: *bad at, similar to, famous for, concerned about*

Sometimes prepositions can begin common phrases: *in advance, out of order, at the time, on one occasion*

Discourse markers

Discourse is a piece of language that is longer and more complex than a sentence.

We use discourse markers to organise our speech/ writing and make clear the relationship between what we have said and what we will say. We also use discourse markers to show our attitude to the subject. The use of discourse markers depends on the function of our speech (e.g. persuading, agreeing, etc., use different markers).

Here are some common discourse markers:

focusing on the main topic: *regarding, as regards, as far as ... is concerned, as for*

returning to the main point (what was said before didn't matter): *anyway, anyhow, at any rate*

returning to a previous line of discussion: *as I was saying, anyway, what I was going to say was ...*

introducing a strong opinion or criticism: *all the same, and yet, still, on the other hand*

Unreal past

Wish/If only

We use *wish/if only* to describe unreal or imaginary situations. These are often regrets.

Wish/If only + past tenses describe imaginary present or future: *If only I was stronger.*

Wish/If only + Past Perfect describes the imaginary past: *I wish I had bought that CD.*

Wish + object + *would* is used to complain: *I wish you would be quiet!*

We cannot use this construction about ourselves. The subject and object must be different.

NOT: ~~I wish I would be more intelligent~~ ✗

It's time/It's high time/It's about time

We use *it's time,* etc. + past tenses to say something should be happening now, but it isn't. It is often used for criticising someone/something.

It's high time you stopped acting like a child.

Would rather/Would sooner

We use *would rather/would sooner* + Past Simple to describe preferences: *I'd sooner she gave me the cash.*

If the person who expresses the preference and the subject are the same, we use *would rather/would sooner* + infinitive without *to*.

I'd rather play basketball than the football.

We often use these expressions to refuse permission: *I'd rather you didn't smoke in my flat.*

What if/Suppose/Supposing

We use *what if/suppose* + past tenses to ask about an imaginary situation in the present or future.

Suppose you asked the bank for a loan?

We use *what if/suppose* + Past Perfect to ask about an imaginary situation in the past.

What if we had arrived earlier?

We use *what if/suppose* + Present Simple to ask about a situation that we think is probable.

What if your plan doesn't work?

Key vocabulary

The arts

plot interval scene orchestra audience novel landscape portraits reviews biography applause conductor rehearsal lead absolute masterpiece critics not one of his best great/difficult read spectacular/dreadful performance breathtaking/ disappointing scenery appalling/poor acting

Describing art

abstract striking avante-garde tranquil colourful plain traditional monochrome disturbing figurative dull stunning I'm a big fan of his stuff It's not my kind of thing at all It's really not my taste I'm really into her work It's not my cup of tea He's one of my all-time favourites I've always admired her work I can't relate to this type of thing

Cameras and photos

close-up out of focus disposable foreground accessories flash features blurred tripod digital holiday snaps

Confusing words

classic/classical opportunity/possibility in the end/at the end fit into/suit vacation/vacancy propaganda/advertising sensible/sensitive at the moment/actually friendly/sympathetic assist/attend reunion/meeting prove/test

1 Match phrases 1–8 to phrases a–h to make sentences.

1 Doris Lessing won the Nobel Prize for literature in recognition

2 Stephen Pinker, a well-known academic, is a master in the fields

3 Many people have drawn inspiration from

4 Kurosawa was one of the greatest film directors of

5 Leonardo's abilities ranged from

6 Thomas Edison succeeded in

7 Madonna's constantly changing image is characteristic of

8 US pilot Amelia Earhart devoted her life to

a) her ability to repackage herself for different generations.

b) of her contribution to the novel.

c) the life of Helen Keller.

d) all time.

e) flying.

f) painting to designing weapons.

g) registering 1,093 patents for new inventions.

h) of both cognitive science and linguistics.

2 Complete the dialogue with the words/expressions in the box.

> more or less   as regards   be honest   in fact
> as far as my work is concerned   kind

A: Rachel, how are you feeling now you've won the Turner Prize?

B: Absolutely delighted. To (1)_____, I never expected to win. I ... er ... (2)_____ of knew I had a chance, but it was a great surprise.

A: How will this affect you?

B: (3)_____, it won't affect me at all. I already have three exhibitions planned. (4)_____ the money, it'll mean I can focus on my work.

A: We hear you'll be making videos, rather than painting. Is this true?

B: That's (5)_____ true. I'll be making videos, but I'll still paint. (6)_____, my next exhibition will be mainly paintings.

A: Thank you, Rachel. We look forward to it.

3 Underline the correct word/expression.

1 What if we *are leaving/left/would have left* really early? Would we arrive on time?

2 I would rather *know/to know/knowing* the truth now than later.

3 I wish I *will/can/could* paint better.

4 It's high time we *had gone/went/go*.

5 She wishes she *had got up/got up/was getting up* earlier yesterday.

6 Supposing you *are running/run/have run* into trouble, what will you do?

7 It's about time they *learn/learned/had learned* to act like adults.

8 We'd sooner you *didn't bring/hadn't brought/wouldn't bring* your cat yesterday.

4 Complete the sentences with suitable words/phrases with meanings similar to those in brackets. Use the letters shown.

1 It was a disaster – a really a_____ performance! (*poor*)

2 The show is quite funny. The characters are really o____ t____ t____. (*exaggerated*)

3 He does have interesting ideas, but his style makes it a rather h_____ read. (*hard work*)

4 The decor hasn't changed since the 1980s, so it's not very c_____. (*modern/up-to-date*)

5 Michelangelo's 'David' is without a doubt his f_____ p_____. (*best work*)

6 The i_____ special effects were what made the film such a success. (*unbelievable*)

5 Complete the text with the words/phrases in the box. You don't need all of the words.

> classic/classical   opportunity/possibility
> in the end/at the end   fit into/suit
> vacation/vacancy   propaganda/advertising
> sensible/sensitive   at the moment/actually
> friendly/sympathetic   assisted/attended
> reunion/meeting   proved/tested

I managed to catch Brett Sankey, director of *Another World*, before he took off on (1) _____. While the film's (2) _____ focuses on Darwar, the (3) _____ hero, the film is (4) _____ about the rights of native peoples. Sankey is (5) _____ to the indigenous people's cause, but what he really likes is the (6) _____ to work with actors.

'All the (7) _____ films have great performances at their heart. *Another World* doesn't really (8) _____ any genre – it's a thriller and a comedy. But it does have great acting,' he says. 'When I (9) _____ an early (10) _____ with the producers, I stressed that the performances would be vital. Anyway, (11) _____ I got what I wanted. We (12) _____ the film with audiences and they liked it.'

10 Feelings

Lead-in

1 Discuss. How do you think the people in the photos are feeling? Why?

2 **a** Check you understand the meaning of the idioms **in bold**. Which idioms apply to the people in the photos?

1 She was **at her wits end** with worry.
2 He failed his exam, so he's a bit **down in the dumps**.
3 They saw the same car at nearly half the price, so now they are **kicking themselves**.
4 She is very **pleased with herself** for getting through the interview.
5 I've been running around all day – I'm **buzzing with energy**.
6 I'm **in two minds** about whether to accept the invitation.
7 Try not to get so **wound up** – it's only a game!
8 They are moving to the Caribbean, and they're **over the moon** about it.

b Match sentences a–h with sentences 1–8 above.

a) It's like **a dream come true**.
b) She deserves **a pat on the back**.
c) Just **chill out**!
d) We should try to **cheer him up**.
e) But they can't **do anything about it** now.
f) We went out to **take her mind off** the problem.
g) I just can't **make my mind up**.
h) When I finish work I need somewhere to **relax and wind down**.

3 Work in pairs. Choose some of the idioms in Ex. 2 and describe a time you felt this way.

I was very pleased with myself when I got my new job ...

Listening

1 Discuss.

1 Do you think your outlook can affect what happens to you in life? How?

2 Do you think some people are luckier than others?

3 Would you call yourself optimistic?

2 **a** 🔊 10.1 Listen to the interview and <u>underline</u> the correct alternative.

1 'Lucky' and 'unlucky' people have a *similar/different* psychology.

2 'Lucky' people have positive expectations, which are often *realistic/unrealistic*.

3 Positive thinking can *help improve/ be a big problem for* business.

4 'Lucky' and 'unlucky' people are genetically *the same/different*.

5 *Extroverts/Introverts* use body language to get people to respond to them.

6 Children who *receive praise/pray regularly* do better at school.

b What do the speakers say about each statement?

3 Listen again. What do the speakers say about:

1 Rhode Island?

2 1993?

3 being robust and resilient?

4 having boundless optimism?

5 failed business ventures?

6 developing drive and focus?

7 sales figures?

8 a particular colour?

9 gifted children?

4 Discuss.

1 Do you agree with what Wiseman says about luck and positive thinking?

2 Do you think business motivational training can improve business?

3 What does the American high school experiment tell us about education?

4 Do you consider yourself lucky or unlucky?

Grammar | modals (and verbs with similar meanings)

5 Look at the way the words **in bold** are used in 1–12 below. Match them to their correct usage in the Active grammar box

1 ... some people **might** seem luckier than others?

2 ... the differences between them **must** be related to their psychology.

3 ... it **will** come as no great surprise that ...

4 They **won't** give up.

5 They didn't **need to** win.

6 You **can't** win the lottery if you don't enter ...

7 ... others **are bound to** go from one failed venture to another.

8 ... **can** I ask you, are some people just born unlucky?

9 You **might** do better if you have a more positive outlook.

10 Lucky people **are likely to** create opportunities ...

11 ... he **is supposed to** speak only to people wearing that colour.

12 You **must** keep your winning ticket to verify the claim.

Active grammar

will

a) for predictions: *Do you think the government will win the election?*

b) for willingness/unwillingness: *I'll get that for you. He won't pay the bills.*

might

c) to talk about possibility: *Majda might phone later.*

d) to make suggestions (polite): *You might try asking your brother.*

must/can't

e) for obligation: *You must be at the office by 8a.m. You can't leave before 5p.m.*

f) for deduction: There *must be some kind of problem. That can't be the manager – he's far too young.*

can

g) for permission: *Can we leave our bags here?*

h) for possibility/impossibility: *We can't all fit in one car.*

(be) supposed to

i) to talk about what you have to do according to the rules/regulations: *We are supposed to be at the presentation.*

(be) bound to

j) for future prediction of certainty: *She's bound to give the secret away.*

(be) likely to

k) for probability: *You're not likely to pass.*

ought to/need to/should

l) for obligation/duty/necessity: *Do you think we ought to let them know we are here? Do we need to book a table? You really should contact the office.*

see Reference page 143

6 Discuss the differences in meaning (if any) between the three options *in italics*.

1 You *might try catching/needn't catch/won't catch* the bus home.

2 *I think I can/I must be able to/You're not supposed to* smoke in here.

3 He *ought/'s supposed/'s likely* to meet us at the theatre.

4 She *can't/must/'s bound* to be older than him.

5 We *didn't need to get/needn't have got/were supposed to get* good marks to get into university.

Person to person

7 Work in pairs. Tell your partner about:

1 three things you should/ought to/are supposed to do this week.

2 what you think your best friend is likely to be doing right now.

3 how you think teachers can best motivate or encourage their students.

4 how you think people's working lives will change in the future.

Vocabulary

8 **a** Check you understand the phrases **in bold** and complete the questionnaire from Professor Wiseman's book, *The Luck Factor*.

HOW LUCKY ARE YOU?

How strongly do you agree/disagree with the statements? Use the scale below.

1 strongly disagree	2 disagree
3 uncertain 4 agree	5 strongly agree

1 I sometimes chat to strangers when queuing in a supermarket or bank. ☐

2 I do not **have a tendency to** worry or feel anxious about life. ☐

3 I am **open to new experiences**, such as trying new types of food or drinks. ☐

4 I often act on my **gut feelings** and **hunches**. ☐

5 I have tried some techniques to **boost my intuition**, such as meditation or just going to a quiet place. ☐

6 I nearly always expect good things to happen to me in the future. ☐

7 I tend to try **to get what I want from life**, even if the **chances of success seem slim**. ☐

8 I expect most people that I meet to be pleasant, friendly and helpful. ☐

9 I tend to **look on the bright side** of whatever happens to me. ☐

10 I believe that even negative events will **work out well** for me **in the long run**. ☐

11 I don't tend to **dwell on things** that haven't worked out well for me in the past. ☐

12 I try to learn from mistakes I have made in the past. ☐

---

b Read the results of the questionnaire on page 151.

c Compare your answers with other students. Do you agree with the rating?

Listening

9 `10.2` Listen to the song and answer the questions.

1 How do you think the singer is feeling? Why?
2 What do you think has happened?
3 What has caused this change of feeling?
4 What does she say about a) her fears b) her opportunities c) her spirit?

10 a Read the song lyrics. Put the lines of each verse in the correct order.

Feelin' so good

__ It became so clear to me that everything is going my way
__ I feel like there's no limit to what I can see
__ When I opened up my eyes today
__ My endless possibilities
__ That's why I'm feeling ...
__ Has the whole world opened for me
__ I felt the sun shining on my face
__ I got rid of fears that were holding me

Chorus:
__ Like I should
__ 'cause not one thing
__ Can bring me down
__ Nothing in this world gonna turn me round ...
__ I knew I would
__ I'm feeling so good
__ Been taking care of myself

__ Call a few friends of mine
__ And everything is still going right
__ Anything I want will be mine
__ Like the stars above I'm gonna shine
__ There's no way you can stop me this time
__ 'cause I'm liking life
__ And tonight's for feeling ...
__ Or break this spirit of mine
__ Now the day is turning into night
__ Tonight I'm gonna have a good time

Chorus (2x)

b Listen again to check.

11 Discuss. Do any of the expressions in Ex. 8 apply to the singer and how she feels?

Speaking

12 a Work in pairs. Think about a dream you would like to realise, or a goal you would like to achieve. Make a few notes about the following:

1 What is the dream?
2 Why is it important?
3 How will you go about achieving it?
4 Who will help you?
5 Will luck play a part in your success?
6 What do you need to help you fulfil the dream?
7 What have you done in the past that could help you?
8 How will you motivate yourself?
9 What can you do <u>now</u> towards realising your dream?

b Tell each other about your dream/goal. Try to offer each other advice on how you might fulfil/achieve it.

10.2 What does it feel like?

Grammar | modals of deduction (past and present)
Can do | make guesses about imaginary situations

Listening

1 Discuss. What is happening in the photos? What would it be like to be there? What problems might there be?

2 **10.3** Listen to three people discussing similar situations. How did they feel?

3 Listen again and answer the questions.

1 Why is it easier for people to get to Machu Picchu these days?

2 When Machu Picchu was discovered by modern explorers, how was the actual site different from now?

3 What difficulties with the first flight does the speaker mention?

4 What doubts does he think the pilot had?

5 What positive/negative emotions does the speaker think Gagarin had?

4 Discuss. Have you ever wondered what it's like to be someone else/ achieve something amazing? Who would you like to have been? Why?

Grammar | modals of deduction (past and present)

5 Complete the tasks in the Active grammar box.

Active grammar

1 Look at the modals of deduction below and read the tapescript on page 175. Can you find any examples?

must be/must have been

might see/might have seen

can't have/can't have had

couldn't take/couldn't have taken

could play/could have played

may live/may have lived

2 Which three verb forms above have similar meanings?

3 Which verb forms mean that something is not possible?

4 Which verb form means we are sure about something (in the positive)?

5 How is the meaning of *must be* and *must have been* different?

We can also use:

will be to make a guess about the present, when we are almost sure that something is true because of habit or deduction.

That'll be John on the phone. He always calls at 6.30.

will have been to make a guess about the past, when we are almost sure that something happened.

That noise will have been the water heater. It always makes a noise in the morning.

see Reference page 143

6 Discuss the difference in meaning (if any) between the two options *in italics* in the sentences below.

1 She *will/must* have felt very upset.

2 He *can't/shouldn't* be happy about his exam result. He *normally does much/could've done* better.

3 You *couldn't/can't* have stayed awake all night. *You never do that/That's not like you!*

4 He *might be/could have been* hungry: that would explain him crying.

5 They *may/might* have found the gold.

Person to person

7 a Look at the photos on page 150. Discuss what you think is happening/has happened and why.

b Read the story behind each photo on page 147. Were your speculations correct?

Reading

8 Read the introduction to a book review below and discuss what you think 'some of the biggest highs' and 'some of the worst lows' might be.

> Esquire magazine interviewed sixty-one people who had experienced some of the biggest highs and the worst lows known to humanity. The result is a book called *Esquire Presents: What it Feels Like*.

9 Work in pairs. Read the rest of the review and discuss whether you think the following statements are true or false. Give reasons.

1 According to the review, the book was published so that ordinary people could read about extraordinary experiences.

2 The book is mainly about famous people's achievements.

3 Buzz Aldrin talks about certain regrets he has.

4 According to the review, Craig Strobeck's experiences are worse than Max Dearing's.

5 Geoffrey Petkovich is probably a fun-liking person.

6 The book is a serious, academic text.

7 A.J. Jacobs researched and wrote the stories in *Esquire Presents: What it Feels Like*.

8 The man who hurt his thumb with a hammer doesn't care because he is physically very tough.

10 Discuss. What motivates people to do the things described in the text? What is the book's 'message'? Would you like to read it? Why/why not?

So what does it feel like ...?

1 As we watch James Bond jump out of a plane, shoot twenty-eight bad guys in five seconds flat, mix a perfect cocktail and get the girl, most of us know that real life just isn't like this. We're never going to win the Nobel Prize, walk on the Moon, win the lottery or get attacked by grizzly bears. And that's why Esquire magazine decided to find out what these things really feel like.

2 Thanks to Buzz Aldrin, we can share the thrill of walking on the Moon. He describes, 'powdery dust ... the sky velvety black ... surreal', and his feelings of responsibility: 'If we made a mistake, we would regret it for quite a while.' Aldrin's account gives us just the right blend of emotion and cold, hard fact. Aldrin's story is, of course, extremely well-known. One of the strengths of *Esquire Presents: What it Feels Like* is that it also covers normal, unexceptional people who find themselves in exceptional circumstances.

3 Max Dearing tells us what it feels like to be struck by lightning: 'I was absolutely frozen, just as cold as I've ever been in my entire life, but then part of me was incredibly hot, too. I saw these red flashing lights, and I kept thinking, "It's a fire truck! A fire truck!" as if I were a little kid. Then there was the most incredible noise I'd ever heard.'

4 If Dearing's experience is shocking (literally and metaphorically) because of its sudden life-changing violence, Craig Strobeck's story is altogether more terrifying because it affects every minute of his life. Strobeck describes what it feels like to have an Obsessive-Compulsive disorder. He has to take two-and-a-half-hour showers. He runs out of hot water but doesn't stop. He cleans every inch of his body a thousand times, and sometimes he gets back in the shower because one area just doesn't feel clean enough.

5 Possibly the strangest experience described in the book, though, is that of Geoffrey Petkovich. He went over Niagara Falls, one of the world's largest waterfalls, in a barrel. He did it 'for a bit of fun', though it was a rather bumpy ride. With him in the barrel were two cans of cola, a packet of cigarettes and two hours' worth of oxygen in tanks, just in case the barrel sank.

6 Petkovich's story is an example of the book's humorous tone, but its editor, A.J. Jacobs, thinks *Esquire Presents: What it Feels Like* has a serious message. 'The guy who was buried under 50 feet of snow in an avalanche says that nowadays he can hit his thumb with a hammer and it doesn't bother him. He's just happy to be here.' The same is true for most of the people in this fascinating book.

Vocabulary | strong feelings

11 Work in pairs/groups. Put the adjectives **in bold** in the correct column in the table. Use a dictionary where necessary.

1 You've just been offered the best job in the world. You must be absolutely **thrilled**!
2 One thing that makes me **furious** is when people drop rubbish in the street.
3 I was **taken aback** when they asked me to be the team captain. I hadn't expected it at all.
4 She was **ecstatic** when she finally passed her driving test.
5 I feel completely **indifferent** about technology; I just don't care one way or the other.
6 They split up after ten years together and now they're both **miserable**.
7 I'm feeling rather **chuffed** because I managed to beat Nikolai at chess!
8 I know Maths isn't your favourite subject, but do you have to look so **uninterested**?
9 She was **terrified** when she saw the spider in her bed!
10 I was absolutely **flabbergasted** when they told me I'd won the lottery.
11 When she was voted Best Actress, she was **dumbstruck**. She just couldn't believe it!
12 He was absolutely **outraged** by your terrible behaviour.
13 I will be **delighted** to attend your party.
14 When the TV repair man didn't show up again I was **livid**. I'd taken the day off work.
15 Stuck in the middle of the avalanche, they were **petrified**. They fully expected to die.
16 We were a bit **upset** that you didn't remember our wedding anniversary.

1 happy	2 unhappy	3 neither happy nor unhappy
4 scared	5 surprised	6 angry

12 Answer the questions.
1 Which word is informal and weaker than the other words (column 1)?
2 Which word usually describes a feeling we have for just a short time (column 2)?
3 Which expression is the most formal (column 5)?
4 Which word means shocked because of some injustice as well as angry (column 6)?

13 Discuss in pairs. How would you feel in these situations? Why? Try to use adjectives you haven't used before.
1 You won the Nobel Prize for Physics.
2 You were chosen by NASA to fly to the Moon.
3 You found a large, unfriendly-looking snake in your living room.
4 You were caught in the middle of a lightning storm while wearing your beach clothes.
5 You were abducted by aliens who gave you a free massage.
6 You were offered a job as a model for a clothing company in Milan.
7 You woke up from a beautiful dream and saw that it was raining outside.
8 You found a large box full of treasure under your floor.
9 You read that a little-known politician in Outer Mongolia had decided to retire at the age of sixty-three.
10 You saw a tiger wandering around your local supermarket.

Lifelong learning

Personalise and memorise!

Write new vocabulary in a personalised sentence about you, your family or your hobbies, etc. This will help you to remember the words. Try this with some of the adjectives in Ex. 11.

Listening

1 Discuss. Which of the situations in the box do you remember from your childhood? How did they make you feel?

> moving house   starting/changing school
> playing/inventing games   making friends
> summer holidays   staying with grandparents
> birth of a brother/sister   spending time alone
> looking after other children   doing sport
> arguing with friends/family   doing exams

2 a **10.4** Listen to people describing childhood memories. Which topics does each speaker mention?

   b Discuss. Do any of the stories remind you of experiences from your own childhood?

3 Listen again and answer the questions.
   1 Did speaker 1 find it easy to get on with the other children? Why/why not?
   2 How has his experience shaped his character?
   3 Where did speaker 2 use to run?
   4 What was bad about the experience?
   5 Is she keen on sports now?
   6 What smells, sensations and colours does speaker 3 mention?
   7 What was different about the breakfasts she used to have on holiday?
   8 How did speaker 4 use to get into the woods?
   9 How did playing in the woods make him feel? How does he describe that time?

Reading

4 a Look at the picture and discuss. Where do you think the story is set? What do you think it is about? How do you think the girl is feeling?

   b Read the text. Were your ideas correct?

5 a Discuss in pairs. What is the significance of the following words/ideas in the story?

   six rent yard noise broom water pipes
   milk gallons stairs trees stories windows

   b How did the story make you feel? What do you think life is going to be like in the house on Mango Street?

The House on Mango Street

We didn't always live on Mango Street. Before that we lived on Loomis on the third floor, and before that we lived on Keeler. Before Keeler it was Paulina, and before that I can't remember. But what I remember most is moving a lot. Each time it seemed there'd be one more of us. By the time we got to Mango Street we were six – Mama, Papa, Carlos, Kiki, my sister Nenny and me.

The house on Mango Street is ours, and we don't have to pay rent to anybody, or share the yard with the people downstairs, or be careful not to make too much noise, and there isn't a landlord banging on the ceiling with a broom. But even so, it's not the house we thought we'd get.

We had to leave the flat on Loomis quick. The water pipes broke and the landlord wouldn't fix them because the house was too old. We had to leave fast. We were using the washroom next door and carrying water over in empty milk gallons. That's why Mama and Papa looked for a house, and that's why we moved into the house on Mango Street, far away, on the other side of town.

They always told us that one day we would move into a house, a real house that would be ours for always so we wouldn't have to move each year. And our house would have running water and pipes that worked. And inside it would have real stairs, not hallway stairs, but stairs inside like houses on TV. And we'd have a basement and at least three washrooms so when we took a bath we wouldn't have to tell everybody. Our house would be white with trees around it, a great big yard and grass growing without a fence. This was the house Papa talked about when he held a lottery ticket and this was the house Mama dreamed up in the stories she told us before we went to bed.

But the house on Mango Street is not the way they told it at all. It's small and red with tight steps in front and windows so small you'd think they were holding their breath. Bricks are crumbling in places, and the front door is so swollen you have to push hard to get in. There is no front yard, only four little elms the city planted by the curb. Out back is a small garage for the car we don't own yet and a small yard that looks smaller between the two buildings on either side. There are stairs in our house, but they're ordinary hallway stairs, and the house has only one washroom. Everybody has to share a bedroom – Mama and Papa, Carlos and Kiki, me and Nenny.

Sandra Cineros

Grammar | uses of *would*

6 Complete the task in the Active grammar box.

> ### Active grammar
>
> Match the example sentences 1–7 to the different uses of *would* in a–g below.
>
> 1 *Each time there'd be one more of us.*
> 2 *The landlord **wouldn't** fix them.*
> 3 *They always told us that one day we **would** move into a real house.*
> 4 *We packed all the books in wooden boxes so that they **wouldn't** get damaged.*
> 5 *We'd have moved to a different area if we'd been able to afford it.*
> 6 ***Would** you shut the window, please?*
> 7 *I wish they **wouldn't** make so much noise at night.*
>
> a) polite request
> b) recurring situation in the past
> c) past purpose/reason (often used after *so that*)
> d) imagined situation
> e) strong wish that someone would/wouldn't do something
> f) past intention/expectation (reported)
> g) refusal

see Reference page 143

7 Add *would/wouldn't* to the following sentences (as appropriate).

1 If you like to follow me, I'll show you to your rooms.
2 I have much more time to do my work, if you looked after the kids a little more often.
3 When we were alone at home, we always cook for ourselves.
4 He never help me with my homework.
5 If only he answer the phone, I could explain what happened.
6 She have liked to see her grandchildren grow up.
7 We hid the parcel in the cupboard so that she notice it.
8 Her parents pay for her to go to university as they didn't believe in education for girls.

Person to person

8 Complete the sentences and compare your ideas with other students.

When I was ten years old I thought ... *I would grow up to be a doctor.*
Would you mind if I ... ?
At school my friends and I would ...
I wish people wouldn't always ...
If I was younger I'd ...
I told (name) that I'd ...
When I was a child my parents wouldn't ...

Reading

9 Read the web extracts and, with a partner, choose a title for each one. Which do you like best?

10 Cover the text. Think of different ways to complete the phrases in the How to ... box. Compare your ideas with the original examples from the extracts.

<table>
<tr><td rowspan="5" style="writing-mode:vertical-rl">HOW TO ...</td><td colspan="2">**describe a childhood memory**</td></tr>
<tr><td>Introducing the story</td><td>One memory that _____ in my mind ...
I have a _____ recollection of .../
I'll _____ remember ...
One of my _____ memories is of ...</td></tr>
<tr><td>Background</td><td>We always/usually/_____ spent ...
We were always _____ .../My parents kept _____ me ...
On Sundays we _____ often ...
I had never .../I thought I'd ...</td></tr>
<tr><td>Specific event</td><td>One time/But _____ night/On this occasion ...
I felt .../I was _____ to death.
However, .../The problem was that ...</td></tr>
<tr><td>Reflecting</td><td>Looking back, ...
I just remember .../It reminds me of ...
It's _____ to believe/I can hardly believe ...</td></tr>
</table>

Speaking

11 a Choose two or three childhood memories/ experiences to talk about. You can talk about any experiences you like or choose from one of the following:

- a song/story from your childhood
- a journey you went on
- a game you played
- a holiday you remember
- a time when you experienced freedom
- an important discovery you made

b Write a few notes and try to use some of the expressions in the How to ... box.

c Tell your stories to other students.

Writing

12 Write a short paragraph describing an early childhood memory using phrases from the How to ... box. Do not give your story a title.

---

http://www.reallifestories.com/childhood.html

Stories from Childhood

We asked you to send in stories about some of your earliest childhood memories:

_____

I have a vivid recollection of walking to school when I was about ten years old and living in Southall, West London. Every morning I would meet my childhood sweetheart at the corner of the street and carry her satchel all the way to the girls' school gate. In the afternoon, I would wait for her outside the same gate at 3.45p.m. and we would walk home together singing, 'You were made for me' by Freddie and the Dreamers.

_____

I'll always remember my granddad bringing a newly born black sheep up to the house one time. He let me hold him without completely letting go because the little ball of curls was wriggling like an eel. I was five years old and had never seen a black sheep. His skull was hard as a rock. Later my granddad told me I was like that little black sheep ... hard-headed and very special.

_____

My earliest memory is of my dad carrying me on his shoulders. On Sundays, we would often go for an afternoon walk, and when I got tired he would carry me. I felt I could see the entire world. And I could ... my three-year-old world, at least.

_____

One memory that sticks in my mind is of me and my brother when we were younger. We generally spent most of our time fighting. We were always chasing each other around the house hitting each other with golf clubs, throwing things. But one night we were staying at my aunt's house, and I was particularly sad about something. I just remember crying into my brother's arms as we were going to bed. I can't even remember now what I was so sad about, but the important thing is that I have this memory of knowing he was there for me, and being comforted by him. Looking back, it's hard to believe what happened that night.

_____

One of my earliest memories was of being scared to death because I thought that I'd been abandoned in the hospital ward. I had my tonsils removed aged two and a half and had to stay overnight by myself. My parents kept telling me that they'd come to take me home tomorrow morning when the sun shines. The problem was that the next morning, it was raining!

b Read your paragraphs to the rest of the class and choose titles for each other's stories.

Phrasal verbs and particles

1 a Discuss. **What do the expressions with** *under* **mean?**

We were working *under pressure*, so we were *under a lot of stress*. The boss needed to work overtime, but his wife wouldn't allow it: he's completely *under her thumb*. Eventually the business *went under*.

b Read the statement and choose (a) or (b).

Expressions with *under* tend to be used with (a) positive and pleasant (b) negative and unpleasant situations.

2 a Look at the ways particles are sometimes used with phrasal verbs.

back	return
on	continue
off	travel to another place
around	do a pointless activity
up	complete something/have no more to do
down	(1) put something onto paper, (2) reduce (speed, number, etc.)
out	(1) distribute something amongst people, (2) lose ability to function

b Complete the sentences with a suitable particle.

I've been handing <u>out</u> leaflets all day. I'm worn <u>out</u>!

1 Bill tried to write _____ everything Tania said, but because she was speaking too fast, he asked her to slow _____.

2 Lisa finally came _____ after several years away from home.

3 Sam decided to carry _____ until she'd finished.

4 Tom and Jo ran _____ together to get married! They set _____ at 6.00.

5 Don is always lounging _____. He's so lazy!

6 The last customer drank _____ and left. Majid counted _____ the money, locked _____ the café and went home.

c What do you think the phrasal verbs mean?

3 <u>Underline</u> the correct word *in italics* using information from Ex. 2.

1 The river dried *up/on/back* completely, so there was no water in the village.

2 I decided to cut *around/down/off* on fatty food and I lost 10 kilos as a result.

3 The blood went to my head and I passed *up/on/out*. I regained consciousness a few minutes later.

4 When the police officer tried to interview him, he clammed *on/up/around*; he didn't say a word.

5 Can you hold *up/on/around* for a few more minutes? We're getting a signal.

6 I applied for the job but they never wrote *up/down/back*.

7 We couldn't get tickets, so we just hung *up/off/around* on the street for hours. It was so boring!

8 The task was difficult, but she soldiered *on/around/off* and eventually finished.

9 Absolutely exhausted, I crashed *up/out/around* on the sofa and slept all night.

10 We had no idea where the party was, so we drove *around/up/down* for an hour and eventually went home.

4 Work in pairs. Explain what the phrasal verbs mean in Ex. 3.

'<u>Dry up</u> means there was no more water. It probably hadn't rained for a long time.'

5 Discuss. Have you (or has someone you know) ever done any of the things in the box? When might you do it/them?

> clam up   soldier on   pass out
> drive around   hang around
> cut down on something
> pack up all your possessions

Lifelong learning

Note it down!

There are thousands of phrasal verbs. It is not necessary to learn them all. The 'rules' here have many exceptions. When you read/hear phrasal verbs that you think are useful, write them down, in context. Look for patterns in the use of particles.

Moan, rave, take a stand!

1 Read the dictionary definitions and discuss. When was the last time you moaned about something, raved about something or took a stand on something?

> **moan** /məʊn/ *v* **1** [I] *informal* to complain about something in an annoying way

> **take a stand** *v* [I] to state publicly a strong opinion about an important issue

> **rave** /reɪv/ *v* [I] **1 rave about/over sth** to talk in an excited way about something because you think it is very good

2 **10.5** Listen to three speakers and answer the questions. What does each speaker talk about? Are they having a moan, raving about something or taking a stand? What are their opinions?

3 Prepare to moan, rave or take a stand about an issue of your choice. Use the pictures opposite to help you if you need inspiration.

4 Work in groups. Take it in turns to speak. As you are listening to other students, write down their topic and one question to ask when they have finished.

TOPIC	QUESTIONS
1	
2	
3	
4	

Modals (and verbs with similar meanings)

don't have to
lack of obligation: *We don't have to be there until 2.30p.m.*

must not
obligation not to do something: *You mustn't talk to him like that.*

should/ought to
advice: *You should see a doctor.*

recommendation: *You ought to see the castle before you leave.*

polite obligation: *Guests should not smoke in the bedrooms.*

uncertainty: *Should we lock both the doors?*

expectation: *They should be here by now.*

should with thinking verbs, to make them less direct: *I shouldn't think the meeting will take long.*

can
permission: *Can I use the telephone?*

can't
impossibility: *This can't be the right place!*

can + be
criticism: *He can be so annoying!*

will
assumption: *They'll be here in a minute.*

won't
refusal: *I won't stop until I get what I want.*

may/might
possibility: *We might need an umbrella.*

might as well
the last option, when the speaker is not keen: *We might as well just pay the bill.*

must
certainty: *They must be hungry by now.*

need
behaves like a normal verb: *Do you need to speak to the doctor?*

is supposed to
obligation: *They were supposed to deliver the parcel this morning.*

be bound to
prediction of certainty: *He's bound to get the job he wants.*

be likely to do/be
probability: *Children living in rural areas are likely to move to the city as adults.*

Modals of deduction (past)

must have (been)
certain: *The crash must have been terrifying.*

might have (been)
possibility: *I might have left my key in the car.*

can't have/couldn't have (been)
impossibility: *He can't have finished already!*

They couldn't have come this far.

could have/may have (been)
possibility: *We could have been left there for ages. There may have been a good reason for the delay, but we were angry nevertheless.*

will have been
when we are fairly certain: *That will have been Jim. He always calls at this time.*

Uses of *would*

polite request: *Would you help me get the files?*

recurring situation in the past: *She would always have a bag of sweets in her pocket.*

past purpose/reason (often used after *so that*): *We took a taxi so (that) we wouldn't be late.*

imagined situation: *I'd like to know what happened!*

strong wish that someone would/wouldn't do something: *I wish he would make more of an effort!*

past intention/expectation (reported): *They asked if we would like anything to drink.*

past refusal: *He wouldn't let go of my bag.*

Key vocabulary

Idioms/Prepositional phrases for feelings/emotions
at her wits end   down in the dumps
fuming with anger   kicking themselves
pleased with herself   buzzing with energy
in two minds   wound up   over the moon

Outlook/Attitude
have a tendency to worry   be open to new experiences
gut feelings and hunches   boost your intuition
to get what I want from life   look on the bright side
dwell on things   chances of success seem slim
work out well in the long run

Strong adjectives to describe feelings
thrilled   furious   taken aback   ecstatic   indifferent
miserable   chuffed   uninterested   terrified
flabbergasted   dumbstruck   outraged   delighted
livid   petrified   upset

Phrasal verbs and particles
under pressure   go under   under the thumb
hand out   wear out   count up   lock up   set off
come back   carry on   lounge around   slow down

1 Rewrite each sentence, using the words **in bold**, so that the meaning stays the same.

1 It won't be a surprise if the manager is angry about the situation. **likely**

2 I'm sure they'll phone us this morning. **bound**

3 The interview is at 10.30, but they asked me to be there half an hour before. **supposed**

4 There must be another way out of the building. **can't**

5 Maybe we'll have time for a quick drink before the meeting. **might**

6 They are refusing to pay the invoice until the dispute has been resolved. **won't**

7 Do you want us to wait for you outside the conference hall? **should**

8 It's better if he brings his own laptop. **ought**

2 Complete each sentence with a suitable past modal phrase.

The mud was up to 5m deep in places.
*It **must have been** impossible to drive through.*

1 There is no reason for her not to come. She ... understood your instructions.

2 You should have seen their reaction! They ... been happier.

3 We were lucky to get out alive. We ... killed.

4 They didn't come home until the early hours of the morning. The party ... good.

5 She could see my face. She ... realised who I was.

6 They'd had such a difficult journey. They ... relieved when they arrived.

7 It's not a very good score. There's no doubt Evans ... disappointed with that.

3 Correct any mistakes in the sentences.

1 If I'd have known, I'd have called you earlier.

2 I wish she won't always tell me what to do.

3 I wouldn't change it for all the world.

4 We left the keys in the office so you will see them when you got there.

5 I'd sit on my grandfather's knee and put tobacco in his pipe.

6 Wouldn't it be easier if we went home first?

7 I told Marcella that we meet her outside the cinema.

8 My parents wouldn't never have dreamed of sending me to private school.

4 Complete the text with a word from the box below.

> worked   end   pleased   terrified
> tendency   minds   moon   calm   aback
> delighted   upset

When I was about ten years old, I remember my father coming in to the room, looking terribly (1)_____ with himself, to tell us that we were going to have another brother or sister. It was unexpected, so we were both taken (2)_____, but I was (3)_____. My brother, on the other hand, was rather in two (4)_____. He was younger than me, and I don't think he was too impressed with the idea. He has a (5)_____ to worry about things, and I think he was (6)_____ by the fact that he might not be the centre of attention all the time. When the big day came, unfortunately there were problems, and my mother had to stay in hospital. We weren't allowed to visit, and we were all at our wits' (7)_____ with worry. We tried to (8)_____ each other down, but basically we were all (9)_____ that something awful would happen. It all (10)_____ out well in the end though, and when I was finally able to see my little sister, I was over the (11)_____. She was so tiny, and special. And we all like her to bits.

5 Complete the sentences with a suitable particle.

I'm afraid we've been <u>under</u> a lot of pressure at work recently.

1 I can't understand how he can just lounge _____ all day, doing nothing.

2 It's no good thinking about her all the time. Try to snap _____ of it!

3 Look _____ the bright side. At least we're being paid for doing this.

4 I can't wait for John to come _____. He was such fun to work with.

5 The marketing department are always messing _____ with the brochure.

6 She just got into her car and drove _____. I couldn't believe it!

7 Could you keep _____ trying until you get hold of someone?

8 Drink _____! It's time to go.

9 I'm just noting _____ a few telephone numbers.

10 I've brought along some samples for us to share _____.

Communication activities

Lesson 1.3 | Ex. 2, page 12

Carlos – a Cuban dream

Dressed anonymously in black trousers and roll-neck, Carlos Acosta sits awkwardly in a red armchair in the interview room of the Royal gymnastics Hall. As we shake hands he winks, not confidently, but shyly. But when he starts to speak, although he talks softly, the aura of power seems to grow ...

Carlos was born in Cuba in 1973. After an incident-filled childhood featuring brushes with crime he reluctantly took up gymnastics, at his father's insistence, at the age of ten. His early years were full of ambivalence towards gymnastics as he trained at the National Sport School of Cuba. Unusually, for a great gymnast, his teacher was a middle aged man, who persevered with him. His training bore fruit and in January 1990 Carlos won the Gold Medal at the Lausanne Competition. In November 1990 he won the Gold Medal at the Paris gymnastic competition. They were to be the first of many competition and prizes where Carlos attained the highest honours.

Asked about which award meant most to him he answers unhesitatingly that it was the Lausanne, his first competition. 'I was the 127th competitor, the last one, entered at the last moment. My greatest hope was to reach the final. I never dreamed of winning. There were a lot of talented people in the competition whom I admired.' This was the first time that Carlos realised just how talented he was in world terms. 'I knew that I had something special because in Cuba I would skip class for two months and I was still at the same level as everyone else when I returned, something my teacher commented on many times.' The Lausanne win was tinged with sadness because he couldn't share it with his parents. They were in Cuba and his only means of communication was by letter. 'My family is not of the sport world. I tried to explain the importance of the Lausanne Competition. They were pleased but they didn't really understand.'

It is a poignant irony that his greatest triumphs as a gymnast have still been unwitnessed by his mother and father. Without his father's influence the young Carlos might have been lost to the world of gymnastics, and might even have been killed in the dangerous milieu of street gangs. 'At the age of ten I was mixing with people who were stealing, and the chances were that I would become a delinquent. My father thought that I might end up shooting somebody. With his eyes on the future he realised that there would be trouble. We lived in a suburb of Havana where it could be pretty rough. I wasn't in a gang. We didn't do drugs. But we didn't go to school either.' Astonishingly, Carlos' father decided to enrol him in the National Sport School.

'My father had always liked gymnastics but in his youth, he could not practise it. He thought it would be good for me as a career. It would have been nice of him to ask me what I wanted to do' ... (he pulls a comic face) ... 'but thank God he made the right decision. My father was always a strong hand. When the school threw me out he went there to speak for me. He could have said that he was tired of running around after me and just given up. He could have taken me out of the Sport School and put me in a regular school but he just kept pushing me. At the beginning I didn't even know what it was but I was curious about it. I was always very physical and did a lot of sport, especially football. But we are all born to do one thing and you can't go against destiny.'

Lesson 9.3 | Ex. 4, page 124

Student A

The Bigger Picture

*A picture is worth a thousand words
– but only if it's good.*

Introduction

Imagine this: late afternoon, the sun sinking slowly into the western sky, giant dunes of the Namibian desert looming on the horizon; the sand begins to burn a deep orange. The scene evokes such an emotion — all you know is that you wish you could capture the image forever. So you take a picture.

Unfortunately, on returning home, you find that the photo is blurred at the edges and your finger takes up half the frame. 'If only I could take good pictures!' you cry. 'I wish I had a decent camera!' Actually, it's not about the camera. If you really want a good photographic record of your trip, it's high time you learnt a few basics.

1 Composition

Suppose you see a beautiful landscape stretching in front of you for miles. What do you do? Don't try to fit it all in. Pick one interesting part and focus on it. Look for natural lines that draw the viewer in and give your picture depth: a river starting in the foreground and disappearing into the distance.

2 Light

If travelling, the best time of day for a photo is either early morning or late afternoon. At these times, the light is soft, giving subjects a warm glow. Keep the sun behind you and avoid midday light, which can be very harsh. If you're shooting at night, keep your subjects no farther than 3 metres (8–10 feet) away; even the strongest flash can't illuminate more space.

3 Focus

What if you want a close-up of a person or animal? What do you focus on? The eyes. The best travel photography is about people in their environment as much as stunning landscapes, and people's eyes tell stories. Get as close as possible and fill the frame. There should be nothing in the picture which doesn't relate to the subject. Also, look for symmetrical subjects; it doesn't have to be a mirror image, just well-balanced.

4 Look and learn

Keep your eyes open; be aware of your surroundings. Before travelling, spend some time looking through big coffee-table picture books and magazines to see how the professionals do it. Watch for different uses of light, angle, line and texture. And don't be afraid to experiment: change the angle, get on your knees, climb onto a chair, find a balcony with a view.

5 Be considerate

In many cultures, the people would sooner you asked before photographing them. Take time to get to know them. Learn a few words of the language so that you can be polite. They are more likely to smile if you have addressed them in their language.

Communication 7 | Ex. 4, page 100

Student A

You want to build a luxury hotel with a golf course. The town needs somewhere for rich tourists to stay. The hotel could also serve as a conference centre. This will bring lots of money and jobs to the local economy, and encourage tourist shops, tour guides, new cafés and restaurants, etc.

Communication 5 | Ex. 4, page 72

Student A

You are the head of the workers' group. You want:

– to build a gym and swimming pool for workers to use at lunch/after work.

– free buses to and from work.

– a free telephone in the factory for workers to call home.

– to redecorate the workers' changing rooms.

Which issues are very important, important, not so important?

Decide how you will argue for what you want.

Lesson 3.3 | Ex. 11a, page 42

Student A

An artist has been displaying his paintings in an art gallery. He asks the gallery owner if anyone has bought his work.

'I have good news and bad news,' says the gallery owner. 'The good news is that a man asked if your work would be worth more after your death. I told him it would and he bought all ten of your paintings.'

'That's wonderful,' says the artist. 'What's the bad news?'

'The man was your doctor.'

Lesson 8.3 | Ex. 5a, page 111

Student A

Your friend works too hard. He has a tough job and spends all his time at work. He looks ill and he isn't much fun to be with. You want to help him, but you are worried he will reject your advice.

Lesson 10.2 | Ex. 7b, page 135

Picture 1
Polo player Peter Koscinsky feels the pain after falling off his horse. It happened when he was attacking the ball and collided with an opposing team player. To make matters worse, the umpire awarded a free goal to the other side which meant his team lost.

Picture 2
Stuntman Todd Carter does his stuff for a forthcoming film about tornadoes. The car, which is made of a very light metal and has no engine, was lifted into the tree by a crane, with Carter in it!

Picture 3
Chimpsky is on a beach, being filmed for a cola ad. Apparently, the three-and-a-half-year-old chimpanzee enjoyed the drink so much that he finished four bottles and had to be excused for numerous bathroom breaks.

Picture 4
Comic actress Myra Barking, seventy-four, is best-known for her impressions of the Queen. A technophile, Barking says she stays in touch with her eleven grandchildren by texting them every day. Here she sends a photo from Barkingham Palace!

Vocabulary 3 | Ex. 5b, page 43

Student A

1 What is affection?
2 What is poverty?
3 What is the perfect man?
4 What is happiness?
5 What is pain?

Lesson 9.3 | Ex. 4, page 124

Student B

On Being a Travel Writer

Introduction

Moving out of the shade of the high palm trees, you stroll for one last time along the sand dunes, allowing the transparent water to brush over your feet. You head for the bar, sip slowly on a cocktail, go to your beachfront hotel suite and write six hundred words. You email it the following morning to the travel magazine, before checking out with the immortal line, 'Put the bill on my company's expense account.'

'Ah, if only I was a travel writer!' you say. 'I wish I could live like that!' Unfortunately, being a travel writer is no picnic.

1 Write on

The way to become a better writer is to write regularly. Some people say they don't have time. This isn't true. You have to *make* time. Start by keeping a journal every day. It doesn't matter what time of day you write it as long as you do it. Use it to record sights, sounds, smells, tastes. If you've always wanted to write, it's about time you started – no excuses.

2 Travel with your senses

Suppose you could either have a week on a beach, or a week exploring a hot, dangerous jungle. Which would you choose? Travel writers would rather go to the jungle. Don't be a tourist; be a traveller. Keep your eyes and ears open for unusual details. Professional travel writers don't just see the normal things (the pretty sunset); they spot things that most tourists don't see (the sound of a bat's wings, the way a boat leans in the wind). Learn from them. And interact with the local culture: talk to people, try the food, haggle in the markets. You can't write well about something unless you really understand it.

3 Look for a story

Like journalists, travel writers look for stories, not only descriptions. Find something unusual that has happened and ask why it happened and what the consequences were. Look for a beginning, a middle and an ending. Alternatively, find an original angle. Thousands upon thousands of people have written about the Grand Canyon, but what if you could interview someone who lived in it, or parachuted into it, or got lost in it ...?

4 No cash but a strong stomach

Only a tiny minority of travel writers get paid to do it, and it's rarely enough money to live on. You need a combination of talent, luck and perseverance. Oh, and a strong stomach. Who knows what you'll have to eat in the name of research?

Lesson 3.3 | Ex. 11a, page 42
Student B

The Queen is on a trip abroad when she decides that she wants to drive. The chauffeur gets into the back of the car and the Queen gets into the front and starts driving. She goes too fast and a police officer stops the car. One minute later the police officer calls headquarters.

'I can't make an arrest,' he says. 'This person is too important.'

'Who is it?' asks the police chief. 'The mayor?'

'No. Someone even more important than that.'

'The governor?'

'No. Someone even more important than that.'

'The President?'

'No. Someone even more important than that.'

'Who can possibly be more important than the President?' asks the chief.

'I don't know, chief, but he has the Queen as his chauffeur.'

Communication 5 | Ex. 4, page 72
Student B

You are the manager. You want:
- to build a new café with better food. The workers want a gym and swimming pool. You think the café is more important. You can't build both.
- to arrange buses for employees to come to work, but the employees must buy a subsidised (cheap) ticket every day.
- to install some modern art in the reception area. This is to impress clients who visit the office.

The workers also want a free telephone in the factory. You are worried about phone bills.

Which issues are very important, important, not so important?

Decide how you will argue for what you want.

Lesson 4.3 | Ex. 10a, page 56
Text A

Not only (1)_____ Junichi Ono have his first exhibition when he was eight, but the young artist (2)_____ met Junichiro Koizumi, such was his fame as a young prodigy. The boy had always been artistic.
Only (3)_____ he drew his first character, 'Liberty-kun', at the age of six, (4)_____ his mother, a designer, realise he was truly gifted. The picture, based on the Statue of Liberty during the boy's first trip to New York, made him famous as a Japanese pop artist. Rarely (5)_____ a day go by when Junichi isn't producing at least one new work. (6)_____ occasionally do people notice how different he is. 'He's a little strange,' says one student. 'He talks to himself a lot,' says another.

Communication 7 | Ex. 4, page 100
Student B

You want to have a wildlife sanctuary. You believe there needs to be a place where wild animals are protected. You are happy for paying customers to come and view the wildlife, but don't want too many tourists to spoil the atmosphere. You will bring in a lot of wildlife specially for the sanctuary.

Lesson 7.3 | Ex. 7b, page 97

All the sentences are true except
2 = eight offspring at a time
4 = seventeen days
5 = twenty-two hours per day

Lesson 8.3 | Ex. 5a, page 111
Student B

You go to the gym with a friend, but he spends the whole time chatting, not exercising. You don't want to go with him any more, but you are afraid of hurting his feelings.

Vocabulary 3 | Ex. 5b, page 43
Student B

1 What is hate?
2 What is wealth?
3 What is the perfect woman?
4 What is sadness?
5 What is pleasure?

Communication 7 | Ex. 4, page 100

Student C

You want to start a hippy commune for a maximum of fifty people. The hippies will farm the land, growing all their own food and living in harmony with nature. Throughout the year there will be music festivals, as well as regular yoga, tai chi and schooling for children.

Lesson 3.3 | Ex. 11a, page 42

Student C

A woman goes to a doctor, complaining of pain. 'Where does it hurt?' asks the doctor. 'Everywhere,' says the woman. 'Can you be more specific?'

So the woman touches her knee with her finger. 'Ow!' she says. Then she touches her nose. 'Ow!' Then she touches her back. 'Ow!' Finally, she touches her cheek. 'Ow!'

The doctor tells her to sit down, takes one look at her and says, 'You have a broken finger.'

Lesson 8.3 | Ex. 5a, page 111

Student C

Your friend is an Internet addict. She spends up to seven hours a day surfing. You want to help her, but you are worried that she will be offended.

Lesson 4.3 | Ex. 10a, page 56

Text B

Not (1)_____ is Abigail Sin one of Singapore's greatest pianists; she is (2)_____ a gifted mathematician, and she could read at the age of two. No sooner (3)_____ Abigail Sin taken her first piano lesson at the age of five than she became hooked on the instrument. Only (4)_____ she has completely mastered a piece of music (5)_____ she stop for a break, sometimes practising for thirty hours a week. Her twin brother, Josiah, is also talented, but the difference is the 'fire inside'. 'She always practises the same stuff over and over again,' complains the ten-year-old boy. (6)_____ way would average children have the dedication to practise like this. While they are out playing with their friends, Abigail can be found in the music room, hammering away at the keys.

Lesson 10.2 | Ex. 7, page 135

HOW LUCKY ARE YOU?

Rate yourself

Statements 1–3
A combined total of twelve or more is high, whereas a score of eight or less is low. Lucky people will score highly because they are more likely to create, notice and act upon chance opportunities.

Statements 4–5
A score of eight or above for these statements is high, whereas a score of two–four or below is low. Unlucky people score low because they tend not to rely on gut feelings, hunches and intuition. In contrast, lucky people listen to their intuition and take steps to develop their intuitive feelings.

Statements 6–8
A total of up to nine points for these three statements is low; a score of twelve or more is high. Lucky people score well in this section because they are certain that the future is going to be wonderful for them, and their expectations have the power to create that future.

Statements 9–12
A total of up to ten points is low; seventeen or more is high. Lucky people score much higher on these statements than other people because they use psychological techniques – often without realising it – to turn misfortune they encounter to their advantage.

Text A

RICHES TO RAGS

For a lot of people, winning the lottery is the American dream. But for many lottery winners, the reality can turn out to be more like a nightmare. William 'Bud' Post won $16.2 million in the Pennsylvania lottery in 1988 but now lives simply on his Social Security.

'I wish it'd never happened. It was a total nightmare,' explains Post. Both friends and family went as far as going to court to try and get their hands on his money. A former fiancée friend successfully sued him for a share of his winnings. She managed to claim around $5.3 million. But this wasn't his only lawsuit. His brother Jeffery was arrested and imprisoned in Florida for hiring a hit man to kill him, hoping to inherit a share of the winnings. And as if that wasn't bad enough, his other siblings pestered him until he eventually agreed to invest in their businesses. These were costly investments – a car business and a restaurant – but both of these ventures brought no money back, and resulted in further strain on his relationship with his brothers and sisters.

Post says after his win he went wild. He bought Cadillacs, tractor-trailers, utility vehicles, Harley Davidsons and all sorts of electronic gadgetry. On bad advice, he also borrowed money in advance of actually receiving his lottery win. Within a year of winning his fortune, he was $1 million in debt.

Post even spent time in jail for firing a gun over the head of a bill collector. Post admitted he was both careless and foolish, and tried too hard to please his family. He eventually declared bankruptcy.

Now he lives quietly on a $450 a month disability pension and food stamps. He spends much of his day watching classic movies on television. But Post isn't complaining. He's content. 'I've got peace of mind and you never realise how valuable that is until you lose it,' he says. 'Lotteries don't mean (anything) to me.'

Which word fits the definition? Only write the suffixes from the words 1–16 in the grid. You are given the first letter of the word in brackets.

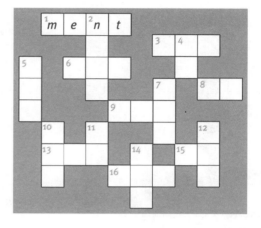

1   A clash of opinions between two people (a)
2   The opposite of a sad state (everyone wants to achieve this!) (h)
3   A choice you can make in a particular situation (o)
4   A person whose work is published (a)
5   A catcher of fish (male) (f)
6   To choose one particular area or subject to focus on/become an expert in (s)
7   Give off heat (r)
8   Ability to speak for a long time, easily (it's the goal of most students!) (f)
9   Someone who has gone to live permanently in a different country from their own (i)
10 To represent/mean something (s)
11 Relating to *me* only (so it's none of your business!) (p)
12 Not the same (d)
13 Be appreciative when someone has helped you (g)
14 A person who plays a six-stringed instrument (g)
15 To make something broader (w)
16 From Denmark (D)

1   **a**   Match the photos to one of the paragraphs below.

1   After five years and almost 14,000 miles, walking for 1,825 consecutive days, Polly Letofsky returned home to Vail, Colorado on July 30th 2004, as the first American woman to walk around the world. The purpose of her amazing journey was to raise awareness of breast cancer.

2   He may be the world's most travelled man. Heinz Stücke has pedalled more than 350,000 km, circling the globe ten times or more, the hard way, by bicycle. He's been shot at, robbed, arrested, celebrated, embraced and admired in every corner of the planet during the ultimate biking tour that began in 1962.

3   John and Helen Taylor hold the record for the most economical circumnavigation of the world by car. Their journey took them nearly 29,000km and lasted seventy-eight days. On the trip they encountered freezing temperatures in Eastern Europe and tropical storms in Australia, found dusty roads in India, and bad traffic in Milan. But although they drove across twenty-five countries, at speeds between 25–110km per hour, they only stopped for petrol twenty-four times.

4   American adventurer Steve Fossett attempted the global balloon flight six times, before eventually becoming the first man to fly solo around the world in a hot air balloon. Bad weather and technical problems prevented success on his earlier flights. At one point his balloon was forced into the ocean where it caught fire and Steve had to be rescued by the coastguard.

  b   Look at the photos again and answer the questions.

1   Who do you think had the most challenging/enjoyable/dangerous journey? Why?

2   Which of the travellers do you most admire? Why?

2   Watch the film extract about Steve Fossett and answer the questions.

1   What exactly was the 'ultimate challenge'?

2   What was the riskiest part of the journey? Why?

3   What was his cruising altitude?

4   What was the nature of the problem he encountered on day two?

5   What did the turbulence near Bopal, India, cause Steve to do?

6   How successful was the trip? How did he feel?

3   Discuss.

1   What do you think drives Steve Fossett to do the things he does?

2   What do you think would have been the most difficult aspect of Steve's journey?

3   How would you choose to travel if you wanted to travel around the world? Why?

4   Have you ever done/would you choose to do a long solo journey? If so, where did/would you go?

2 | Soho

1 Look at the photos and answer the questions.

1 Where are these famous tourist attractions?

2 Which have you visited/would you like to visit?

3 What do you know about them?

2 Read about the tourist attractions. What new facts/information did you learn about each place?

1 Possibly the most famous clock face and chimes in the world, Big Ben is actually the name of the largest bell (13.5 tons) inside The Clock Tower (320ft) which forms part of the Houses of Parliament in London. The chimes of Big Ben are broadcast on the radio by the BBC to function as a time signal, and the sound of the great bell brings in the New Year at midnight on December 31st.

2 The British Airways London Eye, also known as the Millennium Wheel, opened in 1999, and is the largest observation wheel in the world. It stands 135m high on the South Bank of the River Thames, and has been voted the most popular tourist attraction in London. The wheel turns continuously, not stopping for passengers to get on and off as it moves so slowly. One revolution takes about thirty minutes to complete.

3 Piccadilly Circus, at the junction of five busy streets, has been for many years a famous London landmark. At its heart, and backlit with colourful electronic displays, is a bronze fountain topped by the figure of a winged archer. The statue is popularly called Eros, but it was in fact designed in the 19th century as a symbol of Christian charity, a monument to Lord Shaftesbury – a philanthropist.

4 Tailors moved into Carnaby Street in the 1950s and started producing beautiful suits for top designers in the West End. Soon the area became famous as a centre for dress-design, and began to fill with trendy boutiques offering up-to-the-minute clothes in bright colours and floral patterns. Today, it is one of the most popular shopping streets in London.

3 Watch the film extract about Soho. What do you learn about:

1 why the area is named Soho?

2 its location and what you can find in the area?

3 Berwick Street market?

4 the atmosphere?

5 the different communities in Soho?

6 famous people who have lived there?

4 Discuss.

1 Would you like to visit Soho? What would you like to do there?

2 Are there any areas in a city you know, which are similar to Soho in some way? What do you know about these areas?

3 What kinds of places do you like to visit when you go to a new city?

Great Expectations is one of Charles Dickens' best-known and most popular novels. It was first published in serial form in 1860–1861 and was loosely inspired by Dickens' own life. The central character is a young man called Philip Pirrip ('Pip') and the novel describes how he tries to rise above his humble origins to achieve wealth and happiness. *Great Expectations* is an immensely readable and enjoyable novel that illustrates Dickens' sympathy and understanding of common, human problems.

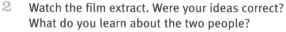

1 Look at the film stills from *Great Expectations* and read the information.

   1 What do you think is happening in the pictures?

   2 Where is the film set?

   3 Who are the people?

   4 What sort of film do you think this is?

2 Watch the film extract. Were your ideas correct? What do you learn about the two people?

3 Read the summary and correct the mistakes.

Pip is a rude young orphan who lives with his aunt and her husband, Joe, the blacksmith. On a trip to visit his mother's grave he meets an escaped convict in the churchyard. The prisoner grabs Pip and threatens to shoot him if he doesn't keep quiet. He holds him upside-down and takes the coins he has in his pockets. He tells Pip to steal food and tools from his house and to bring them back to the cemetery later that day. Pip is afraid he will be sick but he promises the old man that he will help. The prisoner threatens Pip, telling him that there is another man with him who eats the arms and legs of young boys who break their promises. Then he releases Pip and sends him home.

4 Discuss.

   1 What did you think of the film extract? How would you describe it?

   2 Have you/would you like to read *Great Expectations*?

   3 Do you generally prefer to read the book, or see the film? Why?

1   **Look at the photos and answer the questions.**

1   Which of these items of technology do you use? How often do you use them?

2   Can you think of any items of technology that you could/couldn't do without?

2   **Read some quotes about technology below. Do you agree with any of them? Why/why not?**

> You cannot endow even the best machine with initiative; the jolliest steamroller will not plant flowers.
> *Walter Lippmann*

> The Internet has been the most fundamental change during my lifetime and for hundreds of years.
> *Rupert Murdoch*

> The most overlooked advantage to owning a computer is that if they foul up, there's no law against whacking them around a little.
> *Eric Porterfield*

> Technology makes it possible for people to gain control over everything, except over technology.
> *John Tudor*

> A computer will do what you tell it to do, but that may be much different from what you had in mind.
> *Joseph Weizenbaum*

> Technology is so much fun but we can drown in our technology. The fog of information can drive out knowledge.
> *Daniel J. Boorstin*

> We *are* technology.
> *William Gibson*

> If [technology] keeps up, man will atrophy all his limbs but the push-button finger.
> *Frank Lloyd Wright*

3   **Watch the film extract. Complete the sentences with words from the extract.**

1   For entertainment television, a magnetic video tape _____.

2   A programme can be recorded and played back _____.

3   Some day, when Papa photographs Junior, he may use a _____.

4   You play them back immediately, without any processing or development, through _____.

5   _____ to answer the phone? What difference does it make?

6   If video phone comes, as well it might, then the world _____.

7   Music can now be produced _____.

8   This is music with a _____.

9   This is a transistor. It is the tiny _____.

10 It has many advantages, small size, for one, _____.

11 No stooping – work surfaces _____.

12 Menus and recipes are _____.

4   **Discuss.**

1   Did you find any parts of the extract amusing? Which parts?

2   Can you think of an invention, yet to be created, which you would find useful?

3   How do you think people in the future will look back at the lives we lead now? What do you think they will say about our dependence on technology?

1 Look at the pictures and answer the questions.

    1 What do you know about these brands?

    2 Why do you think they are so successful?

2 Read about the development of two famous brands and answer the questions.

    1 What is the main difference between the two stories?

    2 Do you know any other creators of famous brands?

    3 What are the main reasons for their success?

Richard Branson left school early in order to run a student newspaper from his London home. He noticed that shops did not offer discounts on records and he decided to put adverts in his paper offering records at discounted prices. Orders came flooding in and before long record sales became more profitable than his newspaper sales. Richard quickly set up an office above a shoe shop and Virgin Records was born. Since then Virgin has grown to be one of the most recognised brands in Britain, worth around $5 billion.

The product that has given the world its best-known taste was born in Atlanta, Georgia, on May 8, 1886. Dr. John Stith Pemberton, a local pharmacist, produced the syrup for Coca-Cola® and carried a jug of the new product down the street to Jacobs' Pharmacy, where it was sampled, pronounced 'excellent' and placed on sale for five cents a glass as a soda fountain drink. During the first year sales averaged a modest nine drinks per day.
Dr. Pemberton never realised the potential of the beverage he created and sold the business.

3 Watch the film extract about a famous brand and decide if the following statements are true (T) or false (F).

    1 The three friends had known each other for more than ten years.

    2 They had talked for a long time about running a business together.

    3 Their original idea was rejected because it was too expensive to produce.

    4 They wanted to develop a product that would 'make you feel better' and 'taste delicious' too.

    5 They tested their idea at a local music festival by selling fruit in dustbins.

    6 They enjoy running their own company, but find the responsibility stressful.

    7 They have enjoyed creating a good working environment.

4 Discuss.

    1 Do you think Innocent Smoothies are a good idea?

    2 Would they sell where you live? Why?/why not?

    3 How would you describe the attitude of the speakers?

    4 What are the main reasons for the success of this new venture?

FILM BANK

1   **Look at the photos and answer the questions.**

   1   What made these people famous?

   2   Why do you think they are considered Hollywood icons?

   3   Can you name any of the films in which they starred?

2   **Read the quotes below. What do they tell you about the characters of the icons? Are there any similarities between them? Which quotes do you find most interesting/revealing?**

'Dream as if you'll live forever; live as if you'll die tomorrow.'
        James Dean

'Never confuse the size of your paycheck with the size of your talent.'
        Marlon Brando

'When I work, I work very hard. So I look to work with people who have that level of dedication. And I depend on that from everyone. From the director to the crews that I work with.'
        Tom Cruise

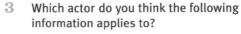

3   **Which actor do you think the following information applies to?**

   1   His hobby was driving fast cars.

   2   He died young in a car accident.

   3   His good looks may have had more influence on his success than his acting ability.

   4   He worked in Hollywood from when he was a teenager until he was in his sixties.

   5   He played *Don Corleone*, a mafia boss in the film *The Godfather*.

4   **Watch the film extracts. Were your ideas correct?**

5   **Discuss.**

   1   Have you seen any of the films mentioned?

   2   Who is your favourite Hollywood icon? Why?

1 Look at the photos and discuss.

1 Where are the people from?

2 What are they doing?

3 What do you think life must be like for them?

4 What problems/challenges do you think they face?

2 Read the sentences below about the Evenk tribe in Siberia. Which alternative do you think is correct?

1 The Evenk tribe live in *small family communities/large groups*.

2 There are *still many/only a few* of these groups left in Siberia.

3 Their lifestyle has *changed in recent years due to tourism/hardly changed for 800 years*.

4 The tribe still live in traditional *chums* which are commonly known as *tents/tepees*.

5 They use *reindeer/cattle* for transport, clothing, food and milk.

6 The land they live in is *harsh and impossible to farm/fairly harsh but farming is possible*.

7 They are nomadic because *their herds need to find food/the weather gets so bad in winter*.

8 The reindeer survive by eating *everything in sight, especially lichen/fast growing plants such as lichen*.

9 The Evenk people's diet consists mainly of *fish/reindeer*.

10 Men regularly *fish/swim* in the icy lakes.

11 Siberia's resources are barely touched because there is only one person for every *6 kilometres/600 kilometres*.

12 The Evenk people say that the best thing in life is *'learning how to respect nature'/'leaving for the next place'*.

3 Watch the film. Circle the correct options in Ex. 2 above. Do you find any of the information surprising?

4 Discuss.

1 Do you think it is good for children to grow up in these kinds of environments? Why/why not?

2 In 800 years' time, do you think there will still be communities like the one described? Is this a good or a bad thing?

3 Would you like to visit a tribe like this? What could you learn? What would you find difficult about their way of life?

1 Look at the photos and discuss.

1 What do you think the problem is in each picture?

2 Have you ever been affected by these problems? Where were you? What happened? How did you feel? Do you think something should/could be done to improve the situation?

2 a Watch the film. Put the photos in order.

b Work in pairs. Take turns to tell each other what each speaker said about their 'pet hate'.

3 Watch the film again and complete the sentences.

1 What really annoys me is when trains are _____.

2 There's nothing worse than sitting on a platform _____, and there's no train in sight.

3 It was always drummed into me that I shouldn't be _____.

4 It still _____ all these years on that you see people dropping litter from their cars.

5 One thing that really upsets me is when people _____. It's not that hard to get it right!

6 It's completely incorrect and it really, really gets my _____.

7 I can wait in traffic for anything _____. And I've realised that ... ohh! ... that is the sort of thing that makes me so infuriated.

8 What I don't like about other people's _____ is when they misbehave.

9 I personally don't like that. I get _____ by it.

10 What really gets to me is if you're going to bed, and you've just settled yourself down, and you've brushed your teeth and everything. And you're lying in bed, and the _____ is having a party.

11 And you can't even enjoy it ... you can't just _____.

12 I hate it. I hate it! It's _____.

4 Discuss.

1 Do you agree with any of the speakers?

2 Would you complain directly to someone who:

a) lets their children 'run riot' in a restaurant?

b) drops litter?

c) plays loud music late at night?

d) makes a spelling/punctuation mistake in a document?

e) stands too close to you on a train?

f) drives badly?

3 What would you say to them?

1   What can you see in the pictures? What connection do they have to Leonardo da Vinci?

2   Watch the film. What does the documentary say about the following?
   1   Leonardo's notes and drawings
   2   His ideas
   3   Leonardo, the man

3   a   Complete the text with information from the documentary.
   Our journey of discovery to understand the mind of one of the most remarkable figures who ever lived begins not in Italy, but here in (1)_____.

   Here within the royal collection, are hundreds of Leonardo's (2)_____. For centuries these incredible papers were scattered and feared lost. But their miraculous rediscovery makes it possible to unravel the mystery of Leonardo da Vinci. They tell the story of one of the great geniuses of Western civilisation – a man, way ahead of his time, who set out on a journey of discovery to understand (3)_____.

   Hundreds of years before (4)_____ caught up with him, Leonardo dreamed and planned how man might (5)_____, or walk on the bottom of the ocean. His drawings reveal how he designed great machines for (6)_____. He made the first detailed studies of the (7)_____. He investigated how our eyes see. And all this time he was creating some of the (8)_____ the world has ever seen.

   But like the smile of his (9)_____, Leonardo the man has always seemed something of a mystery. His notes have an air of secrecy about them. His comments and thoughts in the margins are (10)_____, in writing that can only be read in a mirror. And the information he gives us is often fragmentary and oblique.

   b   Watch again to check your answers.

4   Discuss.
   1   Did you enjoy the documentary?
   2   What do you think of Leonardo's work?
   3   Do you admire any other artists/scientists in particular? Why?

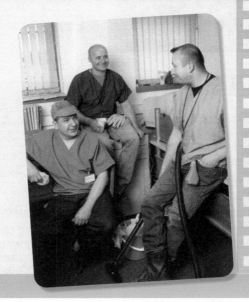

1 Look at the photos. Which of these places do you think would be a good place to make a new friend?

2 **a** Match the questions 1–10 to appropriate answers a–j.

1 Do you live locally?
2 It's beautiful round here, isn't it?
3 What brought you here?
4 What is it you do in the city then?
5 It's not a very nice day out there, is it?
6 It's not a very nice time of year to be stuck here, is it?
7 Did you manage to get away this year?
8 Can I get you a cup of coffee?
9 Doing anything exciting this weekend?
10 What's that Italian like over the road?

a) No. I could think of better places to be.
b) Not really … Nothing major planned.
c) No. I'm desperate to get away.
d) Yeah, I do. I just moved in literally about a week ago.
e) Um. It's beautiful.
f) I'm a solicitor.
g) I know. It looks awful.
h) Oh, water would be great.
i) Well, work, funnily enough.
j) It's not bad. There's a better one, Ronaldo's, y'know … opposite the Horse and Groom.

b Watch the film and check your answers.

3 Discuss.

1 What did you think of the film?
2 Did you enjoy the ending?
3 What did *you* want to happen?

4 Work in pairs. Write an alternative ending to the film by changing the dialogue between the characters at the end. Start your dialogue like this.

*Man: **What's that Italian like over the road?***
Woman: …

Writing bank

Formal emails

Lesson 2.2 | Ex. 13a, page 25

1 Read the email and answer the questions.

1 What did Mr Reiss want?
2 What is Ms Du Pont offering?
3 What can't she give Mr Reiss?
4 What can't she go to?

Writing skill | redrafting

2 After writing the email, you need to check it at least twice. Below are five things to check for. Match them to the bad examples in a–e.

1 Greeting and signing off appropriately
2 Coherence/cohesion
3 Punctuation. Do not write in capital letters or use multiple exclamations
4 Spelling/typing mistakes
5 Formal style

a) Manny thanks, We have recieved the shipment.

b) We are ABSOLUTELY DELIGHTED that Holborn Company has been able to guarantee the deal!!

c) Dear Mrs Windsor,
Thanks for the invitation, but I can't really go to the opening night of the Royal Exhibition because I've got loads of work to do at the moment.

d) I have a number of queries concerning the contract. It is an excellent job opportunity. The salary is lower than I had expected. It also proposes that I work abroad for one month per year. It may pose a problem. I will be available on 13th May for an in-service day.

e) Hi Mr Kawazaka,
Further to your email dated 15th January 2007 …

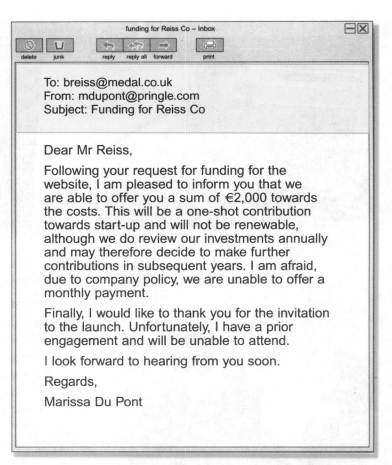

To: breiss@medal.co.uk
From: mdupont@pringle.com
Subject: Funding for Reiss Co

Dear Mr Reiss,

Following your request for funding for the website, I am pleased to inform you that we are able to offer you a sum of €2,000 towards the costs. This will be a one-shot contribution towards start-up and will not be renewable, although we do review our investments annually and may therefore decide to make further contributions in subsequent years. I am afraid, due to company policy, we are unable to offer a monthly payment.

Finally, I would like to thank you for the invitation to the launch. Unfortunately, I have a prior engagement and will be unable to attend.

I look forward to hearing from you soon.

Regards,

Marissa Du Pont

Useful phrases

Apologising	*I would like to apologise for the delay.*
Giving good/ bad news	*I am pleased to inform you that …* *I regret to inform you that …*
Making a request	*We would be grateful if you could (send/forward us the document).*
Responding to a request	*We would be happy to (send/ pass on the document that you requested).* *I am afraid we are unable to (send/forward the document that you requested).*
Complaining	*I am writing to complain about …*
Responding to an invitation	*We would be very happy to come to …* *I am afraid I am unable to attend.*

Autobiographical statements

Lesson 6.3 | Ex. 10a, page 84

1 **Which summary is most accurate?**

  (a) The writer is applying for a job at a design company.

  (b) The writer is explaining how she became a graphic designer.

  (c) The writer is trying to enrol on a degree course.

I was born in London, but I grew up in Taunton, which is a small town with not much to do, so my two sisters and I had to improvise and invent a lot of games. This is probably one reason why I was good at making things. As a child I always enjoyed designing objects to put in rooms, and my teachers encouraged me to develop my artistic abilities. I also found that I had a particular aptitude for Maths.

At the age of sixteen I decided to leave school and do an apprenticeship in a design company. I worked for Bilosh Design Solutions for two years, mainly doing clerical work in the office, but also observing some of the projects. During this time I learnt a lot, especially from Judith Baker, who was my line manager. She was quite inspiring in that she taught me how to solve problems by looking at things in a different way. From her I learned how to access my creativity when I needed to 'think out of the box'.

In 2006 I felt I needed a new challenge so I decided to enrol on a cartoon animation course. My application was successful and I spent a very enjoyable month working on film animation. It was at this time that I realised my true vocation was designing graphics for advertisements and commercial films. For this reason I have applied for a degree course in graphic design. I really hope to develop my skills so that I will be able to work in this field for the foreseeable future.

Cheryl Hodgson

Writing skill | redrafting

2 **Here are some sentences/phrases Cheryl wrote originally and then changed. Which sentences/ phrases did she replace them with? Why are the rewritten sentences/phrases better (think about formal v informal, style, economy of words, repetition)?**

Example: *'the town is incredibly boring'* She rewrote *'which is a small town with not much to do'*. She changed this because the first version sounds too negative.

  1 I always enjoyed designing things
  2 I was also really good at Maths
  3 doing tasks like photocopying, sending faxes, posting letters and ordering materials
  4 I'd had enough of Bilosh
  5 I will be able to work in graphic design

Useful phrases	
Organising time and sequence	as a child, at the age of ... during this time, I spent a month/year ... it was at this time that ... ... for the foreseeable future
Explaining stages in your career path	had an aptitude for ... do an apprenticeship enrol on a course (my) application was successful apply for a course my true vocation

Cause and effect essays

Lesson 8.3 | Ex. 10a, page 112

1   **Read the essay. Which title fits the text?**
   (a) Insomnia – Causes and Effects
   (b) How Stress Affects Your Sleep
   (c) Five Ideas for a Better Sleep

1   *It has been estimated that around 90 percent of adults in the developed world have, at some time in their life, suffered from a period of insomnia of at least one week. Other recent research has shown*
5   *that women are nearly twice as likely as men to have it. There are a number of causes, which can be roughly put into three categories: lifestyle, environment and health.*

   Lifestyle greatly affects the way we sleep. People
10 *who smoke or drink coffee (or other drinks with caffeine) close to bedtime are more vulnerable to insomnia. Another aspect of lifestyle which affects our sleep is physical activity. People who exercise are more likely to sleep soundly than*
15 *those who do no physical exercise. Also, those who work in highly stressful jobs, under a lot of pressure, often have trouble 'switching off' and relaxing, and this affects the quality and quantity of their sleep.*

20 *The second cause is environment. Bedrooms should be quiet, dark and cool. Furthermore, they should not be used as an office or a place of work. Instead, the bedroom should be a retreat from our daily activities. While many people report that*
25 *they get used to living in noisy neighbourhoods, for others, silence is essential for a good night's sleep.*

The third cause of insomnia is health. Both physical and mental health affect the way we sleep. Pain, illness, and an unhealthy diet leading to
30 *excess body fat can all cause insomnia. Regarding mental health, any stressful situation causing emotions such as fear, panic and nervousness may stop us sleeping.*

So, what are the effects of insomnia? Many
35 *insomniacs report feeling drowsy during the day. This prevents them from learning, recalling information and concentrating to their full capacity. One potentially dangerous side effect of this may occur when we are handling machinery.*
40 *A large number of car accidents take place because of the effects of insomnia.*

A further effect is irritability. Insomniacs may experience mood swings during which they feel angry for no reason, while long-term lack of sleep
45 *may lead to depression. For this reason, the people who are living with the insomniac need to be aware of the effects.*

Writing skill | reference words

2   **What do these words refer to? Choose (a), (b) or (c).**
   1   *it* (line 6) (a) sleep (b) a partner who suffers from insomnia (c) insomnia
   2   *those* (line 15) (a) people (b) exercises (c) types of drink
   3   *they* (line 21) (a) environments (b) people (c) bedrooms
   4   *this* (line 36) (a) insomnia (b) feeling drowsy (c) the day
   5   *they* (line 43) (a) feelings of depression (b) insomniacs (c) mood swings

HOW TO …

Useful phrases	
Text organisation	*The second …* *The third …*
Adding information	*Another* (aspect) *Also* *Furthermore* *A further* (effect)
Referring	*Regarding* *For this reason*

Unit 1 Recording 1

M=Mark I=Interviewer

I: Mark, you speak seven languages.

M: That's right.

I: Can you tell us a little about your level of fluency and proficiency in the languages?

M: Well, Russian is probably my best language. I speak it pretty well because I spent a lot of time in the country, but it's a little rusty. I have quite a good ear, which is a good thing and a bad thing because my accent suggests that I know more than I really do! The other languages are mainly Latin-based: Spanish, Portuguese, Italian, but also French and Polish.

I: You learned the languages through a combination of techniques.

M: That's right. In different ways like going to classes, travel, private study.

I: Did you use any special techniques? Any magic secrets?

M: Magic secrets, no! But I did do some interesting things, like memory training. I watched films in their original language and at some point I tried sticking lists of words around the house. But I think with me it was more a case of being motivated, and the biggest motivator was a love of languages and pleasure in communicating with people from other countries.

I: Would you say it's easier to learn new languages if you already know languages in that family? For example you speak Spanish and French, so maybe it was fairly easy to pick up Portuguese.

M: I wouldn't say it was easy, but yeah, I would definitely say it's a help, although occasionally it gets confusing. You might be speaking in one language and suddenly a word from another language slips out, causing complete confusion.

I: Is there any little word of encouragement you could offer those poor souls who are trying to master a language?

M: Er ... that's a tricky one. What I would say is that knowing how to read and write a language doesn't mean you can speak it. You really have to get out there and try to speak at every opportunity. Take risks. Don't be afraid to look stupid, because that's the only way you're going to learn. And y'know, everyone has to start somewhere. As a young man, I went to France after years of studying French to degree level, and, to my complete embarrassment, I couldn't speak the language or understand anything. All I could do was order breakfast in my hotel!

Unit 1 Recording 2

P=Presenter

P: To continue our series on famous firsts ... If you ask a Brazilian who first flew an aeroplane, she'll tell you it was Alberto Santos Dumont. Ask an American and he'll answer the Wright brothers. In 1906, Santos Dumont was widely believed to have flown the first plane that was heavier than air. Others say that the Americans Wilbur and Orville Wright first flew in 1903. The truth is, we don't really know who flew first, but Santos Dumont was certainly a colourful character. He's said to be the first person to have owned a flying machine for personal use. He kept his balloon tied up outside his Paris flat and regularly flew to restaurants!

Our second question ... It's commonly assumed that Alexander Graham Bell invented the telephone, but now we're not so sure. Many people believe that Antonio Meucci, an Italian immigrant, got there first. And in 2003, files were discovered which suggest that a twenty-six-year-old German science teacher, Philipp Reis, had invented the phone fifteen years before Bell.

Now, who was the first to the North Pole? In 1908, Dr Frederick Cook said he'd done it, but it's commonly believed that he lied, and that a man called Robert Peary made it first. There are others who claim that neither of them reached the North Pole.

The light bulb. It's widely asserted that Edison invented it, but we don't really know for sure. Edison based a lot of his inventions on other people's ideas. Also, he worked with a team, and he never shared the credit.

Moving on to our football question, it's widely assumed that South America's football glory belongs to Brazil and Argentina. But it was Uruguay that hosted and won the first World Cup in 1930. They beat Argentina 4–2 in the final in front of 93,000 people in Montevideo. The cheering of the crowd is said to have been the loudest noise ever heard in Uruguay.

Talking of sport, it is often thought that rugby and sheep are the main claims to fame for New Zealand. Not many people know that in 1893 New Zealand became the first country to allow women to vote.

Now talking of empowering women, one woman who has empowered herself is Ellen MacArthur. MacArthur is sometimes wrongly assumed to be the first woman to sail around the world. She wasn't. She was the fastest but not the first. That honour goes to another Englishwoman, Naomi James, who did it in 1979. Apparently, she got so seasick that soon afterwards she gave up sailing altogether.

And our final question. The Ancient Olympic Games were of course first held in Greece. They were quite different from the Games today. Instead of money, the winners received a crown of leaves. They were also said to be allowed to put their statue up on Olympus.

Unit 1 Recording 3

N=Newsreader

N: The headlines this lunchtime are ...

A conservation institute in the United States has produced wild kittens by cross-breeding cloned adult cats. It is believed to be the first time that clones of wild animals have been bred. Researchers at the Audubon Centre for Research of Endangered Species say that the development holds enormous potential for the preservation of endangered species.

An American millionaire has succeeded in his long-held ambition to circumnavigate the world in a balloon. Fifty-eight-year-old Steve Fossett had already made five attempts on the record, but was frequently beaten back by the weather. In 1997 he was forced to land in Russia, in 1998 it was Australia and in 2001 he found himself crash-landing on a cattle ranch in Brazil.

And finally, the story of a man who has entered the record books as the world's most renowned eater of burgers. It is estimated that Don Gorske has eaten over 15,000 Big Macs, and he even proposed to his fiancée Mary in the car park of a McDonald's. In fifteen years, he says, he has missed a Big Mac on only seven occasions, including the death of his mother, a snowstorm and a 600-mile drive without a McDonald's in sight.

Unit 1 Recording 4

1 A conservation institute in the United States has produced wild kittens by cross-breeding cloned adult cats.

2 An American millionaire has succeeded in his long-held ambition to circumnavigate the world in a balloon.

3 And finally, the story of a man who has entered the record books as the world's most renowned eater of burgers.

Unit 1 Recording 5

1 When I was at school, a friend of mine was injured in an accident while playing rugby. He was paralysed and needed to spend the rest of his life in a wheelchair. Together with some friends we decided to organise a sponsored bike ride to raise money for his family, and other people in a similar situation. So we set up a charity called 'One Step Ahead' and arranged to cycle from Scotland to Gibraltar. I'd never done anything like that before, so it was a fantastic learning experience. I'd always thought it would be great to cycle across a whole country, but this exceeded my expectations. There were about twenty or thirty of us on bikes, and the rest of the crew in vans with all the equipment, and camping gear. It was very tough cycling, especially in Spain where we had to battle against the heat. But we had a fantastic time, and at the end, when we arrived, there was a huge party for us, and the media came and took photos. We were even on the news! We felt we'd accomplished something quite important, and we raised lots of money for people with spinal injury too.

2 I've been doing volunteer work here in the rain forest, in Brazil, for a while now. Next week I'll have been here for three months, helping to teach English to the young children in the village. It's been an amazing experience, because I'd never even left Europe before, so you can imagine how different things are here. When I arrived I really didn't know what to expect. It was a real culture shock, and I was here on my own for the first couple of months. Now my fiancée has come out to join me, and things are a bit easier. I've been living with a small tribe of people right out in the forest, and I'd never done any teaching before either, so the whole thing has been quite a challenge, and I've learnt a lot. But some of the children are speaking quite good English with me now, and a few of them are starting to write little stories too, so I feel it's been quite an achievement.

3 I've run a marathon. In fact, I'm planning to run it again this year. I did it last year for the first time and it was great. It felt like a major achievement. I had to train really hard, getting up early in the morning to run before going to work. And as the distances got longer I had to get up earlier and earlier. And it was incredibly hard because I'd never done any training like that before. I've always run, but just for myself, to relax and to keep fit, but this was a chance to be more competitive, and really push myself

to the limit. It is a fantastic run, because London is a beautiful city, and there's such a good atmosphere as you go along the route, with people cheering you on. My parents even came over from New Zealand to see me arrive at the finish. I couldn't move for about a week afterwards last time, but I was glad I'd done it, and I'm looking forward to the next one.

Unit 1 Recording 6

1 Jake, this is my friend Amy, who I've known for absolutely ages.
2 I asked what had happened, but nobody could tell me.
3 I chose this school because I'd heard it was the best.
4 He should have finished by the time we get back.
5 Before I came to the US, I'd never been abroad.
6 I'm so exhausted. I've been working really hard.
7 By the time she retires, she'll have been working there for more than fifty years.
8 I'll phone you as soon as we've arrived.

Unit 1 Recording 7

E=Expert

E: If you ticked mainly (a), then you seem to be very comfortable as you are, and you're not too keen on new challenges. I think you need to make an effort to get off the sofa. Go on! Take a risk – it might have a positive effect!
Now, if your answers were mainly (b), it means you like a challenge and you take advantage of your opportunities. You seem willing to have a go at anything and everything. So, good luck, but be careful!
Those of you who ticked mainly (c), well, you obviously make a habit of checking everything before committing yourself. You are super-cautious. Well, you may live a long, safe life, but a bit of a challenge from time to time won't do you any harm!

Unit 2 Recording 1

1 I'm from South Africa. I spent two and a half years, actually more like two years, living in Vancouver, Canada. Er … my wife and I were trying to set up our own business there as packagers in the publishing industry. Unfortunately, things were not going very well economically. Canada wasn't in a depression, but it was just not a very good time to try and start your own business in publishing. What did I like about Vancouver? Well, Vancouver is one of the most beautiful cities in the world. In fact, Vancouver is regularly named as the best place in the world to live. Stunningly beautiful because of mountains, sea, forests and natural beauty, and for me, combined with a large city. Vancouver is a city where you can walk to the beach. Vancouver is a city where the beaches are right in the city and you can go to the beach for your lunch break. You can take a bus and go skiing in the mountains forty minutes later. Canadian food, of course, is not at the top of the world's list of good food, but Vancouver has got a very large Chinese population, Indian population, and of course as the rest of Canada, people from all over the world, so you can eat extraordinarily good

food in Vancouver. Urm … the only food that people might consider uniquely Vancouverite is what they would call 'fusion' cuisine, which is food prepared by chefs that mix their diverse background from Asia or Europe and integrate it with the local foods and in fact you can have a very good meal that way. My best memories about Canada? Well, the open spaces, vastness and the friendly people as well.

2 I'm from Belfast originally, but over the past ten years I've been living, um I've lived in Spain, Austria, France and other parts of the UK. Um, I lived in Austria for a year when I was about twenty-two, twenty-three. It was a gap year from university. Er, I was studying German so I wanted to spend a year there. I was a teaching assistant there. I worked in a school four days a week, so it was really great because it meant I had long weekends. Um, I usually went travelling with my friends at the weekends. We went to Slovenia, Prague, Italy, Germany, and the best thing was I pretended I was fifteen so that I could get some rail discount. I got half price train tickets which was excellent. Um, the other great things about living there was obviously skiing and ice skating on lakes, which you can't do in Northern Ireland. Um, obviously the scenery is beautiful. The people were nice. The thing I didn't really like was the food, because I'm vegetarian and in Austria they tend to eat a lot of meat, but apart from that everything else was great. Um, I think my favourite memories of Austria are the scenery, being able to go off into the mountain after school every afternoon and go skiing or swimming in the lakes in the summer, and I'd definitely like to go back one day.

3 When I lived in Japan, actually in Tokyo, for about two years – this was about two years ago now – urm, it was, as you can imagine, a completely crazy experience for me, coming from Oxford which is a very, y'know, small, provincial, very quiet kind of town. Er, I was living in Tokyo because I was working as an English language teacher for a really tiny language school run by this nice, nice old lady erm, in a suburb of Tokyo. I thoroughly enjoyed Tokyo. It was such an interesting experience. It was like being, y'know, dropped in the middle of a lifestyle that was completely different to my own. Erm, even going to the supermarket was a massive adventure because of course I couldn't read anything 'cause the writing system's so different, so I'd sort of pick up a tin and think, 'Ooh that looks interesting, I'll take that take that home and, y'know, I'll see what comes out' and got a few surprises of course, a few unidentifiable foods that I'd never seen before, but that's always a good thing. Erm … I think my favourite memories of the country would have to be the people. Because I was teaching English, I knew a lot of Japanese people as students, as colleagues in the school and so on, and I just found them so nice. They were friendly, funny, really interested in what a foreigner like me was doing in Tokyo and very keen to, y'know, share experiences of travelling abroad and to … to tell me all about the social customs in Japan and things like that. So it was a, it was a really rewarding experience, absolutely great.

Unit 2 Recording 2

1 Would you mind shutting the door?
2 I was wondering if you could give me a lift?
3 Could you possibly pass the salt?
4 Would it be possible for me to use your phone?
5 I wouldn't have thought so.
6 Do you think you could keep the noise down?
7 I was hoping you could help us with the luggage.
8 If I were you, I'd leave a bit earlier.

Unit 2 Recording 3

W=Woman M=Man

W: It's made such a big difference to me. I mean, communication is miles easier than it was before. Do you remember the days when we had to go through all that hassle of writing letters?
M: Sure, I'd agree with that. But I'd still say that face-to-face communication is better. Sending an email is nowhere near as personal and meaningful as a conversation.
W: Well, it depends, doesn't it?
M: On what?
W: OK, an email is nothing like as good as seeing someone you like , or your friends or something, but I can tell you this much: rather than going to see my clients every day, or nattering on the phone, I'm much better off sending them an email. It saves time.
M: Yeah, I see what you're getting at, but I just think, the more we use email, the more we need it. It's like an addiction, with people checking their emails every five minutes even in meetings.
W: Fair enough. But I'd still rather have it than not.
M: And, well, the Internet in general, there's so much rubbish on there. Do you use it to do research?
W: All the time. I think it's OK. Maybe it's not quite as good as looking in books. Well, it's not as reliable, though it's considerably faster.
M: I'd say that looking up something on the Internet is marginally less reliable than shouting out of the window, 'Does anybody know the answer to this?' It's not regulated, is it? Anyone can publish anything on the Internet and it may or may not be true.
W: Much the best thing about the Internet is that it lets you do things more cheaply than before, like buying holidays, buying stuff on e-bay.
M: I've never used e-bay.
W: Or Amazon. You can get loads of cheap books.
M: Yeah, but I'd sooner go to a second hand bookshop. I'm not into the idea of giving my bank details over the Internet. No way.
W: There're lots of security measures these days …

Unit 2 Recording 4

1 Erm, I'm a member of an old boys' club erm which is basically when an when you leave school you keep in touch with your old friends and every five or ten years you have a reunion and you get together and party and remember the old days, erm … some good, some bad obviously. Erm, we also get involved in quite a

few charity events in the area where I'm from, erm... and recently we actually did some charity events to save the school that I was at, which was going to be closed. So that was something we did specially. I did it, I didn't join straight after school. Erm, I went abroad for a few years, and I found out about it through a website er called Friends Reunited, where you can find where your old friends are and your old school is. That was great. We probably only meet once every two years as a group. Erm, we have a big party and get to meet all the people that we remember, and some of the teachers as well, er which is fun. What's really interesting about the group is that we've now all known each other for about twenty years, and it's so interesting to meet people every two years and see how they've changed. I'm sure that if I met some of those people in the street now after twenty years, I wouldn't recognise them, and in in a bad sort of way, I suppose, it's, you like to measure yourself against your friends, where they've got to and how have you done in comparison. Um, If there's something I don't like, it's that er... it's very difficult to keep in touch when you are not meeting so regularly. Erm, and you do rely on other people to run the club, and sometimes people aren't as involved as they should be, sometimes you don't hear anything for a year or two, so it is quite difficult to do. But I will definitely stick with it, because it is great to meet people and remember some of the good days.

2 Well, I'm a member of a ... of a kind of society, I suppose. It's a tennis club. Um, it's kind of lessons, but it's also social as well. There's about ... oh I suppose ... it must be about thirty people in the club, and I think I'm quite unusual because I think I'm the youngest there. Urm, I go with a friend of mine, who's ... who's my partner in the tennis. Urm, it's great fun, really great fun. It's kind of fun being the youngest there as well because everyone else is retired and they think we're very cool and exotic for being young. It's been absolutely great. I mean, there's quite a lot of beginners in the class so you never really feel y'know like you're stuck out in the middle of all these wonderful advanced athletes. Urm, we meet once a week and sometimes we meet in a school hall, in a local suburb near to where I live. Um, we meet in the evenings after work and it can be quite hard to get yourself out of the house again ready to do some exercise, but it's fantastic fun.

Unit 3 Recording 1

E=Expert

E: In 1957 a news programme called Panorama broadcast a story about spaghetti trees in Switzerland. While the reporter told the story, Swiss farmers in the background were picking spaghetti from trees. Following this, thousands of people called the show, asking how to grow spaghetti trees.

In 1998 large numbers of Americans went to Burger King asking for a new type of burger. The food company had published an ad in *USA Today* announcing the new 'left-handed Whopper', a burger designed for left-handed people. The following day, Burger King admitted that they had been joking all along. Swedish technician Kjell Stensson had been working on the development of colour TV for many years when he announced in 1962 that everyone could now convert their black and white TV sets into colour. The procedure was simple: you had to put a nylon stocking over the TV screen. Stensson demonstrated and fooled thousands.

Pretending that it had been developing the product for some time, a British supermarket announced in 2002 that it had invented a whistling carrot. Using genetic engineering, the carrot grew with holes in it, and, when cooked, it would start whistling.

Unit 3 Recording 2

1 I'd seen it before.
2 I'd prefer to go home.
3 She'd lost the opportunity.
4 Would you like to play chess?
5 I didn't set the alarm.
6 What would you cook?
7 I'd have done the same.
8 Had she been there?

Unit 3 Recording 3

1 My favourite fictional character has to be *Philip Marlowe*, the detective created by Raymond Chandler. The most famous book and movie in which he appears is, of course, *The Big Sleep*, with erm... Humphrey Bogart playing *Philip Marlowe*. Once you've seen Humphrey Bogart, of course it's very difficult to imagine *Philip Marlowe* as being anybody else other than Humphrey Bogart, because like Humphrey Bogart, *Philip Marlowe* is tall, good-looking, tough, very smart and a smooth talker. I suppose those are also the characteristics that I do like about *Philip Marlowe*. The thing about *Philip Marlowe* is ... like ... unlike most modern characters, he doesn't always say the right thing, although he always has a clever retort and he doesn't always win. *Philip Marlowe* is not always on top of the situation. *Philip Marlowe* sounds like a real guy with real problems who's very clever, very tough and likes to get to the bottom of the problem. Urm, the sort of problems that he has to overcome, of course, as a detective in Los Angeles is generally solving murder crimes, but he's often not so much interested in who did it as to why or how. By the end of the story, you care much about, you care as much about the er ... victim as perhaps the murderer or *Philip Marlowe* himself. This is actually one reason why you can re-read and re-read the Raymond Chandler novels with *Philip Marlowe* in them, because it's not what happens in the story it's how *Philip Marlowe* deals with the problems that matters.

2 I think my favourite fictional character has to be erm the lead character, the heroine if you like, of erm Jane Austen's *Pride and Prejudice*. She's absolutely, I think, one of the best-drawn characters in in English literature. She is of course *Elizabeth Bennett*. Urm, she's

the heroine, she's she's sparky, she's lively, she's feisty, and when you think that this is a book that's set in the 1800s, it's really quite remarkable that you've got such a modern woman as the heroine. I mean she's she's lippy, she talks back to all these men who are older than her and in more authority than her. Fantastic! I think it's er character traits that I'd really quite like to have myself. Urm, I imagine her, and I think I'm quite influenced here by the films and so on that have been made of *Pride and Prejudice*, as being quite tall with a very lively, mobile face and possibly dark hair, as well. Urm ... memorable things that she does: well, the thing that I really like about her erm from the story of *Pride and Prejudice* is the way that she takes control of her own life in a period of history when women really had very little power and very little control over what happened to them in the marriage market, and I think it's great that she erm sort of comes to a self-realisation through the events of the novel and decides to do the right thing and go for the guy that she really likes, and of course she meets lots of problems along the way: people who think she's socially unacceptable or people who erm have very prejudiced views about class and society and of course she succeeds and she wins the day, wins her guy in the end.

3 I think my favourite fictional character was er the old man from *The Old Man and the Sea* by Ernest Hemingway. Er I still have quite a strong visual image of this man. The whole story takes place in a boat off the coast of Cuba, with with just this one character mostly. I imagine him to be quite old. He was a lifelong fisherman. He had quite a tough life, so I imagine he had these really big strong hands that were ... were cut and bruised from hauling in nets his whole life every every night out out in the sea. I imagine him with a little bit of grey hair, er, just old and wise, somebody who had been a fisherman his whole life, took a lot of pride in it and tried to do it as as best he could, and he was down on his luck in the story. He hadn't caught anything for quite a long time, erm but he still dragged himself out every night and cast his nets and hoped for hoped that he would catch something.

In a way, he sort of reminds me of my dad, somebody who had limited opportunities in life, but found a job that he could do and did it to the best of his ability even though there was very little glamour attached to it, and I think this in a way the fisherman was like him. He was a fisherman and he took pride in that, and did the best job he could.

Unit 3 Recording 4

W=Woman

W: Groucho Marx didn't want to be a comedian at first. He liked reading and singing, and he wanted to become a doctor. But his mother had other ideas. She got the boys to start a group called *The Six Mascots*. During a radio show they started making jokes, and this is when they decided to become a comedy act. Their popularity grew quickly. But in 1926 the boys' mother died, and the Great Depression began. In the 1930s a man called Irving Thalberg helped the Marx Brothers to get on television. They made their most famous films, the last of which was called *A Day At the Races*. After this, Groucho became a radio host and he also made more movies, but without his brothers. In the Seventies he toured with a live one-man show, but by now in his nineties he was getting weaker, and he died in 1977 on the same day as Elvis Presley.

Unit 3 Recording 5

M=Man

M: Three colleagues, a photographer, a journalist and an editor are covering a political convention. One day, during their lunch break, they walk along a beach and one of them sees a lamp. He picks it up and rubs it and a magic genie suddenly appears. The genie says 'You can each have one wish.' So the photographer says, 'I want to spend the rest of my life in a big house in the mountains with a beautiful view, where I can take photographs.' Bazoom! Suddenly the photographer is gone to his home in the mountains. Then it's the journalist's turn. 'I want to live in a big house in the countryside with an enormous garden where I can sit and write for the rest of my life.' Bazoom! The journalist is gone. Finally, the genie says to the editor, 'And what about you? What's your wish?' So the editor says, 'I want those two back before lunch. We've got a deadline at 6.00 tonight.'

Unit 4 Recording 1

N=Newsreader

N: Resistance to antibiotics is on the increase. Research out today shows an increase in the number and strength of superbugs, resistant to normal antibiotics. Analysis of particularly resistant strains, kept in laboratory test tubes, shows that in the last twelve months ...
A new virus, developed by hackers in South East Asia has been crashing computer networks around the globe. The virus penetrates standard firewalls to affect computer software and eventually data stored in the microchip. Experts have warned that ...
A breakthrough in genetic engineering technology means that human cloning can now enable scientists to re-build damaged organs in children. Cells taken from skin tissue are used to provide the necessary genes, which are then implanted ...
The on-going budget crisis has been cited as the reason for the latest delay to the space mission. The new shuttle, Discover XVIII, which was originally due to launch last Thursday, is set to orbit Mars, scanning the surface for evidence of early life-forms ...

Unit 4 Recording 2

J=Jane S=Sarah C=Chris

J: It says name four different types of superheroes. Can you think of any?
S: Well, there's ... let's see ... Superman ...
C: Spider-Man, Batman ...
S: The Incredible Hulk ...
C: The Fantastic Four ...
S: The Incredibles ...
J: Well, that's definitely more than four... Shall we move on? The next one is asking about the colour of the Incredible Hulk ...
C: He was green, wasn't he?
S: I heard the original comic book version was

actually grey, but a printing error made him appear green, and the comic's writers decided that it suited him, so they let it stay.
J: Oh ... what do you know? Can you name four of Spider-Man's special powers?
S: Well, he can walk up walls using his spider-grip, he has super-strength ...
C: ... and can lift up to 10 tonnes in weight ...
S: He has webshooters which he can fire to catch villains and erm ... he has spider-sense ...
C: Yes ... a kind of ESP that allows Parker to sense when danger is afoot, and spider-speed so he can run fast to escape danger.
J: Erm ... the name of the planet where Superman was born was ...
C: ... Planet Krypton, wasn't it?
S: 'Course it was! OK, what about the actor who played Superman?
J: Oh, what was his name? Um ... it was the one that was paralysed in an accident wasn't it?
C: Oh, that was Christopher Reeve. Didn't he fall off a horse and suffer a spinal injury ...
S: ... which paralysed him from the neck down. He continued acting and directing though, despite his disability, and also campaigned actively for research into spinal regeneration.
J: Courageous man. OK ... moving on ... what was the name of the film released in 2002 which broke all box office records in the first weekend?
S: Oh, that must be Spider-Man without a doubt!
J: Great! And lastly, the name of the female character who has super-strength, bullet-proof bracelets and ...
C: ... a lasso that makes people tell the truth ... Wonder Woman!

Unit 4 Recording 3

I=Interviewer S=Stan Lee

I: Legendary veteran comic writer Stan Lee co-created Spider-Man and the Fantastic Four, amongst others.
We asked him how he thought of Spider-Man and this was his response.
S: When trying to create a superhero, the first thing you have to think of, or at least the first thing I have to think of, is a super-power. What super-power would be different, that people hadn't seen before? I had already done the Hulk, who was the strongest creature on Earth; I'd already done the Fantastic Four: one of them could fly, one who was invisible, and one whose body could stretch and I was trying to think: what else can I do? And I've told this story so often that for all I know it might even be true! But I was sitting and watching a fly crawling on the wall, and I thought 'Gee – that would be great – what if a character could crawl on walls like an insect?' So I had my super-power, but then I needed a name. So I thought, 'Insect-Man' ... that didn't sound good. Crawling-Man? I went on and on ... Mosquito-Man? ... and then somehow I said 'Spider-Man' and it just sounded dramatic and mysterious to me, so that was my name.
I: When asked why he made Spider-Man a scientist, he replied ...
S: I had always resented that in most superhero stories and actually, in most comic books the hero is some sort of rugged, muscular outdoorsman, a sportsman ... an adventurer. And anyone who was literate

or scholarly they were ... he was always considered to be somewhat of a nerd. And I thought, my gosh, people don't have enough respect for intelligence. So again, in trying to be different, and in trying to be realistic, I thought I would make my teenage hero a scholarship student, extra-bright – he was studying science. And just to show that there's no reason why a hero couldn't also be a kid who likes science and is good at school and is smart ... and that was the thinking behind it.
I: When asked if he was at all scientific, he replied ...
S: I'm not much of a scientist. I like reading science-fiction but when it comes to actual science, I'm ... I'm a dummy. But I like to make things seem scientific!
I: Our final question asked if Stan Lee thought there would ever be real superheroes.
S: I believe that they will be able, through cloning ... through genetics they will be able to find a way to abolish most diseases. They will be able to ... they will have to ... see, once these wars are finished with, if they ever are, we're going to want to go to the planets, they're going to want to go to Mars. Now it's such a long trip, and it'll be so hard to get back again, they're going to have to make human beings adapt to Mars, adapt themselves ... or is it adopt? I never ... I always get those two mixed up. But at any rate, I believe that they will find a way to make people able to live in the atmosphere of Mars, through altering them genetically ... Because of genetics, I think we can do virtually anything.

Unit 4 Recording 4

1 Do you think you'll still be studying English?
2 Do you think you'll have the same lifestyle?
3 Do you think you'll be living in the same place?
4 Do you think your country will have a different government?
5 Do you think you'll have changed much?
6 Do you think you'll have the same hobbies?
7 Do you think you'll have the same close friends?
8 Do you think you'll have seen more of the world?

Unit 4 Recording 5

Dialogue 1
K=Kevin L=Lizzie

K: Hello?
L: Hi, Kevin. It's Lizzie.
K: Oh hi, Lizzie. How are you?
L: Yeah, great. You?
K: Yeah, fine.
L: I guess you're busy as usual this Saturday?
K: Um ... sort of.
L: Yeah?
K: Well, I'm playing cricket.
L: Oh, I didn't know you played cricket.
K: I don't really. Well, once in a blue moon.
L: So that's all day Saturday?
K: Yeah, that'll be ... yeah ... more or less all day.
L: What are you up to in the evening?
K: Well, I might be free. Let me think. Mm, maybe about eight-ish. What have you got lined up?
L: Um, we're thinking of going to Clancy's ...

K: Oh yeah? I used to go there from time to time when I was a student. Do you want me to pick you up?

L: Um, or should I drive?

K: I don't mind driving. Do you want me to?

L: In a way, it's easier if I take my car. Yeah, don't worry. I think I'll drive …

Dialogue 2

L=Lauren A=Andy

L: Lauren James.

A: Hi, dear.

L: Oh hi.

A: Still working?

L: Yep.

A: Bit of a hard day?

L: Kind of. Nothing major, just various bits and pieces.

A: Right.

L: Filling in forms, replying to emails, that kind of thing.

A: Uhuh.

L: Going over the accounts again, checking petty cash, etcetera etcetera. Actually, there were loads of mistakes.

A: Oh really?

L: Yep. But I'm nearly finished.

A: So, d'you want me to get something ready?

L: Yeah, I'm a bit peckish actually.

A: Pasta maybe? Or we've got chicken in the fridge.

L: Chicken sounds good. Um, I'll be home in an hour or so.

A: OK, I'll put the chicken in the oven … [fade out]

Unit 4 Recording 6

1 How many phone calls do you make per day?

2 How many times do you check your emails per week?

3 How many close friends do you have?

4 How frequently do you write letters?

5 What do you do in the evening?

6 How long do you spend studying English at home?

Unit 4 Recording 7

1 <u>Not</u> since <u>Mozart</u> has there been a <u>greater genius</u>.

2 <u>Only</u> after the age of <u>three</u> did she begin to show her <u>gift</u>.

3 <u>Nowhere</u> do the <u>rules</u> say you can't teach <u>advanced subjects to children</u>.

4 <u>Only</u> later did we understand the <u>truth</u> about our gifted <u>child</u>.

5 <u>Not</u> only was he able to <u>write poetry</u> when he was <u>five years old</u>; he also played the <u>violin</u> well.

6 <u>No</u> sooner had we given her a <u>paintbrush</u> than she produced a <u>masterpiece</u>.

Unit 4 Recording 8

I=Interviewer W=Woman

I: Can you tell us a little bit about the case and what made it so special?

W: The case concerned a pair of twins called John and Michael. They were, I suppose in their late teens, but they were absolutely tiny and they wore thick glasses. They used to get laughed at school because, in a conventional sense, they weren't very bright or social.

I: They were outsiders.

W: Well, that's right. Outsiders. But they had an amazing gift. You could name any date in the past or future forty thousand years and they would be able to tell you what day of the week it was.

I: So I could say, for example, 5th June 1376 and they could tell me it was Sunday or whatever …

W: That's right.

I: Or 10th July 2099, and …

W: And they would say 'Monday!' But that wasn't all. During one interview, the psychologist dropped a box of matches on the floor and the twins immediately called out 'one hundred and eleven'. The psychologist counted the matches and there were exactly one hundred and eleven.

I: And the twins hadn't counted them?

W: No. There was no time. As soon as the matches hit the floor, they knew there were one hundred and eleven. Now another thing the twins could do was remember extremely long sequences of numbers. You could say a number of up to three hundred digits, and they were able to repeat it back to you perfectly.

I: So they basically have an extraordinary ability with numbers.

W: Not only with numbers. They have another talent, which is that you can name any day of their lives since they were about four years old, and they are able to tell you what the weather was like, what they did, and other events in the wider world. They can remember absolutely everything about that day.

I: Just any ordinary day.

W: Any and every ordinary day.

I: Obviously the twins, John and Michael, were studied at length by various psychologists, educators …

W: Yes, they were.

I: What progress did these people make in coming up with explanations of their ability?

W: I think the main thing is that we realise that John and Michael's ability is actually a visual one as well as mathematical. If you ask them how they do it, they say they can 'see' the answers. When the box of matches fell, they 'saw' one hundred and eleven. It wasn't a calculation. Similarly, they can 'see' themselves as five year-olds. Somehow they have an ability to record incredible numbers of things in the mind. Of course, we have no idea how it works, but it would be very interesting to learn …

Unit 4 Recording 9

1 Great discoveries of our time … well, in the last one hundred years or so, I guess medical advances, like the use of x-rays in diagnosis, or the discovery of penicillin by Fleming. I mean, he made that discovery almost by mistake, and it changed modern medicine completely. Or perhaps the elucidation of DNA by Watson and Crick in the fifties. That paved the way for the whole area of genetics and genetic engineering …

2 I would say that sending man to the Moon was one of the greatest scientific achievements, learning about space. The man who invented the liquid-fuelled rocket, Robert Goddard, was fascinated by the idea of sending a rocket into space, and he spent years researching his ideas, until he developed the first rocket, called Nell. It was 10 feet tall,

and he fired it from his aunt's farm in the US. At first nothing happened, but when the fuel finally ignited the rocket was launched. It only reached a disappointing 14 metres into the air though and scientists were sceptical of its success. When the newspapers got hold of the story they wrote the headlines 'Moon rocket misses target by 238,799 miles.' But later, engineers in Germany and America used his ideas, and the film footage of Nell, to develop military and space exploring rockets. The New York Times had to write Goddard a public apology …

3 Computers, it has to be. Information technology, and the Internet. The whole way in which information is distributed and kept nowadays. It's just been revolutionised by information technology. And things have happened so quickly. I mean, the first computer was built in 1948, I think. And was so big it took up a whole room! If you think about the latest designs now, and the capacity, it's just amazing. And it has made the world a smaller place, because it is so easy now to get information about anywhere in the world. There are no secrets …

4 I don't think we should underestimate the importance of domestic appliances, like the washing machine, dishwasher, all your electrical goods. And processes like freeze-drying food. These timesaving discoveries have allowed a whole new freedom to women, who previously had to spend their whole lives in the kitchen. It's meant that they could go out to work, and that has had a huge impact on society. Or perhaps it should be the advances in travel, with the bicycle, then the car and the aeroplane. The world must have been a very different place when the fastest way to get anywhere was on a horse! …

Unit 5 Recording 1

1 He can't complain. It's his own fault he lost the money.

2 We are by no means certain that it is the same man committing the crimes.

3 What I really miss is having enough time to spend with friends.

4 They didn't understand what we wanted at all.

5 He didn't even stop at the red light. He just drove straight through.

6 The costs were very high indeed.

7 It was always Sammy who got into trouble.

8 Keith wasn't in the least bit annoyed when we cancelled the meeting.

Unit 5 Recording 2

P=Presenter

P: While we're on the subject of choosing business partners, I cringe whenever I hear that two old friends or family members are planning to start a business together as fifty–fifty partners. It isn't that doing business with friends and family is a bad idea – many very successful businesses are family-owned. It's just that being someone's friend or relative is one of the worst reasons I can think of for making that someone your business partner. One of the problems is that once someone becomes your business partner, there is generally only one way to get rid of them (legally, of course) if things don't work out.

You must buy them out for the fair value of their interest in the business. And that can be an expensive proposition.

There are a few ways to determine if someone has what it takes to be your business partner, however.

Firstly, you need to decide, are you a visionary, or an operations person? Successful partnerships combine those two kinds of people. A visionary is a strategic, 'big picture' thinker who understands the business model, the market and the overall business plan. An operations person is someone who rolls up their sleeves, wades up to their hip boots in the details and executes the strategy that the visionary comes up with. You are either one or the other – it is almost impossible to be both. Once you have determined if you are a 'visionary' or an 'operations person', look for your opposite number. That way your business is more likely to strike the right balance between strategy and tactics.

Do you have all the skills you need on board to make the business work? Perhaps you are an inventor who is excellent at product design but clueless about selling. Perhaps you have a strong marketing background but need someone to help you crunch the numbers and make sure your products or services can be delivered within budget. Your partners should complement your set of business skills, not duplicate them. Keep in mind that you can acquire someone's skills without making them a partner. If a particular skill, such as contract negotiation or bookkeeping, is not critical to the success of your business, you may be better off hiring a lawyer, accountant or consultant to do it for you and keeping ownership of your business.

Can you communicate directly and honestly with this person, without pulling any punches? Communication between partners can often get rough; disagreements and arguments break out all the time. It is difficult to criticise someone harshly, yet sometimes you must be cruel with your business partners in order to do the right thing for your business. Your business may well suffer if you consistently hold back important information for fear of offending your partner or jeopardising the underlying friendship or emotional bond between you. Sometimes the most successful business partnerships are those where the partners do not socialise outside the office. And lastly, is your business partner willing to hang around for the long haul? This is the critical test of a business partner. Many people are happy to help out with a business during its start-up phase, only to lose interest later on when something more attractive (like a job offer from a big corporation) comes along, a life-changing event (like the birth of a new child) occurs, or the going is getting tougher and the business isn't as much 'fun' as it used to be. If you are not sure if someone is committed to the long-term success of your business, make them an employee or independent contractor, with perhaps an 'option' to acquire an interest in your business at a date two or three years down the road ... provided, of course, they are still working for you at that time and you continue to be satisfied with their performance.

Unit 5 Recording 4

I=Interviewer W=Will

I: 98 percent of staff working at Piranha recruitment say they laugh a lot with their team. As many as 95 percent say that they are excited about where the company is going. So what have they all got to smile about? Last month this small London-based company won a prestigious award for being one of the best small companies in the UK to work for. With us today is Will Becks, the Company Director. Will, first of all, tell us a little bit more about the company and what you do.

W: Good morning. Well, Piranha is more than just a normal recruitment agency. The difference is that we actually train and then place graduates in sales jobs. That means we have a lot of young people working for us, so it's a bit like a continuation of university, but with a salary. We're only a small company, with as few as sixty employees, but there's a good atmosphere in the office. There's a great deal of energy.

I: Yes, your employees have said that there is a fun atmosphere, with outgoing, like-minded people. You have regular parties, an annual skiing holiday, a present for the most-appreciated employee of the month, and plenty of other benefits too. I'm not much of an expert on these things. Why such an emphasis on staff incentives?

W: Well, our staff are young and highly qualified. They are good at what they do, and they believe in it. We have trained sales people going into companies to try and place graduates. Quite a few of them get offered the job themselves. If we didn't look after our staff, they would quickly get poached by other companies. So the incentives need to be good to keep people.

I: So how are your salaries?

W: Salaries are good and there are monthly, performance-related cash bonuses. Staff also set their own targets for the coming year, and for the most part they have their say in their incentives too. Our accountant has just got the new Audi A3. He chose it, and he's delighted.

I: And how about the atmosphere in the office. How do you influence that?

W: We have a company café, where we offer free breakfasts, and cappuccino all day long. People spend an awful lot of time in there discussing ideas over coffee, but it's very productive.

I: The vast majority of your staff say that they admire their managers, and feel that they can actively contribute to the future success of the company. How did you achieve this?

W: Well, one of the things is that we help them with finding somewhere nice to live. Rent is very expensive in London, and as lots of our employees are fresh out of university, with a lot of debts, they don't have a huge budget for accommodation. So, we've bought some properties, and quite a few staff rent them from us at reasonable rates. It makes a real difference. It means that working for the company becomes a lifestyle choice. They are involved personally. Also, we like to give people a say in the company. We have monthly meetings to discuss big issues, when we all sit around and talk about things. Initially, only a handful of people would come to the meetings.

So we decided to offer free food, sandwiches and pizza, so now everyone comes, and everyone has something to say.

Unit 5 Recording 5

1   As many as 95 percent say that ...
2   Tell us a little bit more about ...
3   There's a great deal of energy ...
4   plenty of other benefits ...
5   not much of an expert ...
6   for the most part they have their say ...
7   People spend an awful lot of time in there ...
8   The vast majority of your staff say ...
9   quite a few staff rent them ...
10 only a handful of people would come ...

Unit 5 Recording 6

K=Kobus B=Bridget

K: Well, I'd replace these chairs for a start. No wonder I've got backache.

B: Oh come on, we can do better than that. How about blowing it all on an all-expenses-paid jaunt to the West Indies or something?

K: Erm ... would you really want to go on holiday with the rest of the staff?

B: Well, no, but ... um ...

K: I think it should go on day-to-day things that'll make a difference in the long term, like renovating the office.

B: God, how boring.

K: Or maybe ... what d'you mean boring?!

B: Well, it's loads of money – let's have some fun! The company could get a house by the sea that the employees could use whenever they were on holiday.

K: Yeah, but that would only be useful once every few years for each person. I mean it wouldn't make the least bit of difference really. My main priority would be to do something practical with the money ...

Unit 6 Recording 1

E=Expert

E: The Great Pyramid is arguably the most accomplished engineering feat of the Ancient World. Built to house the body of the dead pharaoh, the base of the Great Pyramid in Egypt is 230 metres squared, large enough to cover ten football fields. According to the Greek historian Herodotus, it took 400,000 men twenty years to construct this great monument. They used 2.3 million blocks of stone, some of which weighed as much as 50 tonnes!

'La Tour Eiffel' in Paris was built in 1889 to commemorate the 100th anniversary of the French Revolution. The Industrial Revolution in Europe had brought about a new trend – the use of metal in construction. The tower, built from a lattice made from very pure iron, is light and able to withstand high wind pressures. For 40 years from the time that it was built, it stood as the tallest tower in the world, and still today it is the tallest building in Paris.

The Sydney Harbour Bridge is one of Australia's best known, and most photographed landmarks. It is the world's largest (but not the longest) steel arch bridge with the top of the bridge standing 134 metres above the harbour. Fondly known by the Australians as the 'coathanger', Sydney Harbour Bridge celebrated its 70th birthday in 2002, with its official opening in March 1932. Nowadays, a group of twelve people leave every ten minutes to climb to the top of the bridge and admire spectacular views of the city, and out to the Tasman Sea.

The Pentagon, covering 13.8 hectares, is thought to be the largest office building in the world. It takes a person fifteen to twenty minutes to walk around the building once. It was built in five concentric rings, in record time during the Second World War, in order to relocate employees of the War Department from the seventeen buildings they occupied within Washington D.C.

Built between 1406 and 1420 during the Ming dynasty, The Forbidden City, also called the Purple Forbidden City, or Gugong Museum in Chinese, is located in the centre of Beijing, PRC. Occupying a rectangular area of more than 720,000 square meters, the Forbidden City was the imperial home of twenty-four emperors of the Ming (1368–1644) and Qing (1644–1911) dynasties. It is one of the largest and best-preserved palace complexes in the world, with over a million rare and valuable objects in the Museum.

Opening on 31st December, 1999, the Millennium Dome was built to celebrate the new millennium. The massive dome is over one kilometre round and fifty metres high at its centre. It covers twenty acres of ground floor space. How big is that? Well, imagine the Eiffel Tower lying on its side. It could easily fit inside the Dome. With its 100 metre steel masts and translucent roof, the Dome was meant to paint a portrait of the nation. Unfortunately, the project became one of the most controversial in Britain, due to its enormous cost, and doubts about how to best utilise the space after 2000.

Hassan II Mosque, in Casablanca, Morocco, was built for the 60th birthday of former Moroccan king Hassan II. It is the largest religious monument in the world after Mecca. It has space for 25,000 worshippers inside and another 80,000 outside. The 210-metre minaret is the tallest in the world and is visible day and night for miles around. The mosque includes a number of modern touches: it was built to withstand earthquakes and has a heated floor, electric doors, a sliding roof, and lasers which shine at night from the top of the minaret toward Mecca.

Unit 6 Recording 2

J=Jodie I=Interviewer

J: I think, with technology, it was Microsoft that started it.

I: 'It' being the use of teenagers …

J: Using teenagers really to find out what's in and what isn't, what the market wants next. Around the year 2000, they started observing these kids to find out what they were doing with technology.

I: And this was an American thing?

J: It was … well, no, actually they went all over the place observing these kids: from street markets in Seattle to skating rinks in London, bars in Tokyo, anywhere they thought trends might kick off.

I: So the idea was to watch these children, or teenagers, and learn what they wanted to do with their mobile phones, with software …

J: That's right. Because it's teenagers that really drive technology. Kids have no fear of technology. They experiment and they automatically home in on the new. One thing that became clear is that teenagers want technology they can carry around. Anything bigger than a few inches is out. That's why there was the development of these tiny mobile phones that could be attached to your arm, that type of thing. Text messaging caught on because kids wanted to pass notes to each other during class. The lights that you find on IBM's ThinkPad keyboard are there because IBM noticed that kids take notes in the dark during lectures.

I: So all of these things came about because of the needs of kids.

J: That's right.

I: And what's coming up on the horizon? Is there any big new development that has been led by teenagers?

J: Well, the next big area is collaborative computing, where you have groups of people working together online. This is really going to take off in the next few years, because it has massive potential for working environments in the sense that you may be able to work simultaneously on a project with someone who's on the other side of the world, moving data around together.

I: So is it just technology with these kids?

J: You mean where teenagers are leading the market?

I: Yes.

J: Not at all. I mean, style has been youth-led for years and years, but in particular, trainers. Now, if you want to keep up with the latest style of trainers, who do you ask? You don't ask anyone over twenty, that's for sure. And I think it was Converse trainers who used to do lots of their market research on the streets, on the basketball courts of New York, anywhere you find teenagers. They may still do this, I don't know.

I: And, what, they just talk to these kids?

J: Talk to them, watch what they are wearing, the colours, the style, and maybe bring in a prototype, ask the kids if they'd wear these. If not, why not?

Unit 6 Recording 3

A=Alison J=Jim M=Mark L=Leah

Dialogue 1

A: It depends on the age.

J: Uh huh.

A: 'Cos when they're young teenagers, no I don't think so.

J: What kind of limits would you put on, say, a fifteen year old?

A: Depends. There are some places that are not for teenagers but still they want to go to these places. I wouldn't let my twelve year old go to a cinema alone .

Dialogue 2

A: Teenagers? I don't think so.

J: Really? Why not?

A: Because they … they can't … er, well, they still can't evaluate what they're seeing and how much time they're spending. They could be doing other things.

J: It's not that good for them either, is it, their eyes. And sort of, it's a bit passive, can be a bit passive.

Dialogue 3

M: Oh, definitely, yeah. They're our friends.

L: Me too. If parents can choose who they hang out with, then we should too.

M: What's the difference?

L: Exactly. It's not like we're stupid and can't judge someone's character.

Dialogue 4

L: I think if it's a school day the next day, then it makes sense to have some kind of limit.

M: Yeah, but who sets the limit? If you know you're gonna be OK on six hours' sleep or something …

L: Yeah, you should discuss it, but if you're going to be exhausted in the morning then that's not really …

M: I'm saying it's not up to the parents to dictate it. We know how to switch off the lights, don't we?

Unit 6 Recording 4

1 Whatever you do, don't forget to turn off the power.
2 However good you are at swimming, Thorpe is better.
3 Whenever you feel down, give me a call.
4 Wherever we go, they're always close behind.
5 Whenever I can, I'll see her.
6 Whoever they employ, he'll have to work miracles.
7 However you fix the photocopier, it always breaks again.
8 Whatever those children do, they make a success of it.

Unit 6 Recording 5

1 She's very charismatic.
2 I find him inspirational.
3 He's very dignified.
4 She's rather aloof.
5 He's so idealistic.
6 They are tireless.
7 He's not very trustworthy.
8 She's extremely resolute.
9 She's a bit lacking in drive and energy.
10 He wavers in the face of problems.
11 He's not very approachable.
12 He's corrupt.
13 She's rather nondescript.
14 She's very down-to-earth and practical.
15 She's not very inspiring.
16 She lacks gravitas.

Unit 7 Recording 1

1 Looking after rabbits is really easy. The first thing you need to do, before you even get the rabbits, is to plan where they're going to be and to make sure that you buy urm a hutch that's the right size for your rabbits, so that they're comfortable, and make sure that your hutch is going to be in a position where they're not exposed to anything. So you need to plan well. Once you've got your rabbits, urm, basically you feed them twice a day. Urm, you have to make sure they like the food they're given. It can be a bit tricky because they're a bit picky about what they eat, rabbits, so you need to make sure you give them the right thing. You have to clean them out once a week or more, er, so you need, er, fresh straw and hay. It's best to get it from a farmer because

it's cheaper. Erm ... and you need to have them vaccinated against myxomatosis because they can come in contact with wild rabbits and then they can get ill. Urm, apart from that, that's it really.

2 It seems pretty straightforward, but actually there are lots of things that can go wrong when you choose a cat. A lot of people, for example, just go for the erm ... the cutest cat they can find, which is understandable, but not the right way to go about it. The first thing you've got to do is er, to ask yourself a number of questions. Can you afford a cat? I mean, people often forget that it isn't just food; you also have to pay a vet if the cat gets sick. Do you have enough space in the house? So, once you've answered these questions, the next thing is to think about what type of cat. If you buy a kitten, you need to consider how big and active it will be once it's grown up, and this depends on the breed. But, different breeds have different characteristics.

Unit 7 Recording 2

1 The first thing you need to do ...
2 So you need to plan well.
3 You have to make sure they like the food they're given.
4 It's best to get it from a farmer.

Unit 7 Recording 3

1 A lot of people, for example, just go for the cutest cat they can find.
2 The first thing you've got to do is to ask yourself a number of questions.
3 ... the next thing is to think about what type of cat...

Unit 7 Recording 4

M=Man

M: The first thing I noticed when I entered the bureaucrat's office was that it was bright white, like a doctor's surgery or the cell of a madman. There were a few filing cabinets next to the desk and a huge photo of the king staring at us from the wall. The air was thick and a fan droned weakly, whirring overhead as a gang of flies zig-zagged across the air.

The bureaucrat behind his desk looked up to greet me.

'How can I help you?' he said. I told him I needed a visa for my trip to the Danakil Depression, and he asked me if I'd ever been in a desert. 'I've been in many,' I replied. He shifted in his chair and said, 'The Danakil Depression is the world's hottest place. It's not a tourist site. There's nothing there but hot air and salt.' I told him I knew that, and that's why I wanted to go there. 'Typical British,' he said. 'Obsessed by the weather.'

He asked me what I'd do if I got lost, and I told him I wouldn't. 'And what about the three s's?' he said. 'What three s's?' 'Snakes, spiders and

scorpions. What if you get bitten?' 'I won't.' He stared at me again, glanced at my passport, and with a resounding thump, stamped it. 'One visa,' he said. 'This will get you into Danakil, but it won't get you out.'

Unit 7 Recording 5

M=Man

M: Going to the Danakil Depression means walking into hell on Earth. The land is sunk one hundred metres below sea level and the place is a furnace. The air shakes, warped by the sun. Even the wind brings no relief from the heat. Almost everything around you is dead: stumps of trees, cracked earth, the occasional white glow of animal bones.

Along the way we saw a group of bandits on camels, brandishing their weapons. They waved and went on riding. Salt statues loomed out of the spectacular landscape, three metres high, vibrant colours and shapes from another world. An active volcano was hunched on the horizon, biding its time. We stopped to visit a ghost town, with its abandoned shacks stripped bare by the wind and the nomads and the scavenging animals. This was Danakil, where an American company had tried to set up a business in the sixties and been defeated by the heat. The ruined buildings made of salt blocks were now crumbling away, and there were metal tracks in the ground where they had tried to build a railway but which now led nowhere.

For three days my shirt was drenched and my mouth parched. Even covered up against the sun, my skin baked and burned, and there seemed no escape from the cauldron of heat. They tell you to drink twelve litres of water a day, to remember to drink even when you're not thirsty, but it's never enough.

When we finally arrived at our destination I felt empty, as if everything had been a mistake. I didn't regret going to Danakil, but the land was so inhospitable that permanent settlement seemed impossible, and it felt wrong being there, as if we were trespassing on a place nature had intended only for itself.

Unit 7 Recording 6

I=Intro man S=Sharon

I: Sharon Edwards once spent a day in an aeroplane, looking for a cat. The plane flew around the world for three weeks before she found it. They sent the cat home first-class. Another time, she found two suitcases full of birds from Turkey. But her strangest experience was when she pulled a snake out of a man's clothing.

S: I'm an animal health inspector at Heathrow Airport. I look after the animals that pass through Heathrow. I check that they are healthy and legal and sometimes I look after them when they are waiting for a connecting flight.

Here are the areas for cats, reptiles, birds and fish. Over there is the area for very big animals. The biggest we ever had here was a black rhino, absolutely enormous.

At the Animal Centre here, we receive all types of animals – we've had chimpanzees, wild cats, poisonous spiders, and it's impossible for one person to know about all of these. It keeps you on your toes because you're always picking up new information about different breeds of

animal. But there are twenty people working here and between us we share our expertise. There is also a library and the Internet if we have any problems. I recently had to feed a group of toucans, but luckily, Tesco's is open twenty-four hours, so I had to go out at 2a.m. to buy bananas.

The most common animals are cats and rabbits. They come in all the time. And also lots of little children arrive at Heathrow carrying their pet hamster in their pocket, so I have to look after it for a while. The children always look very contrite when they're caught, but we usually don't take any action. It's not what you'd really call smuggling!

I often work at night. It's very quiet between 1 and 4a.m. because we don't have any night flights. We try and give the animals a night-time. We dim the lights, and it's peaceful. And you never know what the new day will bring.

Unit 7 Recording 7

1 A monkey costs as little as that?
2 It's as big as an elephant.
3 We're as happy as can be.

Unit 7 Recording 8

Example
W: You've got bad eyesight haven't you?
M: I'm as blind as a bat.
1 You're free now, aren't you?
2 You're strong, aren't you?
3 You're quiet, aren't you?

Unit 7 Recording 9

R=Rachel G=Graham

R: Well, it's a piece of land that's about fifty square kilometres, so there's really quite a lot you could do with it, but I mean I don't really know, I don't really have any expertise in managing the land. I don't know about you, Graham, but have you got any ideas what we could do with it?

G: Well, when I see fifty square kilometres of land, I think money. I think ...

R: Ha, that's typical!

G: Well, yeah. I think, y'know, a hotel will be great here. I think there's enough room for it, and as it's in the middle of, y'know, this kind of wonderful environmental area that we could really sell it.

R: Yeah, but the problem with the hotel is that you, I mean, the land's got this, these really beautiful environmental features, you've got these beautiful hilly bits and there's all these beautiful trees, and y'know it's quite a little forest down there. Perhaps it would be nicer to do something that's kind of more sympathetic with the environment, y'know, like um, you could leave it, we could leave it wild and just let the animals roam free, or you could have like a more organised animal sanctuary erm to really, y'know, get the most out of, of the features of the land. There's a lot of wildlife.

G: What would we get out of that?

R: It's good for the environment, Graham. I mean, it's doing something good, and giving something back to, to the Earth, and making sure that they, y'know, these sort of erm animal species are left to, to live in their own environment.

G: Mm. OK. Perhaps not a hotel then, but I think we could think of, y'know, a commercial use that would fit in more with the environment. What about some kind of health resort, maybe?

R: Well that's quite a nice idea because there's, y'know, there's so much land and, y'know, people could go walking in the hills, and we could do nature trails through the forest. We could even have like a little organic garden or, y'know, provide food that's really fresh and healthy because it's... the land's really good for growing vegetables and things like that and it's a great climate in this area, so y'know maybe that's a nice idea, we could have an organic health spa. What do you think?

G: Hm ... yeah, that's a nice idea.

Unit 8 Recording 1

1 That's a good question. Ummm. I think I'd like some kind of gadget that means I don't have to clean the house. Like a machine or a robot that tidies everything away. Does the washing-up, the ironing. Either that or get a maid.

2 A time machine. Not so I could go back and see earlier civilisations and dinosaurs – I mean, who cares about dinosaurs? – but so I could go back this morning and hit that guy who took my parking space.

3 Ooh, that's a difficult question. I'd have to think about it. Well, I wouldn't mind a weather machine, with me in control, of course. So when my friends go on holiday, I could make it rain every day and they'd stop telling me how beautiful the weather was.

4 That's tricky. How about a pill that you can substitute for food, so no one would need to starve? And so I wouldn't have to cook.

5 Let me see. You could have a pill that makes you extremely intelligent. You'd take it just before every exam or whenever the computer breaks down.

6 Well, I'd like to invent a special device that could take you to other places but only in your mind. Like a hat or glasses that give you all the sensations of being there. Then I'd use these glasses to go straight to a beach in Hawaii and spend the week there instead of in the office with all these other idiots.

7 I'd invent a clock that extends hours of the day when you need it. Like every morning when I'm lying in bed and have to get up.

Unit 8 Recording 2

T=Thomas E=Elise

T: I was on a business trip in Rome a few years ago. I'd been having dinner with a client all evening, and afterwards I found myself desperately looking for a late-night Internet café to check my emails from the office. So there I was at midnight, wandering around one of the most beautiful cities in the world, and I was tearing my hair out trying to get access to a computer. Anyway, I went back to the hotel, crashed out on my bed and thought, do I really have to live like this? Are those emails really so important? So I started to reappraise my life. The world is one stressed-out place. When I go to cities now, I see everybody rushing around with their mobile phones and their Personal Organisers and everyone's scared they're going to miss something. Y'know, just before we die, no one ever says, 'Ooh, I wish I'd spent more time working in the office.'

After leaving my job, I moved to the coast. I sell surfing gear now. It doesn't make much cash, but then money isn't the be-all and end-all. I'm happier than ever before because I think living by the sea gives you a certain perspective on life. The waves will be rolling in every morning long after we're gone. And it makes you realise all that rushing around isn't going to make any difference.

E: I've been working in an investment company for about four years. It's a very competitive business, of course, and you have to know about every fluctuation in the market even as it's happening. So I live a very fast-paced, high-pressure lifestyle. Actually, my friends tell me I suffer from a disease called 'running out of time syndrome'.

A lot of my work is done on the move, so I carry my office around with me: laptop, phone, Blackberry, electronic Notepad. I suppose you could call these my weapons of war! They're a security blanket really.

I don't live a particularly healthy lifestyle: I grab a sandwich when I can, and drink far too much coffee. But it's not going to be like this forever. Most people in my profession burn out after three and a half years. In fact, the statistics are getting worse – I think it's under three years now. So by the time I'm forty, forty-five, I'll be slowing down a bit. But I don't think I'll ever live on a farm in the middle of nowhere with my slippers on, growing vegetables. I'd hate that. I enjoy the buzz too much.

Unit 8 Recording 3

M=Man W=Woman

Dialogue 1

M: This stupid thing keeps getting jammed.

W: What, again?

M: I can't get it to make any copies.

W: It happened to me yesterday. Give it a good kick.

Is that better?

M: Well, I feel better, yeah, but it's still not working.

Dialogue 2

W: See? It's always coming up with the same message.

M: You have performed an illegal operation. Ooh, naughty.

W: See? I don't know how to make it shut down normally.

M: Have you tried dropping it onto the floor?

W: What?

M: Or shouting at it? That works sometimes.

W: You're not funny.

Dialogue 3

M: I'm having problems switching it on.

W: Oh really?

M: This thing seems to be stuck. It won't go round.

W: Oh yes.

M: Which means I can't get any air in here. And it's so hot.

W: Right in the middle of summer as well. You can always open the windows.

M: Oh! Yeah, thanks.

Unit 9 Recording 1

I=Interviewer E=Expert

I: What can you tell us about what happens when geniuses relax?

E: Without a doubt, we can be sure that great scientists don't always make their discoveries in the lab. Archimedes's famous Eureka moment came while he was having a bath. Physicist Richard Feynman saw a plate flying through the air in a college cafeteria, and was inspired to calculate electron orbits. He later won the Nobel Prize. And Alexander Fleming was making mould for his hobby, microbe painting, when he accidentally came across Penicillium notatum, later known as penicillin.

I: So what does this tell us?

E: Well, we're looking into the psychology of high achievers. A recent study by Robert Root-Bernstein compared the hobbies of 134 Nobel prize winning chemists to those of other scientists. He found that the Nobel prize winners were accomplished outside the lab. Over half were artistic and almost all had a long-lasting hobby: chess or insect collecting. Twenty-five percent of the Nobel prize winners played a musical instrument and eighteen percent drew or painted regularly. Of the normal scientists, under one percent had a hobby.

I: Fascinating. So should we conclude then, that only a creative person can be a genius?

E: Well, I think that's debatable. Perhaps it's true up to a point, but I don't think it's as clear-cut as that. What we do know is that to a certain extent, creative thinking can help people to solve problems, even scientific ones. That if you are thinking about a problem all the time, often the answer eludes you. But it may come in an inspiration when you are least expecting it – perhaps when you're asleep, or thinking about other things, doing a hobby, for example. It's not 100 percent certain, but it seems that the mind has the ability to make connections from one part of your life to another, so that actually stepping back from a problem can often provide the answer. And people who are good at making these connections, people who pursue creative hobbies and interests, often excel in their particular fields.

Unit 9 Recording 2

Saying what you like

I'm really into her work.

I'm a big fan of his stuff.

He's one of my all-time favourites.

I've always admired her work.

Saying what you don't like

It's not my kind of thing at all.

It's really not my taste.

It's not my cup of tea.

I can't relate to this type of thing.

Unit 9 Recording 3

A=Abby, B=Becs, C=Chris

Dialogue 1

A: What do you think of this one?

B: Um ... it's OK. To be honest, it's not really my taste. I'm not really into this style of portrait. And it sort of looks like a photo to me.

C: Yeah, you have to get up really close to it to see that it's a painting.

A: What do you think of it?

C: I really like it, actually.

A: Me too.

C: I like the colours, and the expression on her face is kind of intense.

A: It's a bit enigmatic, isn't it? You don't really know what she's thinking. And the details too. You can almost see the pores of her skin. Don't you think?

B: Well, as I was saying, it really does look like a photo – the detail is amazing, so as far as the skill is concerned, and the technique, I think it's great, but to tell you the truth, I still wouldn't want it hanging on my bedroom wall.

Dialogue 2

A: I like this one.

C: He's just got such an interesting face, hasn't he? He looks like one of those poets from the Seventies.

A: With that big beard.

C: With that big beard and the shirt.

B: Is it Hawaiian, that shirt?

C: And the medallion.

A: Oh yeah, I didn't notice that.

C: As a matter of fact, I prefer this one to the other one. At any rate, I think it's more interesting visually.

A: How about this one for your bedroom wall?

B: Nope. 'Fraid not. Mind you, I'd put it in the bathroom.

Dialogue 3

B: I think this one's great.

C: It's kind of menacing isn't it?

B: For me, what's interesting is that they are in a group, almost like a gang with this uniform.

C: The jeans and white T-shirt.

B: Exactly, except for the guy sitting in the middle. Now he's the only one sitting and looking directly at us, sort of challenging us, so maybe he's the boss.

A: Well, what I noticed is that, as you said, they're in a group, but somehow they look isolated. They're all facing in different directions and they don't seem to relate to each other at all.

C: And I wonder why it's called La Familia. They obviously aren't a family in any traditional sense. At any rate, they don't look like a family, so it's kind of intriguing. I think this one should win, actually.

A: Me too.

Unit 9 Recording 4

A=Abby, C=Chris

C: So which one won in the end?

A: Which do you think?

C: Well, as I said before, my favourite is La Familia, but ...

A: That one didn't win.

C: Oh really?

A: The winner was *Giulietta Coates*, the one that looks like a photo.

C: Right. Well, I think it's really good too, but it isn't my favourite.

Unit 9 Recording 5

It's highly likely I'd agree.
I would probably agree to that.
I would consider doing that.
I suppose I might do that.
I probably wouldn't accept.
It's unlikely I'd be able to do that.
There's no way I would do that.

Unit 9 Recording 6

E=Expert

E: Clarence Birdseye was a taxidermist from New York. On a visit to the Arctic he saw how the native people preserved their food by putting it in barrels of sea water, which froze quickly. This way, the food maintained its freshness for later. So in 1923 he bought a seven-dollar electric fan, some ice, and some buckets of salt water and experimented by putting food in them. Birdseye's experiments worked, and he went on to become the pioneer of frozen foods in the western world. In 1929 he sold the patent for 22 million dollars and in 1930 frozen food went on sale for the first time in the United States.

As a young man, Chester Carlson's job involved making multiple copies of patent documents by hand. Writing everything down was difficult for Carlson because he was short-sighted and had arthritis, so in 1938 he invented a machine to make copies. He tried to get funding for his idea from all sorts of well-known companies, including IBM and General Electric, but they turned him down. Eventually the company that became Xerox bought his idea, and the first photocopier was manufactured in 1959. Now there's hardly an office in the world that doesn't contain his invention.

Unit 10 Recording 1

I=Interviewer, R=Richard

I: In June 1980, Maureen Wilcox became one of the US Lottery's biggest losers. She bought tickets for the Rhode Island and Massachusetts draws and chose winning numbers for both. But her Massachusetts numbers would have won the Rhode Island lottery, and vice-versa. Meanwhile, lawyer John Woods was one of many to narrowly miss death in the Twin Towers on September 11. Not that unusual, except that he also escaped the 1993 bombing there, and the Lockerbie plane crash in a similar way. So, are some of us just born lucky? Is there a scientific reason why some people might seem luckier than others? With us today in the studio is Professor Richard Wiseman, who has studied 'lucky' and 'unlucky' people, and thinks that the differences between them must be related to their psychology. So, Richard, how are these two groups different?

R: Lucky people are more open to opportunity, and trust their hunches. They tend to be optimistic and expect good fortune. And when things go wrong, they are robust and resilient. They won't give up. We did some research, to see if people who thought they were lucky, actually won the lottery more often, and things like that. Well, it will come as no great surprise that they didn't actually win more often.

I: No? Right.

R: But there was something interesting happening. The lucky people had much higher expectations of winning. They didn't need to win. Their optimism was still boundless. And this is important. It's what psychologists call a positive delusion. Although it's a delusion it's actually good for you because it keeps you trying. You can't win the lottery if you don't enter, and in many areas of life, having positive expectations makes a favourable outcome more likely.

I: Is that really the case? What areas of life are you talking about?

R: In business, for example, some people seem to have the knack for making a business work, while others are bound to go from one failed venture to another. We showed in our research that you can improve your business success by learning how to be 'lucky'. Let me explain. We teamed up with a management firm, and for five months, employees took part in a specially devised programme of lectures, questionnaires, meetings and assessments designed to make them think and behave like lucky people. This was a little different from the usual business motivational training. It was more about looking for opportunities by being relaxed, open and fluid rather than developing drive and focus. The results were impressive, with 54 percent of participants believing that their personal luck had increased, and 75 percent indicating that the company's luck had increased. But perhaps more importantly, this was borne out in hard sales figures – the company's income increased by 20 percent each month.

I: Wow, that is impressive. So Richard, can I ask you, are some people just born unlucky?

R: A survey in the UK showed that 50 percent of the population thought of themselves as lucky, and 14 percent as unlucky. Presumably, these two groups differ, in their behaviour and in their psychology. So I thought we ought to look at that. And our research showed that there were big differences. So, I guess if you say that your genes affect your personality, and your behaviour, which they no doubt do, then, yes, you could be right. Some people are born lucky, or unlucky.

Lucky people are likely to create opportunities for good fortune by being extrovert, sociable, and using open body language that gets people to respond to them. They are relaxed and easy-going, and therefore, more likely to notice chance opportunities that may turn into a lucky break. They also like variety and change. One man, for instance, breaks routine by thinking of a colour when he's on his way to a party. At the party he is supposed to speak only to people wearing that colour. This takes him out of his comfort zone of chatting to those he already knows, and brings him the prospect of new friends and new opportunities. Lucky people also have positive expectations of life and things tend to go their way. A famous experiment illustrates how this can work. Psychologists told American high school teachers that certain children in their class were especially gifted. In fact, there was nothing special about these pupils. The teachers shouldn't have treated them any differently, but they began to shower the 'special children' with extra praise and encouragement. And the children responded by producing better schoolwork, doing better in tests, and generally achieving more than the other children. This study shows the power of positive expectations ...

Unit 10 Recording 2

V=Verse, C=Chorus

Feelin' so good

V: When I opened up my eyes today
I felt the sun shining on my face
It became so clear to me that everything is going my way
I feel like there's no limit to what I can see
I got rid of fears that were holding me
My endless possibilities
Has the whole world opened for me
That's why I'm feeling ...

C: I'm feeling so good
I knew I would
Been taking care of myself
Like I should
'cause not one thing
Can bring me down
Nothing in this world gonna turn me round ...
V: Now the day is turning into night
And everything is still going right
There's no way you can stop me this time
Or break this spirit of mine
Like the stars above I'm gonna shine
Anything I want will be mine
Tonight I'm gonna have a good time
Call a few friends of mine
'cause I'm liking life
And tonight's for feeling ...
C: (2x)

Unit 10 Recording 3

1 It must have been amazing to be the first modern person to see Machu Picchu, after it had been covered by jungle for so long. Urm, I think it must have been pretty hard to get there, actually, because nowadays they've built a train, there's a little village nearby, near Cuzco, and it's ... urm, easier to get to. But, the first people that went there had to climb right up the side of the huge mountain without knowing that there was anything there at the top, so they must have been really driven people to ... to make themselves climb up there. But, although they might have felt the same atmosphere when they were arriving, it couldn't have been quite as spectacular as it is today because the ruins now are all there for you to see as soon as you arrive, but it must have had more of a mysterious air when they discovered it covered in vegetation and all hidden without really knowing what it was.
2 I've often wondered what it was like to have been in the first aeroplane to take off and really fly, not just like the Kitty Hawk going for a ten second or a thirty second hop, but really climbing into the air. It can't have been easy because you have to realise those aircraft were not very sophisticated. They must have been difficult to fly – physically and even mentally – and you would've had to do lots of calculations that no one else has done before, and then of course it would have been incredibly exhilarating as the freedom increases as you go higher and higher, and then just think of all the doubts: how's this going to work out? Are you going to control it? And then coming in for the landing. How would that have been? In a way, you would know that this is going to be a crash, but a crash that you have to control, and that too couldn't have been easy.
3 I think Yuri Gagarin must have had, I think, missed, mixed emotions about being the first person in space. I think, on the one hand, there's that sort of thrill and excitement of ... of space travel, and the absolute awe of what he's experiencing, seeing Earth from space and being the first person to see that, having never even had any concept of what it might look like from space, and sort of, urm, just the complete vastness of space and just how amazing that must be. But on the other hand, sort of being up there on your own, basically in a tin can, y'know, anything could have happened up there, um, he probably didn't know if he would

get back home or not. He must have felt alone and also probably quite scared as well.

Unit 10 Recording 4

1 During my childhood my parents moved quite a lot, so I was always changing schools, and starting new schools. In fact, in about six years I think we changed school three times, so it was quite often. And that was quite difficult, er, because just when you've met new friends and you've got used to the teachers and the lessons, then you're told you've got to do it all again. It's true that I got quite lonely and I found it quite difficult to relate to other children, especially because they all knew the area, they already had their small groups of friends, and I was slightly out of it. Urm, but this also made me very outgoing, because if I wasn't going to be outgoing and energetic, and entertaining, urm ... it was going to ... I was never going to have those friends. So, er, it was difficult. Sometimes I did feel quite lonely, and I did feel as if it was hard work each time, but I'm lucky that I now have a lot of friends because of it.
2 I think one of my worst memories of childhood is probably a sport-related memory because I'm not really a sporty kind of girl. Um, I grew up in central Manchester and my school was kind of in the middle of an industrial estate, and lots of shops and ... and things like that. And they used to make us go cross-country running every week, so we'd be out there, in the rain, and the wind, and the snow in the middle of Manchester with the traffic roaring by, running around in our little shorts and T-shirts, looking like complete idiots – I absolutely hated it. I used to dread Mondays, because I knew PE lessons were coming up, and it was just going to be absolute torture. I'm still the same now. I still hate sports, and running is just one of the sports I hate the most I think. It's just something that I find so uncomfortable and so unpleasurable, so yeah that's probably my worst memory of childhood.
3 When I was a child, er, when I was a very little girl, we used to go to Majorca nearly every year. It was a real family holiday and my grandparents came as well. Erm, the last time I went we must have been about seven, I suppose. I don't remember the first few times in fact. I don't remember catching a plane. The thing I remember most vividly, um, is arriving in Majorca, and the wall of heat that used to hit us every time we got off the plane. Erm, and the smell of the air, that was so different from England. It was a fantastic smell. And I remember the things that um children remember about holidays, rather than anything too cultural. I remember the pool, I remember how blue the pool was – we used to swim every day, and the breakfasts that went on forever. Just the way the routine was completely different from what we did at home. And er the way we met people from all over the world. We made friends with a Norwegian family one year, and kept in touch with them, which was nice. So it's just really the colours and smells that er take me back there. I haven't been there since 'cause I don't really want to spoil it. I think the magic of it might go if I was to see it now as an adult.
4 During the summer holidays, I lived in the back of a wood. Er, my parents' garden backed

onto this small wood, and I used to climb over the garden fence and my friends and I used to play in the wood, literally all day. We used to climb trees, run in and out of bushes and just have a general laugh and it was just great. It was just a great sense of freedom, that you should really have when you're a child. It was just essentially a very good and happy time.

Unit 10 Recording 5

1 Oh my goodness, I went to the most amazing restaurant last night. You would not believe it, I've never seen anything like it in my life. It was called um, it was called The Bentley and it was in South Kensington, and it was the most fascinating building 'cause it was one of those beautiful old Georgian terraces that's been turned into a boutique hotel, so it was all chandeliers and really plush sofas, and incredible service. I mean, they were so polite and charming. The food was kind of French style, but it was very modern haute cuisine, and we had what's called a 'grazing' menu, which was terribly expensive but extremely exciting, because you get little plates of food. Um, I think we had seven courses in total.
2 I just, I can't stand public transport in this country. I mean, despite the fact that it's expensive and unreliable, it's just so ridiculously complicated. Just look at trains, for example. There must be about twenty different ticket types. And it all depends on when you're travelling, what time of day, how far before you booked your ticket, it's just ridiculous. So for example, you could be sitting on a train and the person sitting opposite you could've paid ten times the amount for their ticket just because they happened to buy it on a different day. I don't understand why we don't have systems like in other countries where you just pay per kilometre and then pay perhaps an upgrade if you get on a faster train. As it is now, it's just so complicated and I, I just, personally I choose not to use it.
3 Well, I really hate smoking and I just think it should be banned completely because it's not ... people who don't smoke ... it's so unfair for us, erm, y'know, you go to a restaurant or you go to a café and you're breathing in other people's smoke and you smell of smoke at the end of the day when you've been with a smoker and y'know, it's obviously not good for the smoker, but it's not good for the non-smoker either. Erm and it's really quite repulsive that you have to breathe in somebody's second-hand smoke. And, er, smokers will say, well, y'know, we'll go to a part of the restaurant where it doesn't affect you or we'll go outside, but it does because even if you're outside and you're walking behind somebody who is smoking then you're breathing in their smoke. Erm, and I think they should just ban it because it's one of the few bad habits that really does affect everybody else.

Pearson Education Limited
Edinburgh Gate
Harlow
Essex CM20 2JE
England
and Associated Companies throughout the world.

www.longman.com

First published 2007
Second impression 2007
ISBN 978-0-582-84171-0 (Book only)
ISBN 978-1-4058-4827-5 (Book and DVD pack)

Set in 10.5/13pt Meta Plus Book and 10/13pt Meta Plus Normal
Printed in Spain by Mateu Cromo, S.A. Pinto (Madrid)

We are grateful to the following for permission to reproduce copyright material:
New York Times for an extract 'To masters of language, a long overdue toast' by William H Honan, published in *The New York Times* December 1997 ©1997 The New York Times Co. Reprinted with permission; Matt Rendell for an extract 'Mirror, Signal Manoeuvre' published in *The Observer* May 2004; Mike Dixon for an extract on Carlos Acosta published on www. nationaldanceawards.com , Mike Dixon is chairman of the Dance Critic's Circle; Caroline Green for an extract from 'Special report: superhero science' published in *Focus Magazine* August 2004; Solo Syndication Ltd for an extract 'From behind bars to bouquets' by Rachel Cooke published in *The Daily Mail*; Cliff Ennico for an extract 'Picking the right partner' published on www.entrepreneur.com/article/0.4621.298643.00html; The Boston Globe for an extract from 'Riches to rags' by Stan Grossfeld published in *The Boston Globe* December 2005; Fortune Magazine for the following extracts 'How we pick the 100 best' and 'The 100 best companies to work for' by Robert Levering, 'The Wegmans Way' by Matthew Boyle published in *Fortune Magazine* January 2005 ©2005 Time Inc. All rights reserved; The Australian Government for an extract 'Sydney Harbour Bridge' published on www.culture.gov.au May 2006 © Commonwealth of Australia reproduced by permission; British Broadcasting Company for an extract ' A step-by-step guide to charisma' by Tom Geoghegan published on www.news.bbc. co.uk May 2005; New Scientist for an extract 'Rats' brain waves could find trapped people' by Emily Singer published in *The New Scientist* September 2004; Independent News and Media Ltd for an extract 'Revealed: the illegal online animal trade' by Maxine Frith published in *The Independent* August 2005; Guardian Newspapers Limited for an extract 'Dear Jeremy' by Jeremy Bullmore published in *The Guardian* October 2005© Guardian Newspapers Limited 2005; NI Syndication Ltd for extracts 'The bigger picture' by Doug McKinlay published in *The Times* July 2005 and 'A life in the day' by Richard Johnson published in *The Sunday Times Magazine* January 2004 © Times Newspapers Limited; Susan Aldridge for an extract 'Do you feel lucky? (punk)' published in *Focus Magazine* August 2004; Bloomsbury Publishing Plc for an extract from *A House on Mango Street* by Sandra Cisneros; The Music Sales Group, Reach Global (UK) Limited, Warner/Chappell Music Ltd, Faber Music Ltd and EMI Music Publishing Ltd for the words and music to 'Feelin' So Good' by Sean Puffy Combs, Mark Cory Rooney, Joseph Anthony Cartagena, Christopher Rios, Jennifer Lopez, George Logios, Steven Wayne Standard and Craig L Peyton © 1999 Nuyorican Publishing/Justin Combs Publishing/Cori Tiffany Publishing/Reach Global Inc/Joseph Cartagena Music/Let Me Show You Music/Sony/ATV Music Publishing (UK) Ltd/Jelly's Jams LLC/Warner Chappell Music Ltd/EMI April Music Inc Ltd.

In some instances we have been unable to trace the owners of copyright material and we would appreciate any information that would enable us to do so.

Acknowledgements

The publishers and authors would like to thank the following people and institutions for their feedback and comments during the development of the material:

Robert Armitage, International House, Terrassa, Spain; Joanna Cooke, United Kingdom; Rolf Donald, United Kingdom; Fiona Gallagher, Republic of Ireland; Elizabeth Gregson, Italy; Elizabeth Kalton, Keep Talking, Udine, Italy; Diane Naughton, Spain; John Peebles, Spain; Nancy Pietragalla, Argentina; Agnieszka Tyszkiewicz-Zora, SJA University of Łodz, Poland

Illustrated by: Beach (Beach-o-matic), Mark Duffin, Sally Newton, Amanda Montgomery-Higham (SGA), Roger Penwill and Lucy Truman (New Division)

Cover design by Zeke Design

Photo Acknowledgements
We are grateful to the following for permission to reproduce photographs:

AA World Travel Library for p. 153(tr); AKG Images,London for pp. 118; Alamy for pp.20(ml) (© Leonid Serebrennikov), 39(tm) (Rob Bartee), 53(b) (Bubbles Photo Library), 61(tl) (Jack Sullivan), 64(tm) (Horizon International Images Ltd), 64(r) (Steve Rant), 67(b) (Iconotec), 71(mr) (NOIMAGE), 82(Ali) (Pictorial Press Ltd); 84(Clinton) (Frances Roberts), 93(t) (Ariadne Van Zandbergen), 97(b) (Rob Walls), 98(piano) (Lebrecht Music & Arts Library), 103(bl) (Aliki Image Library), 104(tr) (Kitt Cooper-Smith),109(b) (Frank Chmura), 114(bl), (Terry Harris), 117(ml), (CW Images), 131 (Richard Church), 153(l) (AM Corporation), 155(camcorder) (Judith Collins), 156(tr) (Richard Levine), 156(br) (Jack Sullivan), Courtesy of Apple for p. 9(computer); Ardea for p. 92(t); Art Directors & TRIP for pp. 19(tl), 22(Japanese men), 37(r), 39(b), 57; Anthony Blake Photo Library for pp. 72(b), 142(cake); Steve Bloom Images for p. 89(t); Bridgeman Art Library for pp. 117(t) 'Starry Night' Credit: Starry Night, 1889 (oil on canvas) by Gogh, Vincent van (1853-90) ©Museum of Modern Art, New York, USA, 120(tr) Portrait of Albert Einstein (1879-1955) by Private Collection/ Boltin Picture Library, 120(b) Self Portrait with Straw Hat, 1887 (oil on-canvas) by Gogh, Vincent van (1853-90) ©Van Gogh Museum, Amsterdam, The Netherlands/ J.P. Zenobel, 160(m) Detail of the Mona Lisa, c.1503-6 (panel) Vinci, Leonardo da (1452-1519) / Louvre, Paris, France; Camera Press for pp. 9(glacier, athletes), 14, 19(t), 22(table scene), 61(ml), 64(l), 71(tr), 75(t), 77(dome), 82(Diana), 92(r); Corbis for pp. 25 (Boris Roessler), 33(t) (National Gallery Collection; By kind permission of the Trustees of the National Gallery, London), 33(ml) (Bettmann), 61(t) (Andy Rain), 75(tl) (Karen Kasmauski), 98(honey) (Envision), 103(tl) (David Turnley), 104(ml) (Jose Luis Pelaez Inc), 110(tr) (B. Bird), 110(l), (Creasource), 111 (LWA-Dann Tardif), 128(l) (Bettmann), 131(ml) (Anthony Redpath), 150(4) (Peter Dazeley). 160(r) (Kevin R Morris); Roger Cotgreave /Tao Jones Photography/ Photographersdirect.com for p. 155(studio); Michael Coyle for p. 56(b); DK Images for p. 104(tl); Empics for pp. 6(b), 9(World Cup), 75(bl), 142(street), 152(balloon) / Photographersdirect.com; Victor Englebert / agpix.com / Photographersdirect.com for pp. 26/27(Cali); Mary Evans Picture Library for pp. 33(bl), 119(r); Eye Ubiquitous for pp. 19(bl), 27(Corsica), 37(l), 82(Mandela), 89(tl & bl), 109(t), 158(b), Chris Fairclough Worldwide for p. 28(m); Fernando Freixosa for p. 13; Courtesy of the Garibaldi-Meucci Museum, Staten Island, NY for p. 9(gent); Chris George / Photographersdirect.com for p. 155(phone); Getty Images for pp. 5(tl), 30(b), 34(l & r),71(br), 93(b), 98(jacket), 104(mr), 114(m), 131(t & tl), 142(boxing), 145(t), 158(m), 161(tr); By courtesy of Granada International p. 154; Ronald Grant Archive for p. 157(Monroe); Sally & Richard Greenhill for pp. 80(l), 114(mr), 159(train station); Robert Harding Travel Library for pp. 77(pyramid); International Photobank for pp. 77(pyramid), 94(m & b); Lebrecht Music & Arts Library for p. 120(tl); Londonstills.com for p. 62; Lonely Planet Images for p. 114(tl); Dean Marsh for p. 121(Guiletta Coates); Marvel / Sony Pictures / Kobal Collection for p. 48; Masterfile for pp. 30(t), 42(matador), 161(bl); Delip Mehta / Contact Press / NB Pictures for 55(r); Military Picture Library International for p. 104(bl); Mirrorpix for p. 135(br); Courtesy of NASA for pp. 47(tl), 135(bl); National Geographic Image Collection for pp. 124 (t Stephen L Alvarez, m Jodi Cobb, b Nicolas Reynard) 158(t) (Steve Winter);New Zealand Woman Weekly / Frances Oliver for p. 152(woman); Timothy Okamura for p. 121 (La Familia); Oxford Imaging Ltd for p. 126(m); Courtesy of Panasonic for p. 155(microwave); Photofusion Picture Library for pp. 75(ml), 112(m & l); Photolibrary.com for pp. 5(t), 72(tr); Courtesy of Paula Pryke for p. 63; Punchstock for pp. 20(l), 44, 23(l), 69, 110(br) (Bananastock), 22(shaking hands), 37(m), 39(l), 42(b), 55(l), 79(r), 161(tl) (Blend), 72(tm) (Brand X), 7, 53(br) (Corbis), 104(br) (Creatas), 5(ml), 47(ml & bl), 77(city) 100, 142(commuters), 161(ml) (Digital Vision), 5(ml) (image 100), 39(r) (Image Source), 20(r) (Images.com), 58(t & b), 71(tl), 72(tl) (Photodisc), 98(bag) (Stockbyte), 19(ml), 71(bl), 98(fur coat) (Think Stock), 81(t), 103(ml), 107(l) (Uppercut), 112(r) (WestEnd61); Used by permission of The Random House Group Ltd for p. 151; Redferns Music Picture Library for p. 82 (Mick Hutson); Reuters for pp. 58(cats), 67(br); Rex Features for pp. 9(book & cracked earth), 23(r), 33(tl), 40, 41(b), 42(t), 49(r), 61(bl), 64(b), 67(tr), 77(bridge, mosque), 79(l), 80(r), 82(Reagan), 84(Streep, Lee, Pele), 89(ml), 94(t), 97(t), 98(shoes), 103(t), 107(r), 114(br), 117(tl), 134, 150(2), 152(couple with car, man with bike), 156(m & l), 157(Dean, Brando, Cruise, Taylor), 159(child, litter, traffic); Science Photo Library for pp. 9(airplane), 48/49(b) (Dale Darby), 58(robots) (Pascal Goetgheluck); South American Pictures for p. 28(t); Allan Staley Photography / Photographersdirect.com for p. 155(Skype); Superstock for pp. 14(bl), 22(eating pizza), 76(Eiffel, Pentagon), 91, 150(3), 160(l); Jun Takagi for p. 56(t); Andrew Tift for p. 121 (Daniel); The Travel Library for pp. 26(Cape Town), 28(b); Topfoto for pp, 47(l),78, 81(b), 82(Clinton), 114(tr), 145(b), 150(l); Travel Ink for p. 135(t); UN Photo Library for pp. 6(l) (Paulo Filgueiras), 6(l) (Evan Schneider); Universal Puctures / Ronald Grant Archive for p. 142(King Kong); Warner Bros / Ronald Grant Archive for p. 49(l); Wellcome Trust Medical Photographic Library for p. 119(l); Working Title / Ronald Grant Archive for pp. 41(m), 117(bl); Courtesy of Xerox for pp. 128 (t & gent).

Cover images by Superstock (t), Alamy (l) (Nagelstock.com), Punchstock (b) (Digital Vision).

Picture research by Kevin Brown

Whilst every effort has been made to trace the copyright holders we have been unable to locate the owner of photo page 120(tr) Albert Einstein. We would be pleased to insert the appropriate acknowledgement in any subsequent edition of this publication.

Authors' acknowledgements:

We would like to thank Kate Goldrick and Judith King for initiating Total English, our editors, Bernie Hayden and Kirsten Holt for their attention to detail and excellent ideas, Jo Stevenson (Pearson Education) and Catherine Hollingworth (Pentacor Book Design) for their creative design work, and above all Jenny Colley for her energy, enthusiasm and expertise. JJ also wishes to thank Alexandra Neves, as well as David, Elizabeth, Chris and Jenny Wilson. Antonia would like to thank Andrea for his never-ending support and encouragement, Emilio for his ideas on superheroes, and Giacomo, who has given up so much in order for this to happen.